CIPS STUDY MATTERS

DIPLOMA IN PROCUREMENT AND SUPPLY

COURSE BOOK

Sourcing in procurement and supply

© Profex Publishing Limited, 2012

Printed and distributed by:

The Chartered Institute of Purchasing & Supply, Easton House, Easton on the Hill, Stamford, Lincolnshire PE9 3NZ
Tel: +44 (0) 1780 756 777
Fax: +44 (0) 1780 751 610
Email: info@cips.org
Website: www.cips.org

First edition September 2012

Contents

Preface

Welcome to your new Study Pack.

For each subject you have to study, your Study Pack consists of two elements.

- A **Course Book** (the current volume). This provides detailed coverage of all topics specified in the unit content.
- A small-format volume of **Revision Notes**. Use your Revision Notes in the weeks leading up to your exam.

For a full explanation of how to use your new Study Pack, turn now to page xi. And good luck in your exams!

A note on style

Throughout your Study Packs you will find that we use the masculine form of personal pronouns. This convention is adopted purely for the sake of stylistic convenience – we just don't like saying 'he/she' all the time. Please don't think this reflects any kind of bias or prejudice.

September 2012

The Unit Content

The unit content is reproduced below, together with reference to the chapter in this Course Book where each topic is covered.

Unit purpose and aims

On completion of this unit, candidates will be able to apply a set of appropriate tools and techniques that can assess sourcing options available to organisations when procuring goods, services or works from external suppliers.

This unit identifies sound approaches to sourcing activities that assess the commercial and technical capabilities of organisations to help achieve the right choice of supplier.

Learning outcomes, assessment criteria and indicative content

Chapter

1.0   Understand the main options for sourcing of requirements from suppliers

1.1   Explain the sourcing process in relation to procurement

• Definitions of sourcing	1
• Supplier pre-qualification or criteria for supplier appraisal	1
• Strategic and tactical sourcing	1
• Forming teams with stakeholders for the sourcing process	1
• Vendor or supplier performance management	1

1.2   Compare the main approaches to the sourcing of requirements from suppliers

• Sole sourcing	2
• Single, dual and multiple sourcing arrangements	2
• The use of tendering: open, restricted and negotiated approaches to tendering	2
• Direct negotiations with suppliers	2
• Intra company trading and transfer pricing arrangement	2
• Implications of international sourcing	2

1.3   Develop selection and award criteria that can be commonly applied when sourcing requirements from external suppliers

• Typical selection criteria such as: quality assurance, environmental and sustainability, technical capabilities, systems capabilities, labour standards, financial capabilities	3
• Typical award criteria such as: price, total life cycle costs, technical merit, added value solutions, systems, resources	3
• Balancing commercial and technical award criteria	3

Chapter

How to Use Your Study Pack

Organising your study

'Organising' is the key word: unless you are a very exceptional student, you will find a haphazard approach is insufficient, particularly if you are having to combine study with the demands of a full-time job.

A good starting point is to timetable your studies, in broad terms, between now and the date of the examination. How many subjects are you attempting? How many chapters are there in the Course Book for each subject? Now do the sums: how many days/weeks do you have for each chapter to be studied?

Remember:

- Not every week can be regarded as a study week – you may be going on holiday, for example, or there may be weeks when the demands of your job are particularly heavy. If these can be foreseen, you should allow for them in your timetabling.
- You also need a period leading up to the exam in which you will revise and practise what you have learned.

Once you have done the calculations, make a week-by-week timetable for yourself for each paper, allowing for study and revision of the entire unit content between now and the date of the exams.

Getting started

Aim to find a quiet and undisturbed location for your study, and plan as far as possible to use the same period each day. Getting into a routine helps avoid wasting time. Make sure you have all the materials you need before you begin – keep interruptions to a minimum.

Using the Course Book

You should refer to the Course Book to the extent that you need it.

- If you are a newcomer to the subject, you will probably need to read through the Course Book quite thoroughly. This will be the case for most students.
- If some areas are already familiar to you – either through earlier studies or through your practical work experience – you may choose to skip sections of the Course Book.

The content of the Course Book

This Course Book has been designed to give detailed coverage of every topic in the unit content. As you will see from pages vii–ix, each topic mentioned in the unit content is dealt with in a chapter of the Course Book. For the most part the order of the Course Book follows the order of the unit content closely, though departures from this principle have occasionally been made in the interest of a logical learning order.

Each chapter begins with a reference to the assessment criteria and unit content to be covered in the chapter. Each chapter is divided into sections, listed in the introduction to the chapter, and for the most part being actual captions from the unit content.

All of this enables you to monitor your progress through the unit content very easily and provides reassurance that you are tackling every subject that is examinable.

Each chapter contains the following features.

- Introduction, setting out the main topics to be covered
- Clear coverage of each topic in a concise and approachable format
- A chapter summary
- Self-test questions

The study phase

For each chapter you should begin by glancing at the main headings (listed at the start of the chapter). Then read fairly rapidly through the body of the text to absorb the main points. If it's there in the text, you can be sure it's there for a reason, so try not to skip unless the topic is one you are familiar with already.

Then return to the beginning of the chapter to start a more careful reading. You may want to take brief notes as you go along, but bear in mind that you already have your Revision Notes – there is no point in duplicating what you can find there.

Test your recall and understanding of the material by attempting the self-test questions. These are accompanied by cross-references to paragraphs where you can check your answers and refresh your memory.

The revision phase

Your approach to revision should be methodical and you should aim to tackle each main area of the unit content in turn. Read carefully through your Revision Notes. Check back to your Course Book if there are areas where you cannot recall the subject matter clearly. Then do some question practice. The CIPS website contains many past exam questions. You should aim to identify those that are suitable for the unit you are studying.

Additional reading

Your Study Pack provides you with the key information needed for each module but CIPS strongly advocates reading as widely as possible to augment and reinforce your understanding. CIPS produces an official reading list of books, which can be downloaded from the bookshop area of the CIPS website.

To help you, we have identified one essential textbook for each subject. We recommend that you read this for additional information.

The essential textbook for this unit is *Purchasing and Supply Chain Management* by Kenneth Lysons and Brian Farrington.

CHAPTER 1

The Sourcing Process

Assessment criteria and indicative content

 Explain the sourcing process in relation to procurement

- Definitions of sourcing
- Supplier pre-qualification or criteria for supplier appraisal
- Strategic and tactical sourcing
- Forming teams with stakeholders for the sourcing process
- Vendor or supplier performance management

Section headings

1   Strategic and tactical sourcing
2   The sourcing process
3   Surveying and engaging the market
4   Supplier appraisal and pre-qualification
5   Gathering and verifying supplier information
6   Vendor performance management

Introduction

The first section of the *Sourcing from Suppliers* syllabus gives an overview of the sourcing process and related 'big picture' issues, such as sourcing approaches and strategies, criteria for supplier selection, and the supplier's perspective on the sourcing process. Further learning outcomes go on to look in more detail at specific processes, tools, techniques and frameworks that can be applied to the sourcing of requirements from external suppliers.

In this chapter we begin at the beginning: with the sourcing process, and its role within the overall procurement cycle. We also examine some important distinctions in terminology between supplier appraisal at the pre-contract stage of the procurement process (for the purposes of supplier pre-qualification and selection), and in the post-contract stage (for the purposes of performance management).

Finally, we look briefly at the distinction between sourcing processes at the strategic and tactical levels, since this syllabus addresses aspects of both.

1   Strategic and tactical sourcing

What is sourcing?

1.1   The main stages of a generic procurement process – depicted as a cycle – are shown in Figure 1.1. The process starts with the identification of the need.

Figure 1.1 *A generic procurement cycle*

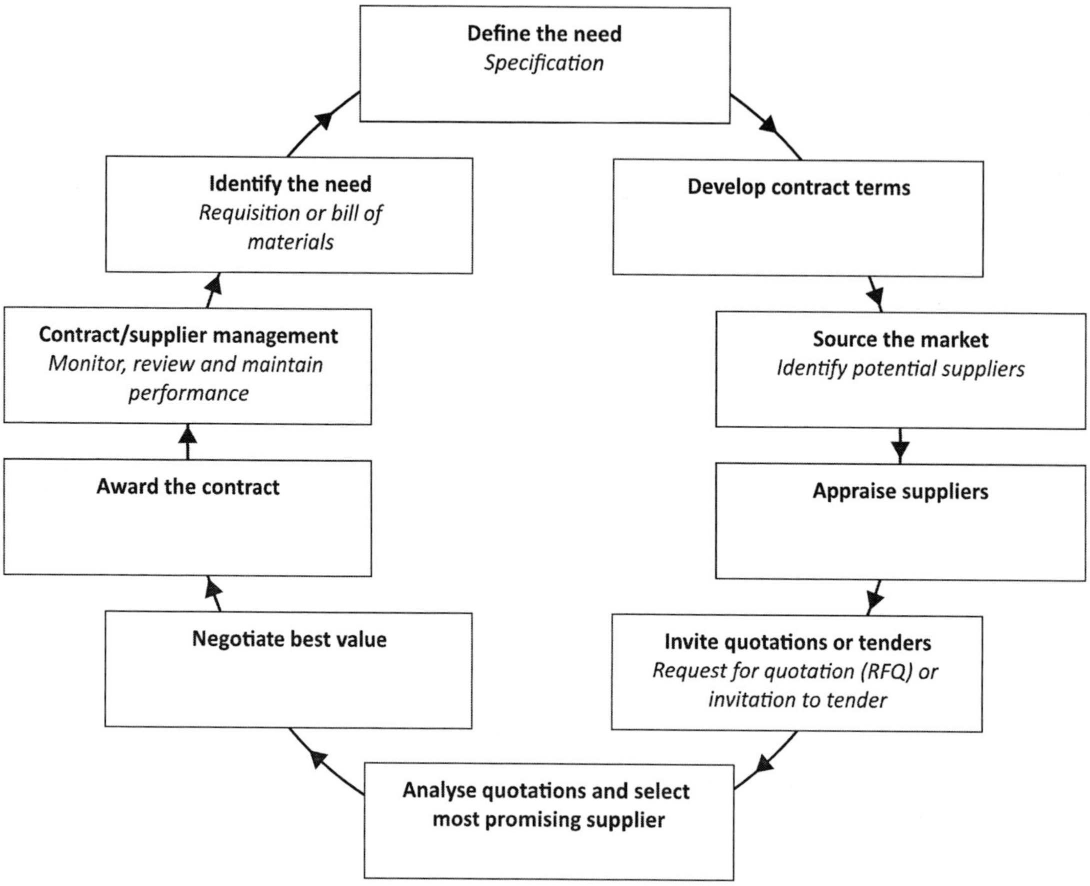

```
                          ┌─────────────────────┐
                          │   Define the need   │
                          │   Specification     │
                          └─────────────────────┘

┌─────────────────────┐                    ┌─────────────────────┐
│  Identify the need  │                    │ Develop contract    │
│  Requisition or     │                    │ terms               │
│  bill of materials  │                    │                     │
└─────────────────────┘                    └─────────────────────┘

┌─────────────────────┐                    ┌─────────────────────┐
│ Contract/supplier   │                    │  Source the market  │
│ management          │                    │  Identify potential │
│ Monitor, review and │                    │  suppliers          │
│ maintain            │                    │                     │
│ performance         │                    │                     │
└─────────────────────┘                    └─────────────────────┘

┌─────────────────────┐                    ┌─────────────────────┐
│ Award the contract  │                    │  Appraise suppliers │
└─────────────────────┘                    └─────────────────────┘

┌─────────────────────┐                    ┌─────────────────────┐
│ Negotiate best value│                    │ Invite quotations   │
│                     │                    │ or tenders          │
│                     │                    │ Request for         │
│                     │                    │ quotation (RFQ) or  │
│                     │                    │ invitation to tender│
└─────────────────────┘                    └─────────────────────┘

              ┌──────────────────────────────────┐
              │ Analyse quotations and select     │
              │ most promising supplier           │
              └──────────────────────────────────┘
```

1.2   The procurement process incorporates both:

- Pre-contract-award stages, including identification and definition of need, procurement planning, development of the contract, market survey and engagement, appraisal and selection of suppliers, receipt and evaluation of offers, and contact award *and*
- Post-contract-award stages, including activities such as expediting, payment, contract or supplier management, ongoing asset management, and post-contract 'lesson' learning.

1.3   **Sourcing** is basically that part of the procurement process that is concerned with 'how and where services or products are obtained' (CIPS). Lysons and Farrington (*Purchasing and Supply Chain Management)* define it as 'the process of identifying, selecting and developing suppliers'.

1.4   The term 'purchasing' is used to refer to post-contract transactional aspects such as ordering, receipting and payment. (This is sometimes called the purchase-to-pay cycle or P2P cycle.) The terms 'supplier management' and 'contract management' are used to refer to post-contract aspects such as the development and performance management of vendors or contractors.

1.5   Remembering the difference between pre- and post-contract stages also helps to distinguish between processes such as the auditing and appraisal of suppliers, which happen *both* pre- and post-contract-award. So, for example, it is important to differentiate between supplier appraisal (evaluating the capability of *potential* suppliers, in the pre-contract sourcing stage) and supplier *performance* appraisal (or 'vendor rating': evaluating the performance of actual suppliers, or vendors, in the post-contract performance stage). We will look at the both these processes later in this chapter.

Strategic and tactical sourcing

1.6 Lysons & Farrington (*Purchasing & Supply Chain Management*) emphasise that sourcing can be carried out at two basic levels: tactical (or operational) and strategic.

1.7 Tactical and operational sourcing processes are concerned with:

- Lower-level decisions relating to low-profit, low-risk and routine items – identified as 'leverage' and 'non-critical' items in the Kraljic procurement positioning matrix (discussed a bit later)
- The formulation of short-range decisions as to how specific supply requirements are to be met, in response to changing or temporary conditions in the organisation or supply market (eg supplier failure, supply disruption or fluctuations in demand)
- Clearly defined requirements and specifications, and transactional sourcing decisions based mainly on open bidding and purchase price (as suits leverage and non-critical items): for example, the operation of tendering.

1.8 Strategic sourcing processes are concerned with:

- Top-level, longer-term decisions relating to items with high profit and high supply risk (identified as 'strategic' items in the Kraljic matrix, as we will see later in this chapter) and items with low profit and high-supply risk ('bottleneck' items)
- The formulation of long-range, high-level decisions eg about procurement policies, the supplier base, supply chain relationships, the purchase of capital equipment and ethical and sustainability issues
- Developing a deep understanding of requirements (eg using value analysis) and of the supply market and individual supplier drivers and capabilities (as suits strategic and bottleneck items).

1.9 CIPS defines strategic sourcing as: 'satisfying business needs from markets via the proactive and planned analysis of supply markets and the selection of suppliers with the objective of delivering solutions to meet predetermined and agreed business needs'.

1.10 Lysons & Farrington argue that 'the status and importance purchasing now has requires a transition from thinking of it as a purely tactical activity to seeing it as a strategic activity.'

2 The sourcing process

2.1 Strategic sourcing is a complex process, involving a number of staged, interrelated tasks. A number of complex models have been developed to map and describe this process in different contexts, but a basic generic model may be as follows.

- **Identification of the requirement**
  This may take the form of purchase requisition from a user department, a stock replenishment requisition from inventory control, or a more complex process of requirement definition via early buyer or supplier involvement in a design and development project. This process may also include a *re-evaluation* of needs, and the definition of requirements in product and service specifications.
- **Sourcing plan**
  Make/do or buy decisions (will the organisation produce the requirement or source it from external suppliers?), and identification of the type of purchase (is this a straight re-buy, modified re-buy or new buy?), together with sourcing policies (eg single or multiple sourcing, local or international sourcing, the use of competition), will feed into a sourcing plan: the process and methodologies that will be used to source the market and select suppliers. A contract may be negotiated directly with an approved or preferred supplier, for example; or the contract may be put up to open tender (competitive bidding). We will discuss various sourcing plans and approaches in Chapter 2.
- **Market analysis**
  Purchasing research into product and supply markets will be used: to forecast long-term demand for the product (of which bought-out materials or components are a part); to gauge market prices

and forecast price trends of bought-out items and materials; to identify a range of potential supply sources; to assess the security or risk of various supply sources; and to evaluate environmental factors impacting on sourcing decisions. An important part of this process will be the identification of new potential suppliers within the supply market. We will discuss the process of surveying the market in Chapter 7.

- **Pre-qualification of suppliers**

  This involves establishing key criteria for supplier suitability, in the light of strategic sourcing objectives, and pre-screening potential suppliers to identify those who can meet the organisation's demands and standards. This is an important opportunity to apply a wide range of quantitative and qualitative criteria as a pre-qualifier, 'weeding out' suppliers who lack necessary values and capabilities – so that the later process of evaluating the bid or proposal and awarding the contract can focus on more easily comparable, quantifiable criteria such as price or whole life cost. The criteria for supplier selection and contract award will be discussed in Chapter 3.

- **Evaluating supply offers and options**

  The offerings of different pre-qualified suppliers may be evaluated in various ways: by obtaining quotations, conducting formal or informal tender (competitive bidding) exercises, or entering into negotiations with one or more suppliers. The 'winning' supplier (which offers the best value solution to the requirement) is selected for the contract.

- **Creation of contract or relationship**

  A purchase order, contract, framework agreement or other form of legal relationship is formulated, to define the terms of sale and purchase or engagement. This may take the form of a one-off purchase; an ongoing contract for the supply of goods, works or services; or a partnership agreement, say.

2.2   Of course, this is really only the beginning of contract management and fulfilment, and potentially ongoing relationship development. Further processes include the delivery of the product or performance of the service; post-purchase performance evaluation; post-contract 'lessons management'; and whole life contract management and supplier relationship management. These processes will be considered in detail in the *Managing Contracts and Relationships* module.

Different purchase contexts

2.3   Not every procurement will follow every stage of the generic sourcing process.

- If a procurement is a **straight re-buy** of items already sourced from a supplier, for example, it will not be necessary to establish a specification, survey and source the market, invite quotations and select a supplier. Preferred or approved suppliers will already be identified, and perhaps contracted on a standing basis (eg using framework agreements or call-off contracts, whereby the buyer contracts to source its requirements from the supplier, and procurement officers or users can simply 'call off' orders on the agreed terms, as needs arise).

- If it is a **modified re-buy**, in that some of the requirement has changed, it may be necessary to re-specify the need or re-negotiate the contract, but the same supplier may be used. Or *vice versa*: the specification may stay the same, but a new supplier will be sought.

- **New buys** are more likely to conform to the full sourcing process, with rigorous market survey, supplier pre-qualification and competitive approaches to contract award.

2.4   Where the item required is a standard or routine one, therefore, 'sourcing' may be largely by-passed. As Baily *et al* summarise the matter:

'The buyer would check first if there is already some commitment by long-term contract, in which case an order could be placed immediately. In the absence of such agreement, the buyer would ask if there is an existing source of supply whose performance is satisfactory; if so, the usual practice is to reorder from that source unless there is reason to review the position. Reasons for reviewing the position include price increase request, failure to meet specification, unsatisfactory performance as demonstrated by vendor ratings, internal pressure to save money, or simply that some time has elapsed since the position was last reviewed.'

2.5   There may, however, be the need to source a new or non-standard product or service – or the buyer may simply wish to stay aware of potential alternative providers in the supply market, if requirements (or existing suppliers' performance) change, or if opportunities arise to investigate better-value or more innovative solutions. In such cases, it will be important to locate, investigate and appraise potential suppliers.

2.6   The extent of this investigation must be proportionate to the importance and value of the item, and the potential risks involved in securing supply. It would not be worth the time and cost of detailed supplier appraisal for light bulbs or toilet paper, say. Systematic, rigorous sourcing processes will be essential, however, for strategic or non standard items; for major high-value procurements (eg capital equipment); for potential long-term partnership relations with a supplier; and for international sourcing and outsourcing exercises (because of the risks involved).

- In the case of low-value, non-critical items, it may be sufficient to conduct desk-based (or secondary) research into basic price, quality and delivery details.
- For more important items, many organisations categorise suppliers as either **approved** (meaning that the supplier satisfies certain basic technical and quality criteria) or **preferred** (meaning that the supplier has a track record of satisfactory performance, and user departments are allowed to order from them without further checking).
- For critical inputs, more rigorous measurement is required before a supplier is considered, or invited to tender, for a contract. This may well involve in-depth research (eg using a Pre-Qualification Questionnaire), with information verified by observation (eg through site visits and capability surveys), reference-checking, output sampling and so on. The buyer may also require external accreditation or certification of the supplier, eg by reference to international standards such as ISO 9001 (quality management systems).

2.7   So how can such priorities be identified? You may have encountered the use of segmentation tools such as Pareto analysis or the Kraljic matrix in your other studies. We will just re-cap them briefly here.

Prioritising sourcing exercises

2.8   Italian economist Vilfred Pareto (1848–1923) formulated the proposition that: 'In any series of elements to be controlled, a selected small factor in terms of number of elements (20%) almost always accounts for a large factor in terms of effort (80%).'

2.9   The **Pareto principle** (or '80/20 rule') is a useful technique for identifying the activities that will leverage your time, effort and resources for the biggest benefits. In a sourcing context, the Pareto principle can be interpreted as 80% of spend, risk or value residing in 20% of supplies or suppliers.

2.10   This elementary form of segmentation can be used to separate the critical few suppliers (who supply important, high-value, high-usage items, which can only be sourced from a limited supply market) from the trivial many (who supply routine, low-value supplies which can easily be sourced anywhere). Most procurement effort and energy needs to be focused on the critical or category 'A' suppliers and the products procured from them.

2.11   Another tool for prioritising is provided by Peter Kraljic (1973). Kraljic developed a **procurement positioning matrix**, which seeks to map:

- The importance to the organisation of the item being purchased (related to factors such as the organisation's annual expenditure on the item, and its profit potential through enabling revenue earning or cost reductions) against

- The complexity of the supply market (related to factors such as the difficulty of sourcing the item, the vulnerability of the buyer to supply or supplier failure, and the relative power of buyer and supplier in the market).

2.12 The matrix therefore has four quadrants, as follows: Figure 1.2.

Figure 1.2 *The Kraljic procurement positioning matrix*

Complexity of the supply market

	Low		High	
High	**Procurement focus** Leverage items	**Time horizon** Varied, typically 12-24 months	**Procurement focus** Strategic items	**Time horizon** Up to 10 years; governed by long-term strategic impact (risk and contract mix)
	Key performance criteria Cost/price and materials flow management	**Items purchased** Mix of commodities and specified materials	**Key performance criteria** Long-term availability	**Items purchased** Scarce and/or high-value materials
	Typical sources Multiple suppliers, chiefly local	**Supply** Abundant	**Typical sources** Established global suppliers	**Supply** Natural scarcity
Importance of the item	**Procurement focus** Non-critical items	**Time horizon** Limited: normally 12 months or less	**Procurement focus** Bottleneck items	**Time horizon** Variable, depending on availability vs short-term flexibility trade-offs
	Key performance criteria Functional efficiency	**Items purchased** Commodities, some specified materials	**Key performance criteria** Cost management and reliable short-term sourcing	**Items purchased** Mainly specified materials
Low	**Typical sources** Established local suppliers	**Supply** Abundant	**Typical sources** Global, predominantly new suppliers with new technology	**Supply** Production-based scarcity

2.13 At a strategic level, the Kraljic matrix is used to examine an organisation's procurement portfolio and its exposure to risk from supply disruption. For the purposes of this syllabus, it can be seen more simply as a tool for assessing what sourcing approaches are most appropriate for different types of procurements, and how a procurement function can add value by leveraging the potential of each.

- For *non-critical or routine items* (such as common stationery supplies), the focus will be on low-maintenance sourcing routines to reduce procurement costs. Arm's length approaches such as vendor managed inventory, blanket ordering (empowering end users to make call-off orders against negotiated agreements) and e-procurement solutions (eg online ordering or the use of purchasing cards) will provide routine efficiency.
- For *leverage items* (such as local produce bought by a major supermarket), the sourcing priority will be to use the buying organisation's power in the market to secure best prices and terms, on a purely transactional basis. This may mean multi-sourcing and opportunistic supplier switching to secure competitive pricing; standardising specifications to make supplier switching easier; and using competitive bidding, auctions and/or buying consortia to secure the best deals.
- For *bottleneck items* (such as proprietary spare parts or specialised consultancy services, which could cause operational delays if unavailable), the sourcing priority will be ensuring control over the continuity and security of supply. This may suggest a rigorous sourcing procedure; approaches such as negotiating medium-term or long-term contracts with suppliers; developing alternative or back-

up sources of supply (multi-sourcing); including incentives and penalties in contracts to ensure the reliability of delivery; or keeping higher levels of buffer or 'safety' stock.

- For *strategic items* (such as core processors bought by a laptop manufacturer), there is likely to be mutual dependency and investment, and the sourcing focus will be on the total cost, security and competitiveness of supply. There will therefore be a need to develop long-term, trust-based, mutually beneficial strategic relationships. A rigorous sourcing process will be required in order to ensure that relationships are developed with the 'right' supply chain partners.

3 Surveying and engaging the market

3.1 'Surveying the market' means identifying or locating suppliers that may potentially be able to supply the requirement. Buyers will constantly be monitoring the supply market(s) relevant to their organisation's requirements, as well as the performance of the existing supplier base. They may also carry out formal supply market research for a given requirement (as discussed in Chapter 7).

Sources of information on potential suppliers

3.2 A number of sources of information may be consulted to identify and research potentially suitable suppliers.

- The buyer's own *database of existing and past suppliers*, including records of their offerings, performance evaluations and so on (discussed in more detail below). This may be supplemented by the buyer's lists of preferred, approved or authorised suppliers, indicating which suppliers have been pre-qualified for use.
- *Formal requests for information (RFI),* often using pre-prepared questionnaires sent to suppliers who might be of interest
- The *marketing communications* of potential suppliers: advertising, direct mail, brochures and catalogues, visits from sales representatives, websites and so on. Catalogues (and their electronic equivalents) may be particularly helpful, with detailed product descriptions, trading terms, price lists and so on.
- *Internet* search for websites including business directories and listings, searchable databases designed to promote exports and specialist purchasing resources (such as the Purchasing Research Service and other sourcing service agencies)
- *Online market exchanges*, auction sites and supplier/buyer forums, which may also allow the posting of requests for quotation and other exchanges
- *Published listings* of suppliers and stockists: general directories (eg the Yellow Pages) and specialist trade/industry directories and registers. Trade directories (eg those published by Dun & Bradstreet) provide information about suppliers' products or services and may also include analysis or rating of the firm's capabilities or financial profile.
- *Trade/industry press* (newspapers, magazines, journals and bulletins) and specialist procurement journals (such as *Supply Management* or *Procurement Professional)* which may carry news and feature articles, supplier advertising, listings, statistical digests and so on.
- *Trade fairs, exhibitions and conferences*, which may provide opportunities for visitors to view competing products and prototypes, meet supplier representatives and contacts, discuss supplier offerings and buyer requirements, and gather relevant literature for the catalogue file. This can often represent cost-effective research, since a number of suppliers are present in one place, and appointments can be made in advance to maximise the use of the time. However, there may also be costs to attending exhibitions, particularly if they are overseas.
- *Organisations promoting trade*, such as trade associations, embassies, chambers of commerce, export associations and so on – and their websites
- *Informal networking* and information exchange with colleagues and other purchasing professionals (eg recommendations and referrals from other buyers, word of mouth about suppliers' reputations).

The supplier database

3.3   Once an organisation has an established supply base, it will usually store information about existing, past and potential suppliers in a *supplier database* or purchasing information system. This might include a range of information: Table 1.1.

Table 1.1 *Supplier information database*

INFORMATION ABOUT EXISTING SUPPLIERS	SOURCES OF INFORMATION
Contact details (including details of account managers, where relevant)	Trade registers and directories, trade/industry exhibitions and conferences
Products and services offered	Supplier literature, websites, corporate reports and accounts
Standard or negotiated terms and conditions of trade, including prices, rates and fees where known	Supplier sales and customer service staff
Approved or preferred status of supplier	Feedback from own staff, vendor managers etc
Average value and frequency of spend with each existing supplier (used to identify key accounts)	Contract and transaction files and records
Special capabilities (eg late customisation capability, EDI) suggesting supplier selection when special needs arise	Reported financial and operational results (eg cost reductions, new product development, lead times)
Results of supplier appraisals, audits and ratings	Supplier appraisal, audit and rating reports
Vendor performance history: quality, lead times, delivery, compliance, disputes	Testimonials or reports from other customers (eg by request or business networking)
Current systems, framework agreements and call-off contracts in place	Electronic performance monitoring (eg goods inwards tracking)

3.4   Having 'surveyed the market' and identified firms that are (theoretically) in the business of supplying the goods or services required, the buyer may choose to find out more about some of the suppliers who are potentially most suitable. Some of this additional 'qualifying' information may be built into the original supply market survey, as outlined earlier. In addition, potentially interesting suppliers may be contacted by telephone or email to request a brochure or catalogue, a visit from the supplier's sales representative, or a visit by the buyer to the supplier (sometimes called a 'site visit').

3.5   However, the buyer may not have been able to gather substantial information about a supplier – or may only have gathered unsubstantiated information: that is, suppliers' claims about themselves (which, as marketing communications, cannot be taken at face value) or the subjective opinions of third parties (which may, likewise, not be entirely accurate or relevant to the buyer's needs).

3.6   For high priority procurements, therefore, a more formal, systematic approach to information gathering about the supplier may be required. This is variously known as 'supplier appraisal', 'supplier evaluation', 'supplier quality assessment' or 'supplier pre-qualification'.

Forming teams with stakeholders for the sourcing process

3.7   In many organisations purchasing is a separate department responsible solely for the procurement of supplies. However, as Lysons and Farrington note, there is an increasing trend towards more integrated structures which take in the wider process of logistics or supply chain management. This includes the whole sequence of activities from the identification of suppliers to the delivery of finished products to end-user customers. 'Such structures emphasise the importance of cross-functional decision-making', because business processes are *horizontal*, cutting across departments and disciplines – and also supply chains.

3.8   There has been a major trend towards the cross-functional and cross-organisational involvement of stakeholders in the sourcing process, often through the formation of project **teams** for sourcing (and other procurement activities).

3.9 A team has been defined as 'a small group of people with complementary skills who are committed to a common purpose, performance goals and approaches for which they hold themselves jointly accountable.' (*Katzenbach & Smith*)

- *Multi-functional* or multi-disciplinary teams bring together individuals from different functional specialisms or departments, so that their competencies can be pooled or exchanged. This is often the case for sourcing and procurement teams, for example.
- *Multi-skilled* teams bring together a number of functionally versatile individuals, each of whom can perform any of the group's tasks. Work can thus be shared or allocated flexibly, according to who is best placed to do a given job when required. This might be the case within a purchasing team, for example, where any member can undertake negotiations, draw up contracts, have knowledge of different categories, prepare investment appraisals and so on, as required.
- *Project teams* and task forces are short-term cross-functional teams, formed for a particular purpose or outcome (eg the integration of information systems, or the review of sourcing strategies) and disbanded once the task is complete. The members of such teams are usually seconded from various functional departments, for the duration of the team's existence, creating a matrix-type structure.
- *Virtual* teams are interconnected groups of people who function as a team – sharing information and tasks, making joint decisions and identifying with the team – but who are not physically present in the same location. Instead, they are linked by ICT tools such as the internet, email, 'virtual meetings' via tele-conferencing, video-conferencing, web-conferencing, shared-access databases and data tracking systems and so on.

3.10 In addition, there may be an opportunity to work in cross-organisational teams: an extension of an internal cross-functional team to include representatives of suppliers or customers. Trent and Monczka argue that supplier participation, in particular, can result in better information exchange; supplier support for the team's objectives; and greater supplier contribution in critical areas (eg product innovation and development).

3.11 Purchasers may participate in permanent or temporary (project based) cross-functional teams dealing with activities such as the implementation of particular strategies for sourcing, global sourcing or outsourcing; quality management and continuous improvement; new product or service development; investment appraisal and capital equipment buying; cost reduction programmes; and research and review.

3.12 Some of the other key stakeholders in the sourcing process would include:

- Users of the items being sourced, who have a clear understanding of desired functionality, operating constraints, training and documentation needs and so on
- The finance function (especially for major capital purchases, for which investment appraisal would be required)
- The product or service design, development or engineering function, which may have prepared the initial specification
- Potential suppliers, who may have resources or expertise to contribute to design and specification, sustainability plans, costing or other parameters in the sourcing decision.

3.13 Dobler and Burt describe four possible approaches to involving stakeholders in design, specification and sourcing processes.

- *Early buyer involvement (EBI).* Management recognises from the outset that purchasing contacts and disciplines are important in product development. Purchasing specialists are involved in the product development team, on an advisory or full-time basis.
- *Formal committee approach.* Management recognises from the outset that preparing a specification is a matter of reconciling conflicting objectives. They appoint a committee with members representing each key stakeholder: design, engineering, production, marketing, quality management and procurement.

- *Informal approach.* Management emphasise the responsibility of all departments to consider both commercial and engineering factors. Buyers are encouraged to challenge the assumptions of users, and to suggest alternative methods and materials for consideration. Designers are encouraged to seek advice from buyers before going too far down any particular design path.
- *Purchasing co-ordinator approach*: a formalisation of the informal approach, with purchasing staff designated as 'liaison officers' to co-ordinate the required communication.

3.14 The concept of **early supplier involvement** (ESI) is that organisations should involve suppliers at an early stage in the product or service development and innovation process: ideally, as early as the conceptual design stage, although this is not always practical. This contrasts with the traditional approach, whereby the supplier merely provides feedback on a completed product design specification.

3.15 The main purpose of ESI is to enable a pre-qualified supplier (with proven supply and technical abilities) to contribute technical expertise which the buying organisation may lack, by making proactive suggestions to improve product or service design, or to reduce the costs of production. There are numerous ways in which suppliers can contribute to the product development process. For example, they can provide constructive criticism of designs, and suggest alternative materials or manufacturing methods at a time when engineering changes are still possible.

3.16 Dobler and Burt cite numerous areas where supplier expertise can benefit the buyer: material specifications; tolerances; standardisation or variety reduction; economic order sizes to reduce costs; packaging and transportation requirements for the product; inventory levels (taking into account lead times); potential changes required in the supplier's manufacturing and/or the buyer's assembly processes to maximise quality or achieve cost savings.

3.17 In service contracting, it is common for the potential service provider to collaboratively develop and negotiate service specifications and service level agreements as part of a cross-functional team with users and purchasers.

3.18 The benefits to be gained from ESI have mainly focused on relatively short-term organisational gains via more accurate and achievable technical specifications, improved product quality, reduction in development time, and reduction in development and product costs. However, there may also be some long-term benefits. ESI can, for example, be a catalyst for long-term partnership relationships with excellent suppliers. It can also improve the buyer's understanding about technological developments in the supply market, with potential for further exploitation.

3.19 As with most approaches, practitioners also need to be aware of potential drawbacks. The product or service may be designed around the supplier's capabilities, which (a) may be limiting, and (b) may lock the buyer into a supply relationship. This may become a problem if the supplier becomes complacent and ceases to deliver the quality or innovation he once did – or if market developments present better alternatives. In addition, ESI may pose confidentiality and security issues (eg the risk of leakage of product plans to competitors).

4 Supplier appraisal and pre-qualification

4.1 The purpose of supplier appraisal, evaluation or pre-qualification is to ensure that a potential supplier will be able to perform any contract or tender that it is awarded, to the required standard. Such a process adds value by avoiding the wasted cost, time, effort and embarrassment of awarding a contract (on the basis of lowest price) to a tenderer who *subsequently* turns out to lack capacity or technical capability to handle the work, or turns out to have systems and values that are incompatible with the buying organisation, or turns out to be financially unstable and unable to complete the work because of cashflow problems or business failure.

Supplier pre-qualification

4.2 'Pre-qualification' in its broadest sense is the definition and assessment of criteria for supplier 'suitability', so that only pre-screened suppliers with certain minimum standards of capability, capacity and compatibility are invited or considered for participation in a given sourcing process. This may be carried out across a range of requirements: to prepare an approved supplier list, for example. Or it may be carried out on a procurement-specific basis, to pre-screen suppliers to receive an invitation to tender or to quote for a contract.

4.3 Having a list of pre-qualified suppliers reduces the investigations needed for individual tenders and purchases: the buyer already knows that any supplier on the approved list has been assessed as capable of fulfilling requirements. This may be particularly helpful where routine purchasing activity is devolved to user department buyers, who may not have the expertise to evaluate or select new suppliers for themselves: instead, they can choose from a list of suppliers pre assessed and qualified by purchasing specialists.

4.4 Pre-qualification is also an important opportunity to embed qualitative selection criteria (such as social and environmental criteria, cultural compatibility or willingness to innovate) in the supplier selection process – without compromising clarity, fairness, competition and economic value in the final selection decision (which can be made primarily on the basis of quantitative criteria such as lowest price or best value).

4.5 Pre-qualification involves two basic processes.

- The development of objective evaluation criteria by which potential suppliers' suitability will be appraised (discussed in Chapter 3)
- The screening of potential suppliers against the defined criteria: for example, using a pre-qualification questionnaire (PQQ) or request for information (RFI).

Supplier appraisal

4.6 Whether or not a separate stage for supplier pre-qualification, screening or shortlisting is applied, there will be a need to appraise or evaluate potential suppliers, in order to assess their capability and suitability, prior to entering into negotiation or other processes for supplier selection and contract award.

4.7 Supplier appraisal is an ambiguous phrase.

- In some contexts (as here) it is used to describe the assessment of potential suppliers as part of supplier selection, prior to contract award or supplier approval.
- In other contexts, it may be used to refer to the assessment of an existing supplier's performance in fulfilling a contract awarded to it. CIPS guidance generally prefers the term 'vendor rating' for this latter kind of assessment, in order to make the distinction clear: the potential 'supplier' has now become an actual 'vendor' (seller) and 'rating' is a common method of carrying out the performance evaluation. (You might also see the term 'supplier performance rating'.) The processes used will be somewhat different (given the better knowledge and access available with an established vendor), but many of the criteria for evaluation are similar.

4.8 Pre-contract supplier appraisal may arise in several circumstances. A supplier may apply to be placed on a list of approved suppliers. Alternatively, a buyer may need to source something that has not been purchased before, or is not available from existing suppliers. In either case, the buyer's aim is to ensure that the potential supplier will be able to perform the contract, if awarded, to the required standard.

4.9 Again, it is worth emphasising that a full-scale supplier appraisal exercise is time-consuming and costly, so it may not be required for all new suppliers (eg for one-off, standardised or low-value purchases). According to Lysons, it will be particularly important, however, for strategic or non-standard items; for major high-value purchases (eg capital equipment); for potential long-term partnership relations; for international sourcing and outsourcing (because of the risks involved); and for supplier development and quality management (in order to identify areas for improvement).

Planning supplier appraisal

4.10 At the planning stage, purchasers will have to consider the following issues.

- The objectives of the appraisal (depending on the purchase situation, the importance of the purchase, the time and budget set aside for the process etc)
- The number of suppliers to be appraised
- The scale, rigour and formality of the process to be used (depending on the information already available, the importance of the purchase etc)
- The time set aside for the process (eg based on the location and feasibility of supplier site visits, the urgency of the purchase situation)
- The resources needed for the process (including personnel eg in a multi-disciplinary appraisal team, information and documentation)
- The likely perspective and response of the supplier(s) to the appraisal process
- Cost-benefit analysis: is the process worth carrying out?

4.11 CIPS have recommended a four-stage approach to assessing suppliers, as part of the supplier selection process.

- Plan and prepare. This could include checking internal policies on supplier selection; checking existing feedback on known suppliers; deciding on the scope of the assessment, depending on the criticality of the proposed procurement; and planning the research or appraisal approach to be used.
- Action and individual assessment: ie accessing available secondary sources of supplier information (such as records, websites and published reports), and implementing appropriate direct assessment methods (such as site visits, capability surveys, output sampling or reference-checking).
- Evaluate and report results
- Recommend and feed back. The end result of the process should be a recommendation on which supplier(s) to adopt, and (in a best practice model) feedback to unsuccessful suppliers on how they can become more competitive, or qualify for contracts, in future.

4.12 Feedback to suppliers is important for a number of reasons. It helps suppliers to improve their performance, and develops the supply market. It helps to build relationships between buyers and potential future suppliers. And it emphasises the important point that the supplier appraisal process is not designed to penalise, but to inform and seek joint benefits.

What should be appraised?

4.13 A supplier appraisal may cover a wide and complex variety of factors that a buyer may consider essential or desirable in its suppliers. One of the main challenges may be to place some kind of practical limit on the number and variety of factors that could form part of the assessment process! The standard procurement literature produces a range of lists of relevant factors: Table 1.2.

Table 1.2 *Potential supplier appraisal factors*

PURCHASING AND SUPPLY CHAIN MANAGEMENT (LYSONS AND FARRINGTON)	PURCHASING PRINCIPLES AND MANAGEMENT (BAILY, FARMER, JESSOP AND JONES)	PURCHASING AND SUPPLY MANAGEMENT (DOBLER AND BURT)
Personal attitudes	Task variables, such as quality, service and price	Results of preliminary survey
Adequacy and care of production equipment	Financial stability	Financial stability
Means of controlling quality	Good management	Good management
Housekeeping	Results of site visits	Results of site visits
Competence of technical staff	Ability to support electronic data interchange	Quality of service
Competence of management	Just in time capabilities	Just in time capabilities

4.14 Criteria should be related to the requirements of the particular buying organisation and procurement type, but another more comprehensive model frequently referred to in the procurement literature is the '**10 Cs'**, which we have adapted (from Ray Carter's original framework) as follows.

- *Competence* (or *capability)* of the supplier to fulfil the contract: whether it can produce the kinds of items, or deliver the kinds of services required; what management, innovation, design or other relevant capabilities it has
- *Capacity* of the supplier to meet the buying organisation's current and future needs: eg how much volume the supplier will be able to handle (its production capacity); and how effectively managed its own supply chain is
- *Commitment* of the supplier to key values such as quality, service or cost management – and to a longer-term relationship with the buying organisation (if desired)
- *Control* systems in place for monitoring and managing resources and risks; eg willingness to comply with procedures, rules or systems required by the buyer; quality or environmental management systems; financial controls; risk management systems and so on
- *Cash* resources to ensure the financial status and stability of the supplier: its profitability, cashflow position (whether it has working funds to pay its bills, buy materials and pay workers), the assets it owns, the debts it owes, how its costs are structured and allocated, and so its overall financial 'health'. These factors will reflect on the ability of the supplier to fulfil its contract with the buyer. They may raise the risk of delivery or quality problems – and more drastic disruption to supply (and complex legal issues) if the supplier's business fails and it becomes insolvent. They will also impact on the prices the supplier will be able to charge.
- *Consistency* in delivering and improving levels of quality and service: eg a 'track record' of reliability, or 'process capability' (robust processes, quality assurance and controls)
- *Cost*: price, whole life costs and value for money offered by the supplier
- *Compatibility* of the supplier with the buying organisation: both cultural (in terms of values, ethics, work approach, management style and so on) and technological (in terms of processes, organisation and IT systems)
- *Compliance* with environmental, corporate social responsibility or sustainability standards, legislation and regulation
- *Communication* efficiency (and supporting technology) to support collaboration and co-ordination in the supply chain.

4.15 Selection and contract award criteria will be discussed in detail in Chapter 3.

5 Gathering and verifying supplier information

5.1 Information about suppliers may be acquired by various means.

- **Self-appraisal questionnaires** completed by suppliers – although the buyer will need to verify the truth and accuracy of supplier-compiled information.
- **Financial appraisal:** analysis of the supplier's financial statements, reports and accounts – or analyses published by credit rating companies (such as Dun & Bradstreet) – providing information on the supplier's financial status and stability; sources of financial risk (such as an excessive debt burden); efficiency; cost structure and profitability; and so on.
- **Checking supplier accreditations,** quality awards and policy statements, in order to assess the robustness of its management systems in areas such as quality, environmental management and corporate social responsibility
- **References,** recommendations, reports and testimonials from existing customers, industry analysts, trade associations, press write-ups or networking with other buyers, to assess the levels of reliability and customer satisfaction attained by the supplier.
- **Work sampling:** checking output samples, prototypes or portfolios of work. This may be done by requesting product samples; randomly sampling production outputs as part of a site visit; making small trial orders; or sampling services with small test contracts or trial periods.
- **Supplier audit** (also called a site visit or capability survey). As this is a more resource-intensive method of appraisal, it might be used for more in-depth investigation of shortlisted suppliers.

5.2 Let's look at some of these approaches in a little more detail. Financial appraisal will be considered separately in Chapters 5 and 6 of this Course Book.

Supplier questionnaires

5.3 Detailed questionnaires should be sent to the potential supplier for completion, posing a range of evaluation questions across the areas discussed in Section 2 above. Many firms use multi-page checklists, similar to vendor rating forms (discussed a bit later in this chapter). The answers are analysed by the buyer, and scored according to a predetermined marking scheme. The supplier can then be rated, for named products or processes, as 'fully approved', 'approved', 'conditionally approved' (requiring improvement) or 'unapproved'.

References

5.4 We noted earlier that one source of information on suppliers is to solicit the opinion of their current or previous customers. One approach to this is to ask potential suppliers for the contact details of selected customers ('references') and to contact those customers to ask about their experience with the supplier ('taking up' the references). Alternatively, the supplier may supply written references or testimonials from customers, which the buyer may follow up by phone (or with a more in-depth questionnaire) to get more details and a less 'prepared' view.

5.5 In either case, you may feel that you are likely to be getting 'positive spin' rather than an unbiased picture, and it may be advisable rather to ask the supplier for its customer list, and permission to contact customers of *your* choice. Suppliers may resist this on quite reasonable grounds (eg to protect the privacy or confidentiality of their customers), but you might still be wary – and choose not to rely solely on any references the supplier provides.

5.6 The purpose of references is to gather a third party (theoretically, objective) view of the supplier's capabilities and performance, and what they are like to deal with. In taking up or following up references (by phone, questionnaire or – for major contracts – personal interview), you might ask a range of questions about areas of interest.

- How would the referee rate the supplier's quality, consistency or service (and how does the referee measure these things)?
- How would the referee rate the supplier's flexibility, responsiveness, innovation, communication?
- What does the referee regard as the supplier's strengths and weaknesses?
- Can the referee cite any critical incidents of excellent or poor quality or service?
- Where there have been quality or service issues, how serious were they, how frequently did they occur, and how co-operative was the supplier in resolving the problems?
- Would the referee use the supplier again, definitely or with some qualification?

Work sampling

5.7   One key way to appraise supplier quality, and/or to verify supplier quality claims, is to evaluate the products or services themselves. This may be done by:

- Requesting samples of the supplier's products, for evaluation
- Randomly sampling the outputs of the supplier's production process, as part of a site visit: that is, inspecting selected items as they come off the production line and/or after they have passed quality control inspection
- Sampling the supplier's products and service with a small trial order
- Sampling the supplier's services with a small test contract, or trial period.

Site visit and capability survey

5.8   Where a potential supplier is accessible, the buyer may use a supplier audit or site visit: a visit to the supplier's premises by a cross-functional appraisal team (eg with experts on purchasing, quality assurance and engineering, say). The team shares responsibility for the decision to approve or reject the supplier on the basis of their observations. A supplier visit can be used for the following purposes.

- To confirm information provided by the supplier in an appraisal questionnaire
- To observe and discuss, in greater detail, the supplier's premises, personnel, equipment, processes (particularly quality management) and outputs
- To enable the buyer to make personal contact with supplier-side account managers and other individuals whose co-operation will be relied on if delivery or other problems occur.

5.9   A *capability survey*, carried out as part of supplier audit, is designed to gather detailed information about the supplier's capabilities.

- *Technical or production capabilities*: its operating capacity, R & D capability, quality management systems, equipment and maintenance, workforce training and productivity and so on
- *Financial capabilities*: financial ratios indicating the company's efficiency, cashflow position, debt and profitability
- *Commercial capabilities*: customer account management, order handling procedures and systems, e-business systems, distribution channels, lead times for delivery and so on
- *Environmental capabilities*: environmental policy, accredited environmental management systems (eg ISO 14001), carbon footprint assessment systems, pollution controls, recovery and recycling procedures, waste/end-of-life disposal methods, 'green' sourcing and so on.

Supplier approval

5.10   Following the appraisal process, one or more suppliers may be officially recognised as being able to meet the standards and requirements of the particular buyer, and therefore eligible for invitations to quote or tender for contracts: this is known as supplier approval. The approval may be for a one-off tender, or may mean that the supplier is put on a list of approved suppliers from which user-department purchasers can source products as required.

6 Vendor performance management

Supplier management

6.1 Many of the value additions (cost savings and improvements) available from procurement are achieved by how a buyer and supplier work together *after* the contract has been awarded. However, buyers have historically given high priority to identifying and evaluating potential suppliers, while paying less attention to the management of supplier relations and performance once contracts have been awarded.

6.2 'Supplier management' is an umbrella term for many aspects of sourcing, contract management and supplier relationship management. Lysons and Farrington define it as:

'That aspect of purchasing or procurement which is concerned with rationalising the supplier base and selecting, co-ordinating, appraising the performance of and developing the potential of suppliers, and where appropriate, building long-term collaborative relationships'.

6.3 There are significant value-adding benefits to the proactive post-contract management of supplier relationships and performance, including the following.

- The company incurs lower costs of identifying, appraising and training new vendors, and lower transaction and contracting costs of multiple sourcing and competitive bidding, by developing a small core group of trusted suppliers.
- Quality and other problems can be ironed out progressively, and continuous improvements made, over a period of feedback, problem-solving and co-operation.
- Goodwill developed with positive relationships may earn preferential treatment or flexibility from suppliers in the event of emergencies (such as materials shortages or underestimated demand leading to urgent orders).
- Suppliers may be more motivated (especially by the promise of long-term, stable business) to give their best performance – and to add value through innovation, flexibility, commitment to continuous improvement and so on.
- Motivated suppliers may be willing to co-invest (eg in research and development, systems integration or staff training).
- There is less risk of supplier failure or poor performance, if performance standards are regularly agreed, monitored and managed.

6.4 After the sourcing, selecting and contracting of suppliers, therefore, it remains the buyer's responsibility:

- To *maintain regular contact* with the supplier, to check on progress and ensure that any issues or problems are discussed
- To *monitor the supplier's performance* against the agreed terms and standards, to ensure that they are being fulfilled: the process of contract management (discussed above).
- To *motivate the supplier*. Of course, the supplier should in any case be motivated by the thought of not gaining repeat business if performance is poor, but this is a somewhat negative incentive. More positively, buyers may introduce systems of recognition for suppliers who achieve consistently high performance.
- To work with the supplier to solve any *performance problems*. Buyers should be ready to accept that their own firm's success depends on the supplier's ability to perform: the process of supporting suppliers in performing well (by sharing information, offering training and so on) is referred to as 'supplier development'.
- To work with the supplier to resolve any *relationship problems* or disputes – ideally, without the costs and damaged relationships arising from taking matters to court (litigation). Constructive and proactive conflict management is essential within long-term partnerships – and to preserve important sources of supply.

Supplier motivation

6.5 'Motivation' is the process by which human beings calculate whether it is worth expending the energy and resources required to reach a particular goal. It is also the process by which one party influences or supports this kind of calculation in another, in order to secure their engagement and effort in pursuit of a goal. Leaders motivate their teams, for example, by offering praise, recognition and perhaps financial bonuses for high-level performance or improvement. Similarly, buyers can motivate suppliers by offering incentives for them to perform to the required standard, or to improve their level of service, or to add value in some other way.

6.6 Motivation can operate positively (the 'carrot' approach), by offering incentives and rewards which are valued by a supplier, and therefore make it worthwhile to put extra effort into attaining the desired behaviour or level of performance. It can also operate negatively (the 'stick' approach), by threatening sanctions or penalties which the supplier will think it worth the effort to *avoid*, by attaining the desired behaviour or level of performance.

6.7 You might wonder if supplier motivation is really necessary, as part of performance management. After all, the buyer usually has an enforceable contract, or service level agreement, with which the supplier is legally bound to comply. Isn't this enough?

6.8 Contracts are themselves part of the process of supplier motivation, because they are legally enforceable: they include sanctions and penalties for non-performance, which the supplier will wish to avoid. However, they only set a minimum level or 'floor' for compliance. If the buyer wants the extra benefits of commitment, flexibility, innovation, proactive problem-solving, continuous improvement and co-operation – over and above what is expressly required by the contract – it will have to make it worth the supplier's while. A purely compliance-based approach to motivation ('Do exactly what the contract requires or else!') creates a compliance-based approach to performance ('You'll get exactly what the contract requires – and no more!').

6.9 **Incentives** for suppliers to perform to the required standard, and/or to improve, are normally built into the contract and other performance management documents. The aim of such incentives is to motivate the supplier by offering increased profit, or some other desirable benefit, as a reward for improved performance or added value.

6.10 Here are some examples of supplier incentives, both financial and non-financial.

- Staged payments (so that the supplier only gets paid in full on completion of the project) or contingency payments (eg part of the payment is linked to results) or faster payment for early delivery (eg pay-on-receipt arrangements)
- Specific key performance indicators (KPIs) or improvement targets linked to recognition and rewards: extension of the contract or the promise of further business; inclusion on the approved or preferred supplier list; publicised supplier awards and endorsements; financial bonuses (eg for extra units of productivity, or each day/week ahead of schedule); and so on.
- Revenue, profit or gain sharing (eg allocating the supplier an agreed percentage or flat fee bonus for cost savings). Where supplier improvements create added value, revenue or profit for the buyer, the 'gain' is shared: a 'win-win' outcome.
- The promise of long-term business agreements or increased business.
- Guaranteed or fixed order levels, allowing the planning of investments and improvements by the supplier
- Opportunities for innovation: eg if the contract gives the provider the chance to implement or devise new solutions that will develop their business and reputation
- A capped price for the product or service that decreases year on year, motivating the supplier progressively to improve efficiency in order to preserve his profit margins

- The offer of development support (eg training or technology sharing)
- Positive feedback sharing, praise and thanks from the buying team for a job well done. (The interpersonal aspects of motivation may not be *sufficient* to secure performance, but they do contribute meaningfully to it. Nobody likes their contribution to be ignored or treated with ingratitude!)

6.11   It is important that incentives are balanced: they should not emphasise one aspect of performance at the expense of other, perhaps less visible, aspects. Otherwise, they might encourage corner-cutting on quality to meet productivity or cost reduction targets, say. They should also be specific (so that it is clear when rewards have been earned) but not so narrowly defined that they stifle flexibility and innovation in pursuit of desired outcomes: focused on results, not on methods and means.

6.12   It is also important that the incentives are fair and easy to administer. Performance criteria must be clear, and objectively measurable in a way that both parties can agree to. Rewards must be given when earned, consistently and without grudging.

6.13   An alternative approach to encourage suppliers to meet performance expectations is to use the threat or fear of being penalised for non-compliance with expectations. Here are some potential **sanctions or penalties**.

- The threat of reduced business for poor performance
- The threat of removal from the approved or preferred supplier list
- Publicised poor supplier gradings ('name and shame')
- Penalty clauses in contracts, entitling the buyer to financial damages in compensation for any losses arising from a supplier's failure to fulfil the contract.

6.14   While penalties support compliance with minimum standards of performance, they usually encourage only short-term improvements at best. Fundamental issues are often not addressed, and the relationship invariably suffers. The 'carrot' is generally acknowledged to be more effective than the 'stick' where the aim is long-term commitment, co-operation and improvement.

Supplier performance evaluation

6.15   There are various good reasons to put effort into the formal evaluation of supplier performance. According to Lysons & Farrington, supplier performance appraisal can:

- Help identify the highest-quality and best-performing suppliers: assisting decision-making regarding: (a) which suppliers should get specific orders; (b) when a supplier should be retained or removed from a preferred or approved list; (c) which suppliers show potential for more strategic partnership relationships; and (d) how to distribute the spend for an item among several suppliers, to manage risk.
- Suggest how relationships with suppliers can (or need to be) enhanced to improve their performance (eg to evaluate the effectiveness of purchasing's supplier selection and contract management processes)
- Help ensure that suppliers live up to what was promised in their contracts
- Provide suppliers with an incentive to maintain and/or continuously improve performance levels
- Significantly improve supplier performance, by identifying problems which can be tracked and fixed, or areas in which support and development is needed.

6.16   Remember that supplier *appraisal* (pre-contract, for the purposes of supplier selection: discussed in Section 4 above) is a somewhat different process from supplier *performance appraisal* (post-contract, for the purposes of management control). The former assesses a potential supplier's *capability* to fulfil the buyer's requirements; the latter assesses a current supplier's *performance* in fulfilling them.

Supplier performance measures

6.17 There are a number of critical success factors in a supplier's performance that a buyer may want to evaluate, and a range of key performance indicators (KPIs) can be selected for each. For a general supply contract, sample CSFs and KPIs are suggested in Table 1.3.

Table 1.3 *General KPIs for supplier performance*

SUCCESS FACTORS	SAMPLE KPIS
Price	• Basic purchase price (and/or price compared with other suppliers) • Whole lifecycle cost of ownership (and/or comparison with other suppliers) • Value and percentage cost reductions (and/or number of cost reduction initiatives proposed or implemented)
Quality/compliance	• Reject, error or wastage rates (or service failures) • Number of customer complaints • Adherence to quality standards (eg ISO 9000) and/or environmental and CSR standards and policies
Delivery	• Frequency of late, incorrect or incomplete delivery • Percentage of on time in full – OTIF – deliveries
Service/relationship	• Competence, congeniality and co-operation of account managers • Promptness in dealing with enquiries and problems • Adherence to agreements on after-sales service
Financial stability	• Ability to meet financial commitments and claims • Ability to maintain quality and delivery
Innovation capability	• Number of innovations proposed or implemented (and/or investment in research & development) • Willingness to collaborate in cross-organisational innovation teams
Technology leverage/ compatibility	• Proportion of transactions carried out electronically • Number of technology breakdowns
Overall performance	• Benchmarking against other suppliers • Commitment to continuous improvement (eg number of suggestions proposed or implemented)

Performance monitoring and review

6.18 Performance monitoring (checking progress and performance against defined key performance indicators or KPIs) and review (looking back at performance over the planning period) may be carried out in various ways.

- *Continuous monitoring* may be possible in some contexts: electronic monitoring tools, for example, allow variance or exception reports to be produced whenever results (eg productivity, costs or on-time-in-full deliveries) deviate from plan, within defined parameters or tolerances.
- More generally, performance may be monitored at key stages of a process, project or contract: for example, at the end of project stages, or production or delivery deadlines.
- *Periodic reviews* are often used: examining results against defined measures or targets at regular or fixed intervals. The purpose of such reviews is generally 'formative': supplying feedback information while it is still relevant for the adjustment of performance or plans. So, for example, a buyer may sample a supplier's process outputs periodically, to check quality and conformance to specification. Buyer-side and supplier-side teams may meet periodically to discuss any issues in contract performance.
- *Post-completion reviews* are often used for projects and contracts, with the purpose of exchanging feedback and learning any lessons for the future.

6.19 There is a wide range of feedback mechanisms for gathering data on supplier performance, and comparing them against relevant performance measures. Which mechanism is used will depend on what kind of quantitative or qualitative data is required, and what aspect of performance is being evaluated. Here are some examples.

- The gathering of feedback from internal and external customers and other stakeholders, using feedback groups, complaint procedures, survey questionnaires and project reviews
- The gathering of performance information through observation, testing (eg quality inspections), and analysis of documentation, transaction records and management reports (eg analysis of inspection reports, and so on)
- Budgetary control: monitoring actual costs against budgeted or forecast costs
- Formal performance reviews or appraisals (sometimes called 'vendor rating' exercises): reviewing performance against benchmark standards, KPIs and/or agreed service levels, and feeding back the information for improvement planning
- Contract management, continually monitoring compliance with contract terms
- Regular meetings between buyer and supplier representatives (or project or account managers) to review general progress, or specific issues such as rates or delivery problems, and exchange feedback on 'how things are going'
- Project management: reports and meetings at the end of key project stages or milestones; periodic 'highlight' reports by the project manager; and post-completion review and reporting, with the aim of extracting learning for the next project
- The use of consultants to monitor compliance with quality standards, benchmarks or ethical standards (eg monitoring overseas suppliers' treatment of their workforces)
- The use of technical specialists to monitor supplier performance (eg on construction or IT projects) beyond the expertise of purchasers.

Vendor rating

6.20   Vendor rating is the measurement of supplier performance using agreed criteria, usually including the following.

- *Price*: eg measured by value for money, market price or under, lowest or competitive pricing, good cost management and reasonable profit margins
- *Quality*: eg measured by key performance indicators (KPIs) such as the number or proportion of defects, quality assurance procedures
- *Delivery*: eg measured by KPIs such as the proportion of on-time in-full (OTIF) deliveries, or increases or decreases in lead times for delivery

Other measurable factors might include: after-sales service, efficiency and accuracy of contract management and administration, willingness to commit to continuous improvement, quality of contacts and communication, contribution to innovation, flexibility and responsiveness to urgent or unusual requests – and so on.

6.21   One common approach to vendor rating is based on the use of a *supplier performance evaluation form*: a checklist of key performance factors, against which purchasers assess the supplier's performance as good, satisfactory or unsatisfactory: Figure 1.3 (adapted from *Dobler & Burt*). A weighting is applied to each factor, so that the supplier's performance in key performance areas, and overall, can be summarised as good, satisfactory or unsatisfactory. This is comparatively easy to implement, once meaningful checklists have been developed, but it is fairly broad and subjective.

Figure 1.3 *Vendor rating form*

SUPPLIER:		DATE:	
Summary evaluation, by department	**Good**	**Satisfactory**	**Unsatisfactory**
Purchasing	☐	☐	☐
Receiving	☐	☐	☐
Accounting	☐	☐	☐
Engineering	☐	☐	☐
Quality	☐	☐	☐
	☐	☐	☐

Performance factors

Purchasing

	Good	Satisfactory	Unsatisfactory
Delivers on schedule	☐	☐	☐
Delivers at quoted price	☐	☐	☐
Prices are competitive	☐	☐	☐
Prompt and accurate with routine documents	☐	☐	☐
Anticipates our needs	☐	☐	☐
Helps in emergencies	☐	☐	☐
Does not unfairly exploit a single-source position	☐	☐	☐
Does not request special consideration	☐	☐	☐
Currently supplies price, catalogue and technical information	☐	☐	☐
Furnishes specially requested information promptly	☐	☐	☐
Advises us of potential troubles	☐	☐	☐
Has good labour relations	☐	☐	☐
Delivers without constant follow-up	☐	☐	☐
Replaces rejections promptly	☐	☐	☐
Accepts our terms without exception	☐	☐	☐
Keeps promises	☐	☐	☐
Has sincere desire to serve	☐	☐	☐

Receiving

	Good	Satisfactory	Unsatisfactory
Delivers per routing instructions	☐	☐	☐
Has adequate delivery service	☐	☐	☐
Has good packaging	☐	☐	☐

Accounting

	Good	Satisfactory	Unsatisfactory
Invoices correctly	☐	☐	☐
Issues credit notes punctually	☐	☐	☐
Does not ask for special financial consideration	☐	☐	☐

Engineering

	Good	Satisfactory	Unsatisfactory
Past record on reliability of products	☐	☐	☐
Has technical ability for difficult work	☐	☐	☐
Readily accepts responsibility for latent deficiencies	☐	☐	☐
Provides quick and effective action in emergencies	☐	☐	☐
Furnishes requested data promptly	☐	☐	☐

Quality

	Good	Satisfactory	Unsatisfactory
Quality of material	☐	☐	☐
Furnishes certification, affidavits, etc	☐	☐	☐
Replies with corrective action	☐	☐	☐

6.22 Another approach is the *factor rating method*, which gives a quantified, numerical score for each key assessment factor. For example, the measure of quality performance might be '100% *minus* percentage of rejects in total deliveries': a supplier whose deliveries contained 3% rejects would score 97% or 0.97 on this measure. Each of the major factors is also given a *weighting*, according to its importance within overall performance, and this is applied to each score, to end up with an overall score or rating: Figure 1.4.

Figure 1.4 *Factor rating method*

Performance factor	Weighting	Score	Supplier rating
Price	0.4	0.94	0.376
Quality	0.4	0.97	0.388
Delivery	0.2	0.72	0.144
Overall evaluation	1.0		0.908

6.23 The supplier in our example has achieved a rating of 0.908 out of a possible 1. This score can be compared with that achieved by other suppliers, and gives a good measure of exactly where each stands in the order of preference. It may also be used year on year, to provide a measure of whether a supplier's performance is improving or declining.

6.24 Of course, neither approach to vendor rating diagnoses the *causes* of any performance shortfalls identified, nor what needs to be done to address them. A vendor rating should therefore be seen within the whole process of performance management: Figure 1.5.

Figure 1.5 *Vendor rating*

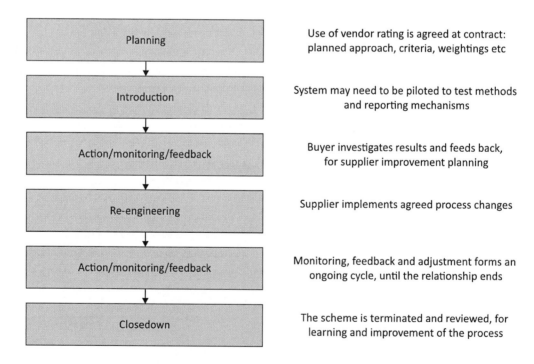

Planning	Use of vendor rating is agreed at contract: planned approach, criteria, weightings etc
Introduction	System may need to be piloted to test methods and reporting mechanisms
Action/monitoring/feedback	Buyer investigates results and feeds back, for supplier improvement planning
Re-engineering	Supplier implements agreed process changes
Action/monitoring/feedback	Monitoring, feedback and adjustment forms an ongoing cycle, until the relationship ends
Closedown	The scheme is terminated and reviewed, for learning and improvement of the process

6.25 Lysons and Farrington note that supplier 'performance scorecards' are increasingly being superseded by more integrated supplier performance management systems, using available information and communication technology (ICT) packages, which provide:

- Real-time visibility into performance across all products and suppliers
- Complex supplier evaluations, utilising data from all areas of the supply chain and performance

- Alert notifications if supplier performance varies from key performance indicators beyond acceptable pre-determined tolerance ranges
- Immediate communication to suppliers regarding performance – as opposed to waiting for periodic reviews, by which time problems may have escalated.

Chapter summary

- The main stages of a generic procurement process can be represented as a cycle, from identification of a need through to management of the contract and the supplier.
- Sourcing is the process of identifying, selecting and developing suppliers.
- Stages in a strategic sourcing process include: identification of a need; forming a sourcing plan; market analysis; pre-qualification of suppliers; evaluating supply offers and options; creation of contract or relationship.
- The extent of a sourcing exercise will be determined partly by the priority of the required supply. Pareto analysis and the Kraljic matrix are two methods of prioritising.
- To survey the market a buyer has a wide range of formal and informal information sources.
- It is usual to pre-qualify suppliers to ensure that they have the capacity and capability to carry out any contract that may subsequently be awarded to them.
- Carter's 10Cs provide a useful framework for appraising suppliers before contract award.
- Information about suppliers may be gained from sources such as: self-appraisal questionnaires; financial appraisal; checking accreditations; references from other customers; work sampling; and supplier audit.
- The buyer's work is not complete once the contract is awarded. Buyers must continue to manage the supplier and the contract to achieve a successful outcome.
- Buyers can motivate suppliers by means of incentives, penalties, or a mix of both.
- Monitoring of supplier performance must be made against key performance indicators and may involve a formal system of vendor rating.

Self-test questions

Numbers in brackets refer to the paragraphs where you can check your answers.

1   What are the main stages in a generic procurement process? (Figure 1.1)

2   Distinguish between strategic sourcing and tactical or operational sourcing. (1.7, 1.8)

3   Distinguish between straight re-buy, modified re-buy and new buy. Why is the distinction important in relation to sourcing? (2.3)

4   Sketch Kraljic's matrix. (Figure 1.2)

5   List sources of information on potential suppliers. (3.2)

6   What items of information might a buyer store in a supplier database? (3.3)

7   What are the four stages in the approach to assessing suppliers recommended by CIPS? (4.11)

8   List Carter's 10Cs. (4.14)

9   Explain how customer references may be used in supplier appraisal. (5.4–5.6)

10   What are the benefits of post-contract relationship management? (6.3)

11   Give examples of supplier incentives. (6.10)

12   List benefits of supplier performance evaluation. (6.15)

13   List mechanisms for obtaining feedback on supplier performance. (6.19)

CHAPTER 2

Sourcing Strategy

Assessment criteria and indicative content

1.2 Compare the main approaches to the sourcing of requirements from suppliers

- Sole sourcing
- Single, dual and multiple sourcing arrangements
- The use of tendering: open, restricted and negotiated approaches to tendering
- Direct negotiations with suppliers
- Intra company trading and transfer pricing arrangement
- Implications of international sourcing

2.3 Produce a plan for the sourcing of goods or services from external suppliers

- The structure of a plan for sourcing goods or services from external suppliers

4.2 Explain the main processes used for obtaining quotations and tenders

- Decision criteria for dispensing with tendering

Section headings

1. The supplier base
2. Different approaches to letting contracts
3. Intra-company trading
4. Other aspects of sourcing policy and strategy

Introduction

In the previous chapter we looked at sourcing as a generic process or sequence of stages.

In this chapter we look at some of the different 'approaches' to the sourcing of requirements from suppliers, depending on strategy, policy and context.

We start by exploring the implications of having a sole source, or multiple sources, of supply to draw on – and, where there are multiple suppliers, the factors to take into account in deciding how many suppliers to use. What is the 'best' size for an organisation's supplier base? What are the benefits and drawbacks of switching between suppliers for ongoing requirements, rather than developing closer relationships with a smaller number of suppliers?

Next, we look at different approaches to letting contracts, depending on the size and complexity of the contract and the buying situation.

We give some consideration to the particular case of intra-organisational supply (that is, sourcing from other units within the buying organisation), and how this differs from sourcing from external suppliers.

Finally, we raise briefly the implications of international sourcing – although this topic will be dealt with in detail in Chapters 11 and 12.

1   The supplier base

1.1   The 'supplier base' is all the vendors that supply a given purchaser. Supplier bases are often described in terms of their size or range (broad, narrow, single-sourced); location (local, national, international or global); and characteristics (eg diversified or specialised).

1.2   Let's start with the issue of range. How broad should the supplier base be?

Multiple sourcing arrangements

1.3   One approach to managing supply risk is by having *more* potential suppliers of a given item or category of purchases, pre-qualified and approved as being able to meet the buyer's requirements.

1.4   One advantage of multiple sourcing is that if there are supply shortages or disruptions (eg because of political unrest or bad weather in one supplier's area), or unforeseen peaks in demand (creating a need for extra supply), or a supplier failure, the organisation has established relationships with a wide range of approved alternative suppliers.

1.5   Another advantage of multi-sourcing is that as circumstances change – for both buyer and supplier – suppliers may become more or less compatible with the buying organisation, and more or less competitive in terms of their offering. Increasing the range of pre-qualified potential suppliers enables the buyer to be more *opportunistic*: taking advantage of the best available price, trading terms, quality, innovation and flexibility on offer at any given time.

1.6   Such a policy is also likely to keep the supplier base competitive, as each supplier knows that it is competing for contracts with a number of other sources of supply.

1.7   However, there are disadvantages of multiple sourcing arrangements.

- They can lead to unnecessarily high procurement costs. A large supplier base usually means more small orders and higher transaction and administration costs: giving larger orders to fewer suppliers, on the other hand, would secure volume discounts and other savings (eg through systems integration with key suppliers)
- They fail to exploit the value-adding and competitive potential of concentrating on more collaborative relationships with fewer suppliers (eg continuous improvement over time, co-investment in innovation and quality, better communication and integration and so on)
- They can lead to waste, by retaining suppliers who cannot (or can no longer) meet the firm's requirements, or are otherwise not often used – and perhaps by increasing stock variety and proliferation, where different suppliers have slightly different products (so that ordering from multiple suppliers works against standardisation, variety reduction and inventory reduction)

Supplier base optimisation

1.8   More commonly these days, however, strong collaborative supplier relationships are used to 'narrow supply', enabling purchases to be concentrated on a smaller group of developed and trusted supply partners. Supplier base optimisation (or rationalisation) is concerned with determining roughly how many suppliers the buying firm wants to do business with.

1.9   Optimising the range of the supply base enables the firm to:

- Avoid the drawbacks and inefficiencies of multiple sourcing (highlighted above)
- Leverage the potential of closer, long-term, collaborative relationships with a few trusted, high-capability supply chain partners
- Maintain the security of supply by ensuring that there are *enough* approved suppliers to cover supplier failure, shortages or other supply risks.

1.10 'The aim of supplier base optimisation is to leverage the buying power of an organisation with the smallest number of suppliers consistent with security of supplies and the need for high-quality goods and services at competitive prices.' (Lysons & Farrington)

1.11 In order to develop this opportunity, existing suppliers will have to be evaluated on performance, cost, service, quality, volume of business and potential or compatibility for closer relationship. An approved or preferred supplier list will usually be drawn up, weeding out unnecessary suppliers.

1.12 From our emphasis on security of supply, you might be able to infer the possible downside risk of reducing the supplier base. A very narrow supplier base opens the buyer to the risks of:

- Over-dependence on a few suppliers, in the event of supplier failure (eg financial collapse or reputational damage)
- Supply disruption (eg due to strikes, technology breakdown or natural disaster affecting the supplier or *its* suppliers)
- The loss of preferred suppliers' goodwill and co-operation
- Preferred suppliers growing complacent (because of the stability of the relationship and the buyer's comparative dependence), and ceasing to offer competitive value
- Being 'locked in' to long-term relationship and co-investment with suppliers who turn out to be under-performing or incompatible with the culture, ethics or objectives of the buying organisation
- Missing out on seeking or utilising new or more competitive suppliers in the wider supply market.

Single and dual sourcing arrangements

1.13 At the very narrow end of the scale, a single supplier may be selected for the development of closer partnership relations or an 'exclusive supply' contract: an approach called **single sourcing**.

1.14 Such an arrangement might be suitable for procurements for which the buyer hopes to gain supplier commitment and co-investment (eg for strategic or critical items) or preferential treatment (eg on price, for leverage items), by offering the supplier exclusivity.

1.15 Buyers now increasingly recognise that multiple sourcing is not the only way to minimise supply risk or secure competitive supply. Single sourcing may be considered appropriate where:

- The total requirement is too small to justify splitting orders among several suppliers, because the unit costs of handling and processing would rise as a result
- One supplier is so far ahead of others in terms of reputation, quality, price etc that it would make no sense to use anyone else
- Expensive set-up costs (eg tooling or systems integration) are required to enable supply: it may not make sense for the buyer to pay for such tooling several times over by using several different suppliers
- The requirement is subject to supply risk, or in short supply: the buyer is likely to be treated more favourably by an exclusive supplier than by any one of several lower-volume and lower-value suppliers.

1.16 This is, of course, the most risky approach on the supplier base spectrum: if a single supplier fails, the buyer is left completely exposed. It might pre-qualify a 'back-up' supplier, as part of a contingency plan, in order to manage the risk of supply or supplier failure – but this may not provide sufficient incentive for the contingency supplier, or any guarantee that the contingency supplier will be ready or willing to supply when required.

1.17 For this reason, many organisations prefer the option of sharing supply between two suppliers: an approach called **dual sourcing.** This enables the buyer to maximise the advantages of narrow supply – while managing the risks of over-dependency on a single supplier.

1.18 Supplier complacency is a key issue in both single and dual sourcing. When suppliers have the business wrapped up under a long-term agreement, they may not be motivated to innovate, continuously improve or provide competitive value. The buyer must be confident in the supplier's commitment before entering such a deal, and must manage incentives, service level agreements and continuous improvement programmes effectively to maintain competitive performance.

1.19 Supplier failure can have severe consequences, particularly if the organisation is tied into a single-sourcing agreement. The financial stability and risk factors of sole suppliers should be monitored closely, and highlighted in the supply chain risk management process.

1.20 Effective contingency planning can mitigate the impact of supplier failure. Back-up or alternative suppliers should be provisionally pre-qualified and accredited where possible. It may be difficult to keep a back-up supplier interested if no business is being offered, but many suppliers are aware that being considered as a contingency is better than not being considered at all! There may also be a risk of undermining the confidence of the main supply partner – and the arrangement will need to be carefully handled.

Partnership sourcing

1.21 The key point about single or dual sourcing is that (a) it *enables* buyers to focus on developing more collaborative value-adding relationships with the selected suppliers, and (b) it *requires* buyers to develop more collaborative, committed long-term relationships with selected suppliers, in order to minimise supply risk. Single-source and dual-source arrangements are generally accompanied by a strong emphasis on mutual commitment, co-investment and relationship building, sometimes identified as 'partnering' or 'partnership sourcing'.

1.22 Partnering has been defined as: 'A commitment by both customers and suppliers, regardless of size, to a long-term relationship based on clear, mutually agreed objectives to strive for world class capability and effectiveness.'

1.23 Partnership Sourcing Limited has identified a number of contexts in which partnership sourcing, in particular, may be most beneficial.

- Where the customer has a high spend with the supplier
- Where the customer faces high risk: continual supply of the product or service is vital to the buyer's operations, regardless of its market value
- Where the product supplied is technically complex, calling for advanced technical knowledge by the supplier (and making the cost of switching suppliers high)
- Where the product is vital and complex, requiring a lot of time, effort and resources ('high hassle') to manage
- Where the supply market for the product is fast-changing, so that an up-to-date knowledge of technological or legislative changes in the market is essential
- In a restricted supply market, where there are few competent and reliable supplier firms – and closer relationships could therefore improve the security of supply.

1.24 The key characteristics of partnership sourcing (according to the CIPS reference paper *Partnership Sourcing*) are as follows.

- Cultural compatibility between the partners
- A high level of trust, knowledge sharing and openness between customer and supplier, extending to the sharing of cost data by both parties (cost transparency)
- Mutual acceptance of the concept of win-win within the supply chain: that is, collaborating to add value and achieve competitive advantage which benefits all participants
- Relevant expertise, resources or competencies in complementary areas (so that each party brings something valuable to the collaboration)
- Clear joint objectives and meaningful performance measures for assessing supply chain performance (focused on quality, cost and service)

- The use of cross-functional teams to enhance co-ordination, process focus and continuous improvement.
- A total quality management philosophy, focused on co-operative efforts to maximise quality and secure continuous improvement
- A high degree of systems integration.

1.25 Lysons and Farrington note that: 'Partnering aims to transform short-term adversarial customer-supplier relationships focused on the use of purchasing power to secure lower prices and improved delivery into long-term co-operation based on mutual trust in which quality, innovation and shared values complement price competitiveness'.

1.26 However, they also quote Ramsay on the downside view.

'As a sourcing strategy, partnerships may be generally applicable to only a small number of very large companies. For the rest, although it may be useful with a minority of purchases and a very small selection of suppliers, it is a high-risk strategy that one might argue ought to be approached with extreme caution. In Kraljic's terms, the act of moving the sourcing of a bought-out item from competitive pressure to a single-sourced partnership increases both supply risk and profit impact: thus partnerships tend to push all affected purchases towards the strategic quadrant. Strategic purchases offer large rewards if managed successfully, but demand the allocation of large amounts of management attention and threaten heavy penalties if sourcing arrangements fail.'

1.27 The advantages and disadvantages of partnership sourcing, from both the buyer's and the supplier's perspective, can be summarised as follows: Table 2.1.

Table 2.1 *Advantages and disadvantages of partnering*

ADVANTAGES FOR THE BUYER	DISADVANTAGES FOR THE BUYER
Greater stability of supply and supply prices	Risk of complacency re cost/quality
Sharing of risk and investment	Less flexibility to change suppliers at need
Better supplier motivation and responsiveness, arising from mutual commitment and reciprocity	Possible risk to confidentiality, intellectual property (eg if suppliers also supply competitors)
Cost savings from reduced supplier base, collaborative cost reduction	May be locked into relationship with an incompatible or inflexible supplier
Access to supplier's technology and expertise	Restricted in EU public sector procurement directives (eg re-tendering after 3–5 years)
Joint planning and information sharing, supporting capacity planning and efficiency	May be locked into relationship, despite supply market changes and opportunities
Ability to plan long-term improvements	Costs of relationship management
More attention to relationship management: eg access to an account manager	Mutual dependency may create loss of flexibility and control
ADVANTAGES FOR THE SUPPLIER	DISADVANTAGES FOR THE SUPPLIER
Greater stability and volume of business, enabling investment in business development	May be locked into relationship with an incompatible or inflexible customer
Working with customers, enabling improved service, learning and development	Gains/risks may not be fairly shared in the partnership (depending on power balance)
Joint planning and information sharing, supporting capacity planning and efficiency	Risk of customer exploiting transparency (eg on costings, to force prices down)
Sharing of risk and investment	Investment in relationship management
Cost savings from efficiency, collaborative cost reduction, payment on time	Dependency on customer may create loss of flexibility and control
Access to customer's technology and expertise	Restricted by EU public sector procurement directives
More attention to relationship management: eg access to a vendor manager	May be locked into relationship, despite market changes and opportunities

Sole sourcing

1.28 The term 'sole sourcing' (as distinguished from 'single sourcing') refers to a situation in which there is only one supplier available in the supply market for a given procurement. The market may be dominated by a single supplier: a market structure known as a monopoly.

1.29 The conditions for a monopoly are as follows.

- Only one supplier of the good or service exists in the supply market. It may be a single organisation, or a group of producers acting together to control supply (eg a cartel such as the Organisation of Petroleum Exporting Countries, or OPEC).
- There are high 'barriers to entry', preventing other competing firms from entering the market. Examples include: high business set-up costs; sole ownership of copyrights, designs, patents, proprietary technology or processes; or the existing producer monopolising available sources of supply and/or distribution channels.
- There are no close substitutes for the good or service available (which would enable buyers to switch solutions – and therefore switch suppliers).

1.30 If these conditions are met, the monopolist essentially controls supply, and has absolute power to determine the price of the good in its market: it is said to be a *'price maker'*. It is this feature which can lead to customers and consumers being over-charged, which is why monopoly markets (as a potential abuse of a dominant market position) are regulated by anti-competition law in the UK and EU.

1.31 The main concern for buyers will be a monopoly supplier's absolute power in the market: there will be no opportunity for the buyer to take its business elsewhere, so the monopolist will be able to dictate terms and conditions of trade. The only alternatives will be to seek substitute goods or services which would meet the same business need, *or* to seek new supply markets, perhaps internationally: this may even be a helpful spur to strategic thinking and innovation.

1.32 Prices will generally be higher in the absence of competition, and the buyer will not be able to exert pressure to reduce prices – nor to improve quality or service levels: its business may represent only a small part of a large supplier's revenue. However, some monopolists enjoy *economies of scale:* that is, cost savings due to their large size. Large-scale operations make greater use of advanced machinery and efficient mass production techniques; are able to access finance more cheaply; are able to benefit from bulk discounts on input purchases; and so on. Some of these cost savings *may* be passed on to buyers in the form of reasonable prices – although this may have to be achieved by regulation. Regulation limits the prices that monopolists are allowed to charge, in the case of privatised industries in the UK, for example.

1.33 Another issue of concern is that buyers may be unable to specify their exact supply requirements, since the monopoly supplier has little incentive to tailor its product range to the needs of buyers. There may be little or no choice, customisation or innovation – and this might be a serious problem for buyers whose own competitive market is highly specialised or fast-changing. Again, however, this is not *necessarily* the case: monopolists may have more resources to invest in customisation, flexibility and innovation, with the incentive of even higher profits.

2   Different approaches to letting contracts

2.1 There are a number of different approaches to letting a purchase contract, depending on the type of purchase and company policy.

2.2 The organisation may already have negotiated a **framework agreement** or standing contract with a supplier, to meet a requirement of a certain type. In such a case, the requirement will simply be notified to the pre-contracted supplier by a purchase or call-off order, on the pre-agreed terms. Alternatively, buyers may be authorised to make purchases up to a certain value from the **catalogues** of pre-approved suppliers: catalogue purchasing is often used for low-value purchases and routine supply replenishments, for example.

2.3   As we have seen, there may be only one available supplier, or the organisation may have negotiated a preferred supplier or sole supplier agreement with a dependable supply partner. In such a case, the buyer may simply negotiate a contract with the preferred or designated supplier.

2.4   The organisation may send an 'enquiry' to one or more shortlisted suppliers, in the form of a request for quotation (RFQ), a request for information (RFI) or request for proposal (RFP). Such enquiries will typically set out the details of the requirement: the contact details of the purchaser, the quantity and description of goods and services required, the required place and date of delivery, and the buyer's standard terms and conditions of business. It will then invite the supplier(s) to submit a proposal and price for the job. These may be evaluated:

- As a basis for negotiation of price and other terms with the supplier or suppliers
- On a competitive basis: eg the best value offer or proposal 'wins' the contract (as in competitive bidding or tendering).

2.5   The organisation may have different procedures in place for orders of different volume or value. For order values under £100, say, there may be no formal requirement for supplier selection. For orders between £100 and £5,000, there may be a negotiation process, or three suppliers may be requested to provide quotations, to test the market and ensure competitive pricing. For orders over £5,000 in value, a full competitive bidding or tendering process may be required.

2.6   The syllabus addresses two main approaches: direct negotiation with suppliers, and the use of tendering or competitive bidding.

Direct negotiation with suppliers

2.7   Negotiation may be the main approach by which contract terms are arrived at, or may be used in support of tendering (eg to improve aspects of the preferred tender, or to ensure that all aspects of the requirement, bid and contract are understood).

2.8   Negotiation is a massive area of study in its own right, and you will cover it in detail as part of your studies for *Negotiating and Contracting with Suppliers*. Basically, negotiation is defined by Dobler *et al*, in the purchasing context, as: 'A process of planning, reviewing and analysing used by a buyer and a seller to reach acceptable agreements or compromises [which] include all aspects of the business transaction, not just price'.

2.9   The process is summed up by Gennard and Judge *(Employee Relations)* as one of:

- *Purposeful persuasion*: each party tries to persuade the other to accept its case or see its viewpoint and
- *Constructive compromise*: both parties accept the need to move closer to each other's position, identifying the areas of common ground where there is room for concessions to be made.

2.10   In a contract negotiation, the buyers' main objectives may be as follows. *(Dobler et al)*

- To obtain a fair and reasonable (or advantageous) price for the quantity and quality of goods specified
- To get the supplier to perform the contract on time
- To exert some control over the manner in which the contract is performed
- To persuade the supplier to give maximum co-operation to the buyer's company
- To develop a sound and continuing relationship with competent suppliers.

Where a relationship is ongoing, one particular issue may have come to the fore, but more often there are multiple objectives, especially in negotiations with a new supplier or potential supplier.

2.11 Negotiation objectives should be ranked as high priority, medium priority or low priority. Most negotiations depend on concessions from both sides, and this ranking procedure will help negotiators to determine where they can best afford to give ground or make concessions (low priority objectives) and which areas are non-negotiable (high priority objectives). If one side's low priority (easy to concede) objectives coincide with the other's medium or high priority (valuable to gain) objectives, there is significant potential for constructive bargaining.

2.12 There are two basic approaches to the negotiation of contract terms with suppliers.

- *Distributive bargaining* involves the distribution of limited resources, or 'dividing up a fixed pie'. One party's gain can only come at the expense of the other party: this is sometimes called a zero-sum game, or a win-lose outcome. If the buyer pushes the price down, for example, the supplier's profit margin will be eroded.
- *Integrative bargaining* involves collaborative problem-solving to increase the options available (or 'expanding the pie'), with the aim of exploring possibilities for both parties to find a mutually satisfying or win-win solution. This may also be called 'added value negotiating' (AVN): the aim is to add value to the deal, rather than extracting value from or conceding value to the other party.

2.13 The foundation for win-win or integrative approaches in supply negotiations is the belief that co-operation along the supply chain can lead to elimination of waste and performance improvements, benefiting all parties. A buyer who focuses exclusively on one objective – say, gaining a 5% price reduction – may miss opportunities to widen the discussion fruitfully. For example, by co-operating with the supplier in improved quality assurance measures, the costs of quality may fall for both parties: this may be enough in itself to achieve the desired improvement in profits, without squeezing the supplier's margins.

Tendering: decision criteria for adopting it or dispensing with it

2.14 The organisation may prefer to use a competitive bidding or tendering procedure, in which potential suppliers are issued with an invitation to tender (ITT), or an invitation to bid for a contract, with the buyer intending to choose the supplier submitting the best proposal or the lowest price.

2.15 When should a procurement function use competitive bidding rather than a negotiation? Dobler and Burt (*Purchasing & Supply Management*) give guidelines for making the decision: Table 2.2.

Table 2.2 *The use of competitive bidding*

FIVE CRITERIA FOR THE USE OF COMPETITIVE BIDDING	FOUR SITUATIONS IN WHICH COMPETITIVE BIDDING SHOULD NOT BE USED
The value of the procurement should be high enough to justify the expense of the process	It is impossible to estimate production costs accurately
The specifications must be clear and the potential suppliers must have a clear idea of the costs involved in fulfilling the contract	Price is not the only or most important criterion in the award of the contract
There must be an adequate number of potential suppliers in the market	Changes to specification are likely as the contract progresses
The potential suppliers must be both technically qualified and keen to win the business	Special tooling or set-up costs are major factors in the requirement
There must be sufficient time available for the procedure to be carried out	

2.16 We might add that competitive bidding should be used where it is *required* by organisational policy (eg for particular procurement categories or contracts of a certain value) or by external regulation. Competitive tendering is compulsory in the UK public sector, for example, for procurements by public bodies over a certain financial threshold, under the EU Public Procurement Directives (enacted in UK law by the Public

Contracts Regulations 2006). We will discuss the particular requirements of the regulations in Chapter 10, in the context of public sector procurement.

2.17 There are several value-adding advantages to competitive bidding or tendering. It ensures fairness and genuine competition between suppliers. It ensures that procurement decisions are soundly based on cost and value for money. It also engages a wide choice of suppliers (particularly if open tendering, or open advertisement of the tender, is used) – which may encourage innovative solutions to requirements.

2.18 However, there are also drawbacks, particularly to open tendering processes.

- Wide competition may discourage some potentially suitable bidders.
- There may be inadequate pre-qualification of bidders, creating the risk of capability or capacity problems emerging late in the process.
- Competition based primarily on the lowest price may put insufficient focus on important criteria such as quality and sustainability: the lowest-price bid may not represent the best long-term value.
- Tendering places a potentially large administrative burden on buyers.
- Contract award may be a one-off, not leading suppliers to expect further business. In other words, competitive tenders do not result in deepening buyer-supplier relationships. This may lead to a widening of the supplier base – whereas the trend (as we have seen) is to develop closer value-adding collaborative relationships with fewer suppliers. There may also be little incentive for suppliers to perform to the highest standard (as a committed, loyal supply chain partner might do), over and above compliance with the minimum standards set by the contract specification.

Tendering procedures

2.19 There are several approaches to tendering, and we will discuss them in detail in later chapters. However, to give you an initial overview:

- **Open procedures** are open to any potential bidder on the basis of a widely advertised invitation to tender (eg in an open reverse e-auction). All bids are evaluated against the requirements set out in the ITT and associated tender documentation, and the contract is awarded on strictly competitive criteria (such as lowest price or best value).
- **Selective or restricted procedures** add a pre-tender qualification stage. Potential suppliers who respond to the tender advertisement are pre-qualified (eg on the basis of their technical competence and financial standing, often using a pre-qualification questionnaire). A relatively small number of suppliers (typically 3–10) are then shortlisted for invitation to tender and participation in the tender process.
- **Restricted open procedures** involve inviting prospective suppliers to compete for a contract on an open basis, but the tender 'pool' is partly pre-qualified by restricting the advertising of the tender to selective media (eg appropriate technical journals or trade/industry web portals).
- **Negotiated procedures** involve the selection of a small number of suppliers to enter into direction negotiations with the buyer. At the end of the negotiation process, suppliers submit their 'best and final offers' – and these are competitively evaluated and compared to select the best-value offer. In other words, this is similar to direct negotiation with suppliers – but with the added element of direct competitive bidding at the end of the 'dialogue' phase.

2.20 Where the buyer has a choice, *selective* tendering will often be used for the following reasons.

- It is less time-consuming and costly for both buyer and suppliers than either open tendering (with its potentially vast number of bids) or negotiated procedures (involving labour-intensive negotiation and dialogue)
- It is less likely to present later problems with technical capability or capacity than open procedures, since special consideration is given to pre-qualification (non-price) criteria
- It is less frustrating for non-pre-qualified suppliers who may incur the trouble and expense of tendering under open procedures, without having a realistic chance of succeeding.

2.21   Pre-qualification of potential bidders on defined criteria provides a systematic means of eliminating suppliers that should not advance to the more time-consuming and costly tendering stage because they:

- Lack recent experience in the relevant kind of work
- Lack secure financial or economic resources to complete the work
- Lack personnel or managerial resources to complete the work successfully
- Lack required technology, facilities or capabilities (eg design capability, quality or risk management systems, reverse logistics arrangements)
- Rely heavily on subcontracting, and lack adequate controls to manage the supply chain effectively
- Represent a high risk (eg if they have convictions for fraud or a history of unethical dealings, say).

2.22   Negotiated procedures may be particularly useful for complex requirements or projects, where the requirement cannot be specified in detail or priced in advance; price may not be the most important variable in a complex requirement; specifications may change over time; and solutions may have to be developed in collaboration with suppliers.

2.23   However, both supplier pre-qualification and negotiation add extra layers of time and cost to the tender process and may not be required for standard, low-risk, low-value requirements. As with so many procurement decisions, it will be helpful for buyers to use segmentation, prioritisation and risk analysis tools (such as the Kraljic matrix or Pareto analysis) to determine which procurements are sufficiently high-value or high-risk to warrant the extra effort.

3   Intra-company trading

3.1   Intra-company trading refers to commercial relationships between entities which are part of the same organisation. One company, division or strategic business unit (SBU) in a large enterprise or conglomerate (eg a group of companies) may supply goods or services to another.

3.2   The general purpose behind intra-company trading is:

- To support capacity utilisation in the supplying entity or unit (ie to maintain production operations, where external orders are low)
- To help the supplying entity or unit to cover its fixed costs in times of recession and low external orders
- To support the profitability of the supplying entity or unit
- To support the profitability of the group as a whole.

3.3   Intra-company trading policies may direct buyers to purchase selected items exclusively from internal suppliers – regardless of price or other criteria. Alternatively – and, arguably, more effectively – they may require that buyers obtain quotations from internal suppliers, which will be competitively evaluated with quotations from external suppliers, and the order placed with the best value source (whether internal or external).

3.4   This highlights the key risk of intra-company trading, which is that internal supply may not be genuinely competitive with external supply – placing procurement professionals in a difficult position, in terms of fulfilling their own objective to secure the best possible purchase value for the organisation. Clearly, it is in the interest of a group of companies *not* to buy externally, if a company within the group can provide what is required. But undue pressure to buy from internal suppliers can lead to sub-optimal decisions, cause (internal) supplier complacency, alienate the external supply market, and – if quality is compromised – alienate customers as well.

3.5   There are also relational and contractual complexities in an intra-company trading arrangement. By way of illustration, consider an extreme case in which the internal supplier is in serious breach of contract: perhaps because it supplied significantly defective goods, which damaged the buying unit's production process. If this situation arose in a normal commercial context, the buyer would seek compensation, if necessary through legal action. But in an intra-company context, this would be almost inconceivable: by accepting intra-group supply, the buyer is effectively accepting limitations in its normal rights of redress against breach of contract.

3.6 There should be clear policy statements on intra-company trading. Baily *et al* offer the following contrasting examples.

- 'The use of materials and services from other group companies is encouraged. Where a group company submits a quotation which is less advantageous than a competitor, it is to be given the opportunity to meet this competition on equal terms.'
- 'Group companies should be given the opportunity to quote against our requirements when they are able to satisfy our needs. It is understood by all concerned, however, that they cannot be allowed advantage simply because they are group members. In all cases they should be treated as any other suppliers.'
- 'Buyers are reminded that companies in the group provide the following materials and services... Please utilise these when and where possible.'

Transfer pricing arrangements

3.7 A transfer price is an amount charged by one division or unit to another within a single organisation, for the purposes of intra-organisational trading. For example, in a very simple case a company might consist of just two divisions: a manufacturing division and a sales division. The manufacturing division produces output which it transfers to the sales division at an agreed transfer price. This price represents revenue to the manufacturing division and a cost to the sales division.

3.8 Why bother to do this? After all, the transfer price is purely an internal mechanism which has no effect on how much the business can charge its external customers.

3.9 One reason for bothering is so that each division can be regarded as a 'profit centre' for accounting and performance evaluation purposes. This may help to stimulate improved performance, particularly if divisional managers are appraised on the basis of the profits earned by their divisions. The level of transfer price may have a significant effect on the profitability of both the transferring division and the receiving division. If the transfer price is very high, for example, the transferring division will appear very profitable, whereas the high cost of 'purchase' in the receiving division will depress its profits. A very low transfer price would have the the opposite effect.

3.10 Historically, this situation has led to a possibility of profit manipulation within multi-national conglomerates. Such companies have been able to set transfer prices not so much with the idea of achieving fairness between their respective divisions, as to achieve tax advantages. The basic idea is to set transfer prices in such a way that group companies operating in countries with low rates of corporate tax should enjoy high profits; while group companies operating in countries with high rates of corporate tax should have low profits. Nowadays, such abuse is subject to tough regulation and policing by tax authorities.

3.11 When one division transfers goods to another division we refer to the goods transferred as an 'intermediate product'. The 'final product' is what the receiving division sells on to external customers: it may or may not be identical with the intermediate product, depending on whether or not the receiving division further processes the goods.

Setting transfer prices

3.12 There are three main considerations for a firm when setting the transfer price for goods.

- *Goal congruence.* It is the task of the management accounting system in general, and the transfer pricing policy in particular, to ensure that what is good for an individual division or SBU is also good for the company or group as a whole – rather than supporting sub-optimal decisions on behalf of separate units.

- *Performance measurement.* The transfer pricing system should result in a report of divisional profits that is a reasonable measure of the managerial performance of a division or SBU.
- *Maintaining divisional autonomy.* One of the purposes of creating SBUs is to allow greater flexibility and responsiveness through managerial autonomy. This should not be undermined by having transfer prices which significantly erode the SBU's profitability.

3.13 If there is a perfectly competitive market for the intermediate product (ie the supplying division could sell its entire output on the open market, and the buying division could meet all its requirements on the open market), the optimum transfer price will be the **market price** for the good (less any savings achieved by internal supply as compared with external market transactions).

3.14 When transfers are recorded at market prices, divisional performance is more likely to represent the real economic contribution of the division to total company profits. If the supplying division did not exist, the intermediate product would have to be purchased on the open market at the current market price – and if the receiving division did not exist, the intermediate product would have to be sold on the open market at the current market price.

3.15 When there is surplus capacity within the firm (ie external demand for the good can be fully satisfied, and the firm still has spare capacity to produce more), the optimum transfer price is the **marginal cost** incurred by the supplying division: that is, the amount it costs to make the extra goods for internal consumption.

3.16 Transferring at marginal cost is unlikely to be 'fair' to the supplying division, because it does not allow for a profit margin. There are various ways around this difficulty.

- *Cost-plus pricing:* the transfer price is the marginal cost or full cost *plus* mark-up. This method often causes conflict over an acceptable mark-up, and may not encourage goal congruence.
- *Dual pricing:* one transfer price is recorded by the supplying division and a different transfer price is recorded by the buying division, with the differences accounted for in a holding company 'adjustment account'. This can be difficult to control effectively.
- *Two-part tariff:* the transfer is recorded at marginal cost, but an additional fixed sum is paid to the supplying division (eg on a per annum basis) to go at least part of the way towards covering its fixed costs, and possibly even to generate a profit. This method often proves to be popular and acceptable to the divisions.

3.17 When there are 'binding production constraints' (eg the selling division has insufficient capacity to meet demand, or resources are scarce), the optimum transfer price is the **marginal cost** incurred by the supplying division to satisfy the internal customer *plus* the **shadow price**: the opportunity cost of lost contribution from external sale of the product, or the extra contribution that would be earned if more of the scarce resource were available.

3.18 If the internal supplier can only meet internal demand by forgoing external sales, the shadow price reflects that lost contribution: the resulting transfer price is therefore fair for the purposes of performance evaluation. However, if the supplier's entire capacity is sold internally, all contribution will appear in the supplier's books and none in the buying division's – which is unfair in evaluation of the buying division's performance. Again, a two-part tariff approach may be used to address the balance.

4   Other aspects of sourcing policy and strategy

Make/do or buy?

4.1   The nature of the make/do or buy question can be stated in fairly simple terms. At one extreme, a firm could make its products (or develop its services) entirely in-house, buying in perhaps nothing but raw materials: the value of the final product arises almost entirely from the work done by the firm. At the other extreme, a firm could minimise its own activities, buying in almost everything from outside suppliers or subcontractors (who would therefore be adding almost all the value in the finished product).

4.2   In most cases, firms will occupy a middle position somewhere between these two extremes. This is the nature of the make/do or buy decision: where exactly should the firm position itself along this spectrum of possibilities? Where is the 'boundary of the firm'?

4.3   Make/do or buy decisions depend on a range of strategic and operational factors.

- The effects on total costs of production of buying-in work (such as subassemblies) and services (such as procurement, IT or logistics) from external suppliers
- The availability of in-house competencies and capacity; how readily they can be acquired or expanded; and whether they will be consistently available in future. (Lack of adequate competence, capacity or resources will push the firm towards the 'buy' end of the spectrum.)
- The availability of suitable external suppliers. A lack of suitable suppliers would push the firm towards the 'make/do' end of the spectrum.
- The need to retain resources, knowledge and skills in-house for future applications.
- Risks of giving control over key activities (and associated intellectual property, quality controls and reputational assets) to external providers.

4.4   The modern focus on 'core competencies' (Hamel & Prahalad) has led many companies to buy in products, components or assemblies previously produced in-house, and to **outsource** or **subcontract** a range of support functions (such as maintenance, catering, warehousing and transport, and staff recruitment and training) and even core functions such as sales and customer service (eg in call centres).

4.5   Lysons and Farrington (*Purchasing and Supply Chain Management*) explain the difference between outsourcing and subcontracting as a long-term strategic versus a short-term tactical approach: 'If you want a beautiful lawn in the neighbourhood and you hire someone to take responsibility for every aspect of lawn care, it's strategic outsourcing. But hiring someone to cut your lawn is subcontracting.'

4.6   Key sourcing issues in outsourcing and subcontracting include:

- The need for the outsource decision to be based on clear objectives and measurable benefits, with a rigorous cost-benefit analysis
- The need for rigorous supplier selection, given the long-term partnership nature of the outsource relationship to which the organisation will be 'locked in'. In such circumstances, selection should not only involve cost comparisons but considerations such as quality, reliability, willingness to collaborate, and ethics and corporate social responsibility (since the performance of the contractor reflects on the reputation of the outsourcing organisation).
- Rigorous supplier contracting, so that risks, costs and liabilities are equitably and clearly allocated, and expected service levels clearly defined
- Clear and agreed service levels, standards and key performance indicators, with appropriate incentives and penalties to motivate compliance and conformance
- Consistent and rigorous monitoring of service delivery and quality, against service level agreements and key performance indicators
- Ongoing contract and supplier management, to ensure contract compliance, the development of the relationship (with the aim of continuous collaborative cost and performance improvement), and the

constructive handling of disputes. This is essential if the organisation is not to gradually surrender control of performance (and therefore reputation) to the contractor.

- Contract review, deriving lessons from the performance of the contract, in order to evaluate whether the contract should be renewed, amended (to incorporate improvements) or terminated in favour of another supplier (or bringing the service provision back in-house).

4.7 Some of the potential advantages and disadvantages of outsourcing can be summarised as follows: Table 2.3. (You should be able to convert this data into the corresponding arguments for and against *internal* service provision or in-sourcing.)

Table 2.3 *Advantages and disadvantages of outsourcing*

ADVANTAGES	DISADVANTAGES
Supports organisational rationalisation and downsizing: reduction in the costs of staffing, space and facilities	Potentially higher cost of services (including contractor profit margin), contracting and management: compare with costs of in-house provision
Allows focused investment of managerial, staff and other resources on the organisation's core activities and competencies (those which are distinctive, value-adding and hard to imitate, and thus give competitive advantage)	Difficulty of ensuring service quality and consistency and corporate social responsibility (environmental and employment practices): difficulties and costs of monitoring (especially overseas)
Gives access to specialist expertise, technologies and resources of contractors: adding more value than the organisation could achieve itself, for non-core activities	Potential loss of in-house expertise, knowledge, contacts or technologies in the service area, which may be required in future (eg if the service is in-housed again).
Access to economies of scale, since contractors may serve many customers	Potential loss of control over areas of performance and risk (eg to reputation)
Adds competitive performance incentives, where internal service providers may be complacent	Added distance from the customer or end-user, by having an intermediary service provider: may weaken external or internal customer communication and relationships
	Risks of 'lock in' to an incompatible or under-performing relationship: cultural or ethical incompatibility; relationship management difficulties; contractor complacency etc.
	Risks of loss of control over confidential data and intellectual property

4.8 Outsourcing should only be applied to:

(a) Non-core competencies which, if outsourced:
- Will benefit from the expertise, cost efficiency and synergy of a specialist supplier
- Will enable the firm to leverage its core competencies
- Will not disadvantage the firm with the loss of in-house capability or vulnerability to market risks
- Will enable the firm to exploit technology or other operational capabilities which it lacks (and would find too costly to develop) in-house

(b) Activities for which external contractors have required competence and capability.

(c) Activities for which value for money is offered by outsourcing (due to the supplier's cost and profit structure, economies of scale, or potential for the buyer to divest itself of assets), in relation to the service levels that can be obtained.

Local or international sourcing?

4.9 Another important strand in the development of sourcing strategy and policy is the question of whether to choose suppliers locally or internationally, and the implications of international sourcing.

- Local sourcing implies using suppliers who are 'based within easy reach of the buyer' (*CIPS Knowledge Summary: Using Local Suppliers*), whether geographically or by other measures of accessibility.
- International sourcing implies the sourcing of goods and services from 'overseas' or other-country suppliers: essentially, 'importing'.

- The term 'global sourcing' has a more strategic flavour, involving the development of an international supply network, from which the company's sourcing requirements can be met flexibly, competitively and in a co-ordinated way.

4.10 Certain obvious advantages of sourcing *locally* present themselves immediately. With shorter distances or 'lines of supply', communications are likely to be easier; delivery costs should be lower, and delivery lead times should be faster and more reliable. Unforeseen 'rush' orders are easier to cope with, and just in time (on-demand) supply may be possible, to minimise stockholding. There are likely to be few problems of language, cultural or legal differences.

4.11 However, there are also major advantages in international sourcing – notably in the area of cost savings and access to geographically-specific supply markets (eg for minerals and agricultural produce). We will be looking at these factors in detail in Chapters 11 and 12. Here, we will merely offer an overview of some of the arguments for and against different sourcing strategies: Table 2.4

Table 2.4 *Arguments for/against local and international sourcing*

BENEFITS OF INTERNATIONAL SOURCING	DRAWBACKS OF INTERNATIONAL SOURCING
Availability of required materials and/or skills: increased supply capacity and competitiveness	Exchange rate risk, currency management issues etc
Competitive price and cost savings (scale economies, low labour costs)	High sourcing and transaction costs (risk management, tariff and non-tariff barriers)
Less onerous constraints and costs re environmental and labour compliance	Cost savings and lower standards may create sustainability, compliance and reputational risk
Leverages ICT systems (eg for virtual organisation, e-sourcing)	Different legal frameworks, time zones, standards, language and culture
International trade (arguably) promotes development, prosperity, international relations etc	Additional risks: political, transport (lead times, exposure), payment, supplier standards monitoring
Public sector: compulsory to advertise contracts within the EU	Environmental impacts of transport/haulage (especially by air freight)
BENEFITS OF LOCAL SOURCING	DRAWBACKS OF LOCAL SOURCING
Investment in local community, employment, skills etc (plus reputational and brand benefits)	Materials, skills or capabilities may not be available locally (or may be more costly)
Accessibility for supplier development and contract management (eg site visits)	Ethical and reputational risks of close social ties with suppliers, common spheres etc
Supplier knowledge of local market, sustainability issues, regulatory standards etc.	Smaller suppliers: no economies of scale (higher costs), greater dependency issues
Reduced transport, payment, cultural risks and costs	Local sourcing policy may make local suppliers complacent/ un-competitive
Short supply chain eg supporting JIT, fewer environmental impacts of transport	*Public sector*: not allowed to discriminate on basis of geography
Avoids 'evils' of globalisation	*Public sector*: may not offer 'value for money'

4.12 There has been a notable increase in international sourcing in recent decades, driven by factors such as the following.

- Improvements in transport technology, creating the 'shrinking' of distance (and related risks) for logistics
- Improvements in ICT, abolishing distance for the purposes of communication, relationship development, delivery tracking and performance monitoring
- Progressive reductions in trade barriers (eg through trading blocs and agreements), facilitating direct investment and the movement of goods and labour
- Sourcing efficiencies: with the ability to select the lowest-cost supplier from anywhere in the world
- Country or region-specific supply factors: some goods (especially raw materials and commodities)

may only be available from particular countries, or may be supplied more efficiently by particular countries, owing to specialisation (eg of call centres and IT services in India)

- Harmonisation of technical standards, which has enabled the sourcing of standardised components, compatible systems and so on.

The 'right relationship'

4.13 Supplier relationship strategies are not explicitly mentioned in this syllabus – and will be covered in detail in the *Managing Contracts and Relationships* module. However, it is worth emphasising that some reliable suppliers will be used again and again for on-going requirements: the buyer may decide not to go through the sourcing stages of the procurement process for each contract, but instead may choose to develop a relationship with a preferred – or even a sole – supplier for certain types of procurement.

4.14 There is a broad 'spectrum' of relationships that a buyer may seek with its suppliers, from one-off transactions (placed on a purely competitive arm's length basis) to close partnership relations with a trusted supplier of strategically important items or services (for which competitive bidding will no longer be relevant or appropriate). On the scale from distant to close, these approaches may cover:

- *Spot buying*: making one-off procurements to meet requirements as they arise, taking advantage of best available terms at the time
- *Regular trading*: giving repeat business to a group of preferred (known, trusted) suppliers
- *Fixed or call-off contracts*, framework agreements or blanket ordering: establishing agreed terms of supply with suppliers for a defined period
- *Single sourcing*: giving exclusivity to one preferred supplier – implying a high degree of trust and commitment
- *Strategic alliance*: agreement to work together with a supplier for long-term mutual advantage in a particular area (eg systems integration or joint new product development)
- *Partnership*: agreement to work closely together long-term, and on a range of issues, for collaborative problem-solving and development.

4.15 Which relationship is the 'right' one? Again, you will cover this in detail elsewhere in your studies, but essentially the decision depends on:

- The *nature and importance of the items being procured*: low-value, routine or one-off procurements are unlikely to justify heavy investment in long-term collaboration – whereas complex, customised, high-value procurements in unstable supply markets may well justify such investment, in order to secure control over the supply specification, quality and availability
- The *competence, capability, co-operation and performance* of the supplier (and reciprocal conduct of the buyer), and therefore the degree of trust developed between them: trust being a necessary foundation for closer relationship
- *Geographical distance*: close relationships may be more difficult to establish and maintain with overseas suppliers, especially if there is little communication infrastructure
- The *compatibility* of the supply partners: if their strategic aims, values and systems are incompatible, it may be too costly to attempt to bridge the distance or overcome the barriers (as long as more compatible alternatives are available)
- The organisation's and procurement function's *objectives and priorities*: best available price (suggesting a competitive, opportunistic or transactional approach) or security and quality of supply, whole life value for money and long-term added value through improvement or innovation (suggesting a more collaborative, long-term approach)
- *Supply market conditions*: if supply is subject to risk (eg through weather or economic conditions), the buyer may wish to multi-source; if prices are fluctuating, it may wish to use opportunistic spot-buying; if the market is fast-changing and innovative, it may want to avoid being locked into long-term supply agreements; if there are only a few quality, capable, high profile suppliers, it may wish to enter partnership with them – and so on.

Supplier switching

4.16 One sourcing policy issue related to supplier relationship strategies is the extent to which the buying organisation is prepared to engage in supply switching: that is, 'dropping' an existing supplier, or deciding not to renew a supply contract, in favour of a new or alternative supplier.

4.17 There may be a range of reasons for changing or switching suppliers.

- Problems with the performance or reliability of the existing supplier
- A new supplier offering a more competitive bid (eg a better solution or better value), when an existing contract comes up for renewal
- A new supplier being better able to capitalise on emerging opportunities (eg new technology, lean or agile supply) through capabilities that the old supplier does not possess
- Low-risk, widely-available, standardised items being sourced through arms' length, transactional purchasing approaches – making opportunistic switching easy, in order to take advantage of price competition.

4.18 However, buyers need to be aware that switching suppliers causes upheaval and cost (identified as 'switching costs'), especially where strong relationships have been established, and relationship-specific plans and investments made (eg on integrated IT systems or collaborative planning). Some of the costs and risks of switching can be summarised as follows: Table 2.5.

Table 2.5 *Costs and risks of supplier switching*

RISKS OF SUPPLIER SWITCHING	COSTS OF SUPPLIER SWITCHING
The new supplier may fail to perform (eg if it made exaggerated claims to win contract...)	Identifying and qualifying new suppliers
Process incompatibility (eg if integrated systems and relationship-specific modifications were made with the old supplier)	Initiating and administering tendering exercises or other sourcing and contracting processes
Cultural/inter-personal incompatibility (eg where patterns of understanding and behaviour developed in the old relationship)	Settlement of not-yet-delivered items from old supplier; settlement of outstanding claims; payment of 'exit' (eg early cancellation) fees
Loss of knowledge (eg where collaborative processes with the old supplier were undocumented)	Change of internal systems and processes to align with the new supplier
Learning curve: time for the new supplier to achieve peak performance, teething problems	Familiarising and training the new supplier in systems, procedures and requirements
Exposure to new and unfamiliar supply risks (political instability, labour unrest, CSR issues, exchange rate risk, transport risk)	Contract development and contract management (perhaps with more intensive monitoring and contact in the early stages of the relationship)
Exposure of intellectual property, confidential data (without trust having yet been built up)	Risk mitigation measures (eg insurances) and corrective measures (eg re teething problems)
Problems of adversarial hand-over from the old supplier to the new: trouble accessing designs, documents, assets, work-in-progress etc.	

4.19 Even if the potential benefits of switching are substantial, there may be barriers to switching. The time and effort invested in developing long-term supplier relationships and integration can cause a psychological 'lock-in' to the current supplier. The existing provision, especially where a satisfactory and proven relationship exists, could lead to future competitive advantage through continuous improvement over time, or co-investment in innovative supply solutions.

4.20 Relationship confidence is also a strong factor in preventing switching. Buyers are comfortable with suppliers they know, and which have been proven over time. Trusting a supplier's quality assurance, for example – and not having to re-inspect all in-coming supplies – may be a disincentive to switching, and having to revert back to expensive and inefficient goods inwards inspections.

4.21 If switching does take place, here are some key issues for buyers.

- The need for early flagging of contracts up for renewal, so that buyers can discuss renewal and switching options with key stakeholders (including users who may have feedback on the impact of supplier performance and risk)
- The need for proactive transition planning and risk management, including contract clauses and supplier KPIs providing for transition and hand-over to new suppliers.

Consortium buying

4.22 A buying consortium is a group of separate organisations that combine together for the purpose of procuring goods or services. A buying consortium might be created when a group of organisations see mutual benefit in aggregating their requirements: creating larger contracts, for economies of scale and increased bargaining power to secure advantageous terms. This might be especially beneficial if one organisation's requirements, on their own, are insufficient to attract attention – or discounts – from high-quality suppliers.

4.23 The consortium is represented in discussions with suppliers by a centralised or shared procurement unit, which may be the procurement function of one of the members, or a third party procurement service. The cost is shared by the consortium members.

4.24 With a buying consortium, the relationship with a supplier is more likely to be transactional, because it could be difficult for a supplier to develop long-term partnership relationships with a group of different organisations. This is particularly the case when the members of the consortium change over time, with some new members joining and existing members leaving the group.

4.25 Buying consortia can be found in both the public and the private sectors, but is particularly encouraged in the public sector, in order to maximise value for money. In the UK, several local government authorities might form a consortium with a centralised buying unit. Similarly, there are buying consortia in parts of the automotive industry.

4.26 The benefits of consortium procurement may be summarised as follows.

- By means of enhanced bargaining power, the consortium can obtain discounts that would not be available to individual members – although there may be difficulties in allocating such discounts fairly among them.
- A consortium can establish framework agreements, simplifying purchase administration for members. This can lead to significant reductions in transaction and contracting costs, especially in the case of low-value items where the administrative cost is disproportionate to the purchase price of the items.
- Consortium members can pool expertise, knowledge and contacts, where these would be beneficial for particular procurement categories or exercises.

4.27 However – as ever – it is not all good news. There are some costs and disadvantages associated with consortium purchasing.

- There are costs and effort associated with communication and coordination, staff development and policy development.
- There is an issue of transparency between consortium members. Buyers need full information about plans, processes, designs and costs in order to make informed procurement decisions: this may expose some members of a consortium to commercial or intellectual property risk.
- Consortia may suffer from lengthy negotiation and decision processes, which are inefficient – and may

deter some suppliers from dealing with the consortium.

- Aggregated demand may create very large contracts, which might disadvantage small or medium sized enterprises (including local and minority-run businesses) from accessing the business: this may be contrary to social sustainability or corporate social responsibility policies – and may also suppress supply market innovation (since SMEs are often more entrepreneurial and innovative).
- Members are not obliged to purchase to the agreed specification.
- Very large consortia may fall foul of laws and regulations designed to prevent dominant market players from abusing their dominant market position (eg by dictating pricing).

The structure of a sourcing plan

4.28 We have not been able to find discussion of this topic in the purchasing literature and do not know what it means. If the meaning becomes apparent from exam questions we will post material on the internet as part of the student online resources. In the meantime, if a question is asked on this subject we can only suggest that candidates refer to a number of variables in the sourcing process.

- The various issues that we have discussed in this chapter: single, dual and multiple sourcing; partnership sourcing (and more general considerations relating to the 'right' relationship with suppliers); the choice between negotiation and tendering; the possibility of intra-company trading; the make/do or buy decision; the choice of local, national or international sourcing
- The various approaches suggested by the Kraljic matrix (refer back to Chapter 1)

Chapter summary

- Multiple sourcing has advantages for buyers, but modern thinking has emphasised a policy of supply base optimisation through collaborative relationships with a small number of suppliers.
- At the collaborative end of the relationship spectrum an argument can be made for dual sourcing, single sourcing, and partnership sourcing.
- Approaches to letting contracts include direct negotiation with suppliers and tendering ('competitive bidding').
- Tendering procedures include open tendering, selective tendering, restricted open procedures and negotiated procedures. In the public sector, the use of such procedures is tightly regulated.
- Intra-company trading refers to situations when one SBU supplies another SBU in the same group.
- There are particular complexities attached to intra-company trading, including the need to set appropriate transfer prices.
- A key strategic issue is the make/do or buy decision. How much should the organisation do internally, and how much should it subcontract or outsource to other organisations?
- Another important decision is whether to source locally or internationally.
- There may be good reasons for switching suppliers in particular cases, but the costs and risks of doing this should be carefully weighed.

Self-test questions

Numbers in brackets refer to the paragraphs where you can check your answers.

1   List disadvantages of multiple sourcing arrangements. (1.7)

2   List risks of a narrow supply base. (1.12)

3   In which circumstances may partnership sourcing be most beneficial? (1.23)

4   What are the conditions in which a monopoly may exist? (1.29)

5   What are the buyer's main objectives in a negotiation with a supplier? (2.10)

6   Distinguish between distributive bargaining and integrative bargaining. (2.12)

7   Suggest four situations in which competitive bidding should not be used. (2.15, Table 2.2)

8   What are the main objectives of intra-company trading? (3.2)

9   What is a transfer price? Why do organisations set transfer prices? (3.7, 3.9)

10   List factors to be considered in the make/do or buy decision. (4.3)

11   List advantages and disadvantages of outsourcing. (4.7, Table 2.3)

12   What factors have driven the increase in international sourcing in recent years? (4.12)

13   List reasons why a buyer might consider switching suppliers. (4.17)

14   What are the benefits of consortium procurement? (4.26)

CHAPTER 3

Selection and Award Criteria

Assessment criteria and indicative content

1.3 Develop selection and award criteria that can be commonly applied when sourcing requirements from external suppliers

- Typical selection criteria such as: quality assurance, environmental and sustainability, technical capabilities, systems capabilities, labour standards, financial capabilities
- Typical award criteria such as: price, total life cycle costs, technical merit, added value solutions, systems, resources
- Balancing commercial and technical award criteria

2.1 Choose appropriate selection criteria to inform the identification of appropriate external suppliers in the sourcing plan

- Typical selection criteria such as: quality assurance, environmental and sustainability, technical capabilities, systems capabilities, labour standards, financial capabilities

2.2 Choose a balance of commercial and technical award criteria in the sourcing plan

- Typical award criteria such as: price, total life cycle costs, technical merit, added value solutions, systems, resources
- Balancing commercial and technical award criteria

Section headings

1. Selection and contract award
2. Supplier appraisal and selection models
3. Selection criteria
4. Award criteria

Introduction

In this chapter we return to one of the core topics mentioned in Chapter 1, in the context of supplier appraisal and pre-qualification: the use of pre-determined criteria against which supplier capability, suitability and acceptability can be measured.

It is important to distinguish, as the syllabus does, between criteria used for supplier selection (or pre-qualification) and criteria used for contract award, so we will start with a discussion of this distinction.

The bulk of supplier investigation and evaluation will generally be done as part of a pre-qualification or supplier selection process. We therefore devote most of the chapter to exploring the typical criteria that may be applied. We have already discussed the process of supplier appraisal and pre-qualification in Chapter 1, together with how information about suppliers can be monitored and gathered. Refresh your memory of these topics, if you need to – and, as you read on, consider (a) what information would be needed to evaluate each selection and appraisal criterion, and (b) how it could be gathered.

Finally, we look at typical criteria for contract award, and how these may be constrained by organisational, ethical and regulatory considerations.

1 Selection and contract award

1.1 Competitive sourcing methods (such as compared quotations or competitive bidding) are often used in sourcing high-value and leverage items from external suppliers, to ensure the competitiveness of supplier's prices and proposals. In such cases, there is usually a concern to minimise the number, complexity and subjectivity of the criteria used in contract award, in order to ensure that the comparison of bids, and the final decision, are objective, justified, fair and seen to be fair. This is important both for the buyer (to secure the optimum, rational outcome for the business) and for suppliers (to ensure that, having spent time and effort on bid preparation, they are fairly judged and ethically treated).

1.2 Contract award decisions are therefore generally taken on the basis of a few objective, quantifiable (numerical) criteria – such as price or best value – which can be directly, unambiguously and consistently compared from one quotation or bid to another.

1.3 However, as we saw in Chapter 1, this presents a risk, because the lowest-price or best-value bid may *not* represent the most innovative, reliable or easily-implemented solution – and the supplier may (or may not) turn out to be technically or organisationally capable of fulfilling the buyer's requirements to the required standard. Pre-qualification (or supplier selection) criteria are therefore designed to ensure that *all* suppliers invited to quote or tender are capable, suitable and acceptable – so that competitive contract award criteria can simply be applied to select the 'best of a good bunch' for a given requirement.

1.4 It is therefore helpful to distinguish between criteria for supplier selection or pre-qualification, and criteria for contract award.

1.5 Criteria used for **supplier selection:**

- Focus on whether or not prospective suppliers are suitable, acceptable and capable of fulfilling requirements
- Are primarily *evaluative:* how suitable, acceptable and capable is each supplier – and is it suitable, acceptable and capable *enough* for the buyer's needs?
- May focus beyond any particular or immediate requirement, to the ongoing future supply needs of the organisation.

1.6 Criteria used for **contract award:**

- Focus on which supplier or bid – out of an available pre-qualified shortlist – is the 'best' or 'winning' option for the specific requirement
- Are primarily *comparative:* which of the shortlisted options represents a better solution or better value than the others?
- Focus on the immediate requirement: the placing of a particular contract.

1.7 It may be worth reminding you of a third category of appraisal and evaluation criteria: the use of performance measures and standards, for supplier **performance management and vendor rating**, once the contract has been awarded (as discussed in Chapter 1).

- Performance measures (or criteria for vendor rating) should be based on contract award criteria, since these are the reason why the supplier was chosen – and provide a clear indicator of whether the buyer's expectations are being met.
- It is important for prospective suppliers to be informed, clearly and in advance, of the criteria on which the contract will be awarded, in order to enable them to compete for the business to the best of their ability (and without wasted time, cost and effort) and in order for them to confirm or challenge the fairness of the award decision. It is arguably even *more* important for suppliers to know the criteria on which their performance will be measured, since post-contract-award, there is a contractual and commercial relationship – and possibly, performance-based incentives and penalties – at stake.

- Performance measures, and key performance indicators (quantified statements of the expected level of performance in a given area) are generally more specific than contract award or supplier appraisal criteria, in order to provide meaningful standards for performance management. Where contract award criteria might include 'optimal lifetime costs' or 'best available quality standard', KPIs might specify target costs or cost reductions to be achieved, and detailed quality standards, tolerances and targets.

1.8 We will start by looking at typical criteria for supplier selection or pre-qualification. Remember that these are only generic examples. Organisations will formulate specific criteria to suit:

- Their own **strategic priorities** (eg for innovation, corporate social responsibility, quality leadership or supply chain integration)
- Particular **process requirements** (eg for reverse logistics capability, late customisation and agile supply, lean or cost-efficient supply, or IT systems compatibility)
- Any **identified risk factors** in the sourcing situation (eg international delivery problems, very low quality and engineering tolerances, high regulatory intervention or reputational risk arising from ethics-aware consumers)
- Different **types of procurement** (eg prioritising price, or quality, or speed of delivery, according to the nature of business need)
- Different **supply relationships** (eg more rigorous criteria on issues such as financial stability, compatibility and corporate social responsibility for ongoing, long-term supplier partnerships than for one-off, short-term price-driven transactions).

1.9 If you are asked to recommend and/or justify selection criteria for a sourcing requirement in an exam case study, remember to take such variables into account – as far as possible from the data given.

2 Supplier appraisal and selection models

2.1 As we noted in Chapter 1, the initial challenge of formulating selection criteria is to place some kind of practical limit on the number and variety of factors that could form part of the assessment process.

2.2 Lysons and Farrington (*Purchasing & Supply Chain Management*) recommend evaluation of potential suppliers from eight perspectives: Table 3.1.

Table 3.1 *Eight perspectives for supplier selection*

Finance	• Financial stability (to support business and supply continuity), measured using a number of indicators and financial ratios (discussed in detail in Chapters 5 and 6 of this Course Book).
Production capacity and facilities	• Production capacity: how much volume the supplier will be able to handle, and how many units it can produce within a stated time period • Innovation and design capability (where relevant): reputation, track record, resources and facilities, willingness to collaborate • Production facilities: machinery type, capacity, state of maintenance and efficiency; health and safety record and systems; efficiency of factory layout and design; use of systems such as CAD/CAM.
Human resources	• Numbers, quality/skills and utilisation of human resources • Quality of management, teamwork, staff motivation, quality focus and employee relations (eg days lost due to industrial disputes)
Quality	• Standards accreditation (eg ISO 9000, BSI Register of Firms of Assessed Quality, Kitemark, etc) • Quality management methods and systems (inspection and testing, process controls, quality assurance of outgoing deliveries etc) • Awareness of total quality management: quality 'culture'
Performance	• Experience of similar projects and accounts; track records; completed projects; customer testimonials; lessons learned from past experience. This will be particularly important for complex requirements (such as construction projects or IT development).
Environmental and ethical considerations	• Compliance record • Policy and value statements; guidelines and codes of conduct; accountabilities for management; progress reporting • Management of the supply chain in these areas • Accreditation eg under ISO 14001 (environmental management systems)
IT development and leverage	• Potential for e-business (use of the internet or extranets) • Leverage of technology to reduce or eliminate paper transactions; shorten order cycles; provide real-time information on product availability; support collaborative planning; manage the supply chain
Organisation structure	• Defined accountabilities • Flexibility (eg cross-functional communication and short decision chains to facilitate swift, responsive decision-making; or ability to redeploy human resources as required to meet fluctuations in demand) • Account management (supplier-side contract and relationship management; points of contact with the buyer)

2.3 Another popular overview model, which we reproduce from Chapter 1, is Ray **Carter's '10 Cs'** model, which we have adapted and expanded in Table 3.2.

Table 3.2 *Ray Carter's 10 Cs for supplier selection*

Competence (or capability)	• Whether the supplier has the resources and expertise to fulfil the contract • Whether it can produce the kinds of items, or deliver the kinds of services required • What management, innovation, design or other relevant capabilities it has to offer
Capacity	• Whether the supplier can meet the buying organisation's current and future needs • How much volume the supplier will be able to handle (its production capacity) • How effectively managed its own supply chain is
Commitment	• Demonstrated commitment to key values such as quality, service, cost management or continuous improvement • Willingness to commit to a longer-term relationship with the buying organisation (if desired)
Control	• Systems in place for monitoring and managing resources and risks: eg willingness to comply with procedures, rules or systems required by the buyer; quality or environmental management systems; financial controls and fraud prevention mechanisms (good governance); risk assessment and management systems; and so on
Cash	• Resources and management capability to ensure the financial status and stability of the supplier eg: profitability; cashflow position (whether it has working funds to pay its bills, buy materials and pay workers – and therefore continue in business); the assets it owns, the debts it owes, how its costs are structured and allocated, and so its overall financial 'health'.
Consistency	• Demonstrated consistency in delivery and improving levels of quality and service: eg a 'track record' of reliability, or demonstrated 'process capability' (robust processes, quality assurance and controls, so that problems are identified and prevented before they impact on the buyer)
Cost	• The price, whole life costs and value for money offered by the supplier
Compatibility	• Strategic, operational, technological and cultural 'fit' between the supplier and the buying organisation. • Strategic and cultural fit involves aligned values, ethics, work approach, management style and strategic objectives and priorities. • Operational and technological fit involves compatible processes, organisation and IT systems.
Compliance (or corporate social responsibility)	• Demonstrated compliance with environmental, corporate social responsibility (CSR) or sustainability standards, law and regulation • Environmental, CSR and risk management systems to ensure consistent compliance • Willingness to comply with buyer policies and standards on ethics, CSR and sustainability (where relevant)
Communication	• Efficiency (and supporting technology) to support collaboration and co-ordination in the supply chain eg: the use of e-business, extranets or EDI; account management structures (for supplier-side contract management); willingness to share information (eg on demands, plans, costs); and so on.

2.4 One final model, which is easy to remember and popular with CIPS examiners, is the FACE 2 FACE checklist (originally developed by Dawn Dadds): Table 3.3.

Table 3.3 *The FACE 2 FACE model of supplier appraisal*

Fixed assets Physical resources to meet buyer needs	**Financial stability** For continuity of supply
Ability to deliver the goods Production capacity and reliability of delivery/quality/service	**Ability to work with the buyer** Compatibility of culture, contacts, willingness to co-operate
Cost Competitive total acquisition costs, willingness to negotiate terms	**Commitment to quality** Reliability of quality standards and systems, willingness to improve
Efficiency Use of resources, minimisation of waste	**Environmental/ethical factors** Policies and practices re CSR, ethics and environmental management

2.5 Let's now look at some of these criteria in more detail, focusing on areas specified by the syllabus.

3   Selection criteria

Financial capabilities, status and stability

3.1   The assessment of a supplier's financial position is often a very straightforward exercise, and should therefore be undertaken at an early stage. If there are doubts about financial stability, the supplier can then be eliminated from consideration without the need for more elaborate appraisal.

3.2   Financial status and stability are measured by factors such as the supplier's profitability, its cashflow position (whether it has working funds to pay its bills, buy materials and pay workers), the assets it owns, the debts it owes, how its costs are structured and allocated, and so its overall financial 'health'.

3.3   These factors will reflect on the ability of the supplier to fulfil the current contract with the buyer – and to maintain secure flows of supply for the future. They may raise the risk of delivery or quality problems – and more drastic disruption to supply (and complex legal issues) if the supplier's business becomes insolvent (a scenario called 'supplier failure'). They will also impact on the prices the supplier will be able to charge the buyer, and their ability to pass on cost efficiencies to the buyer.

3.4   Dobler and Burt cite three typical nightmare scenarios that can arise if dealing with a financially weak supplier.

- You need to insist on maintaining quality, but the supplier is forced to cut costs.
- You have a financial claim against the supplier, but he does not have sufficient working capital to meet it.
- You need to insist on speedy delivery to meet a promised delivery date, but the supplier cannot afford to pay overtime.

3.5   The most accessible source of information on a supplier is their published financial accounts, which offer useful data on factors such as profitability, financial gearing (the extent to which the supplier relies on loan capital), and working capital levels (the extent to which the supplier has liquid assets in the form of cash and debtor balances, rather than tied up in long-term and inaccessible assets).

3.6   Lysons and Farrington cite a document by the UK Department of Trade and Industry (*Sourcing and supplier appraisal*), which recommends a range of financial checks when sourcing suppliers and evaluating tenders.

- The assessed turnover (total revenue) of the supplier enterprise, over a three-year period
- The profitability of the enterprise, and the relationship between its gross and net profits (highlighting cost efficiency), over a three-year period
- The value of capital assets, return on capital assets and return on capital employed (indicating the efficiency with which the enterprise utilises its assets and capital resources)
- The scale of the supplier's borrowings, and the ratio of debts to assets (indicating areas of risk and cost associated with debt finance)
- The possibility of a takeover or merger, which might affect the supplier's continuing ability to supply (eg if the business will be broken up, or if it is acquired by a competitor of the buying organisation)
- The firm's dependency on a small number of major customers (indicating a risk that if one or more withdrew their business, the supplier might face financial difficulties)
- Whether or not the organisation has sufficient resources and capacity to fulfil the order.

3.7   We won't go into further detail here, as financial appraisal is the topic of separate learning outcomes, and will be discussed in detail in Chapters 5 and 6.

Technical capability and production capacity

3.8 Production capacity and technical capability refer to factors in the supplier's operational capacity and facilities, which act as indicators of its ability to fulfil the buyer's current and future requirements. Technical or operational capability factors include:

- Whether the supplier produces (or can produce) the kinds of items, or deliver the kinds of services, required
- What innovations would be required for the supplier to meet current or future requirements – and whether the supplier has, or is willing to develop, innovation capability
- How much volume the supplier will be able to handle, and how many units it is able to produce in a given production period (its production capacity)
- What capabilities the supplier has in operational areas such as engineering, innovation, design, just in time (JIT) supply, late customisation, reverse logistics and recycling – and so on
- Whether the supplier has the capability to respond swiftly and flexibly to urgent or additional requirements
- What type of plant and machinery it has, and whether it is capable of producing items within the tolerances set by the buyer's specification
- How old and how well maintained the plant and machinery is, reflecting the risk of production 'down time' if machinery breaks down or wears out
- The efficiency of factory layout and processes (which will impact on productivity and also cost).

3.9 The term 'production capacity' refers to how much volume the supplier will be able to handle, and how many units it can produce within a stated time period. Production capacity will be evaluated taking into account a range of factors including:

- Maximum productive capacity in a given working period
- Whether capacity is currently over-committed (in which case the supplier may not be able to accept additional work, or may be unreliable in estimating lead times) or under-committed (possibly raising doubts about its quality or efficiency, risks of deterioration or obsolescence of its stocks and so on)
- Potential to increase existing capacity if required by future demand (eg by acquiring additional plant, increasing shifts or overtime, subcontracting and so on) – and the supplier's willingness to do this (given the reliability of demand forecasts, the relationship with the buyer, costs and benefits of expansion and so on)
- The percentage of capacity that is utilised by existing major customers, and/or that would be utilised by adding the buyer's business (raising possible issues of supplier over-dependency on a few major customers, with financial risks if one of them withdraws its business).

3.10 Let's take the example of high-volume order requirements. How can the buyer evaluate or verify the supplier's capacity to supply high volumes on demand, without compromise on quality, and at a price that reflects the expected economies of scale?

- Estimated volumes and maximum potential volumes should be discussed with the potential supplier from the start.
- Suppliers should be asked to provide evidence of any claim to be able to support high-volume production. This may take the form of productivity records, reports of output volumes for previous similar projects, the opportunity to talk to previous or existing high-volume-purchasing customers, or the opportunity to view and audit production outputs at the supplier's factory.
- Test contracts or pilot projects may be used to verify the supplier's capacity in a controlled area.
- The supplier's infrastructure to support volume production (eg its supply chain management) should be examined.
- The contingency plans of the supplier for co-opting extra capacity if required (eg available quality-assured subcontractors) should also be examined.

Systems capabilities

3.11 The supplier's development of, and adherence to, efficient systems and procedures for operation may embrace a number of criteria.

- *Compatibility* of the supplier's systems and procedures with those of the buyer (or its ability and willingness to adapt to the buyer's requirements)
- *Willingness to comply* with any procedures, rules or systems specified by the buyer. Examples include: development of a quality management system (such as ISO 9000) or an environmental management system (such as ISO14000); third party monitoring of the supplier's labour management practices (particularly in low-cost labour economies); protocols for the protection of confidential information and intellectual property; sound capacity planning and production control – and so on.
- *Quality management systems*: the supplier's standards accreditation (if any); its quality management methods (ideally based on quality assurance, not just quality control); its awareness of and willingness to adopt total quality management principles (eg aspiration for 'zero defects', involvement of employees and supply chain partners in quality issues); its willingness to commit to continuous improvement programmes; and so on.
- *IT development*: the potential for e-business and systems integration with the supplier, for more efficient procurement processes (eg whether the supplier is connected to EDI or extranet systems, or willing to be so; whether the supplier uses RFID technology to enable electronic tracking of deliveries and inventory and so on).

Quality and quality assurance

3.12 'Quality' will mean something different for the purchase of computer equipment, engineering components, building materials, cleaning supplies, accountancy services or catering services. A buyer's definition of quality may therefore focus on a range of different dimensions.

- *Excellence*: the degree or standard of excellence of a product; the design, workmanship and attention to detail put into it; and the extent to which finished products are free from defects.
- *Comparative excellence*: how favourably a product is measured against competitive benchmarks (other products), best practice or standards of excellence
- *Fitness for purpose or use*: that is, the extent to which a product does what it is designed and expected to do; or, more generally, the extent to which it meets the customer's needs.
- *Conformance to requirement or specification*: that is, the product matches the features, attributes, performance and standards set out in a purchase specification. Conformance therefore also implies lack of defects, and therefore reflects on the quality of the supplier's processes.
- *Acceptable quality and value for money*: buyers may be willing to sacrifice some performance and features in order to pay a lower price for a product, as long as it is still fit for purpose.

3.13 Quality may be more difficult to define and measure in the case of service procurements, because of their variability and intangibility (non-inspectability). Researchers Parasuraman, Ziethaml & Berry developed an approach to the measurement of service quality which they called **SERVQUAL**. The SERVQUAL model suggests that there are five generic dimensions on which customers evaluate service.

- *Tangibles*: physical products, facilities and results related to the service (eg the smartness of service providers' uniforms and the maintenance of their equipment; the professionalism of documentation provided with the service; the observable state of the office after the cleaners have left)
- *Reliability*: the ability to perform the service accurately, dependably and consistently
- *Responsiveness*: the willingness to help the customer and provide a good level of service
- *Assurance*: the extent to which trust and confidence is inspired in the customer (eg by the competence and conduct of service staff, and the credibility, capability and security of the organisation's systems and procedures)
- *Empathy*: the ability to understand customers' needs, to be approachable, and to offer individual care and attention.

3.14 For a buyer looking to appraise the quality of a supplier's products or services in a commercial setting, the most important definitions of 'right quality' are likely to be fitness for purpose and conformance to specification. The British Standards definition of quality is: 'the totality of features and characteristics of a product or service that bear on its ability to satisfy a given need.'

3.15 Ideally, a buyer would like to transfer as much of the cost and effort of quality management as possible to the supplier. Instead of just appraising the quality of the supplier's **outputs** (which might not be a reliable measure, if based on process or output sampling at a particular moment in time), the buyer will want to be assured that the supplier *itself* has robust **systems and procedures** in place for monitoring and managing the quality of its outputs.

3.16 Systems for the *detection and correction of defects* are known as **quality control**. This is an essentially reactive approach, focusing on: establishing specifications, standards and tolerances; inspecting delivered goods, often on a 'sampling' basis; identifying items that are defective or do not meet specification; and scrapping or re-working items that do not pass inspection.

3.17 There are a number of limitations in such an approach. Inspections are non-value-adding activity. Defective items may slip through in unacceptable numbers (especially under budget or schedule pressures). The process identifies errors once they have already been made – and associated costs incurred (eg on wasted labour and materials). And inspection activity tends to be duplicated at each stage of the supply process (eg re-inspection by the buyer on delivery).

3.18 Systems for the *prevention of defects* are known as **quality assurance**. This is a more proactive and integrated approach, building quality into every stage of the process from concept and specification onwards. It includes the full range of systematic activities used within a quality management system to 'assure' or give the organisation adequate confidence that items and processes will fulfil its quality requirements. In other words, quality assurance is a matter of 'building in quality' – not 'weeding out defects'.

3.19 The term **quality management** is given to the various processes used to ensure that the right quality inputs and outputs are secured: that products and services are fit for purpose and conform to specification; and that continuous quality improvements are obtained over time. Quality management thus includes both quality control and quality assurance. A quality management system (QMS) can be defined as: 'A set of co-ordinated activities to direct and control an organisation in order to continually improve the effectiveness and efficiency of its performance'. The main purpose of a QMS is to define and manage processes for systematic quality assurance: the supplier's QMS will be a key focus of pre-qualification and appraisal investigations.

3.20 A QMS is designed to ensure that:

- The buyer can have confidence in the supplier's ability reliably to deliver products and services which meet its needs and expectations
- The supply chain's quality objectives are consistently and efficiently achieved, through improved process control and reduced wastage
- Staff competence, training and morale (and therefore productive capacity and capability) are enhanced, through clear expectations and process requirements
- Quality gains, once achieved, are maintained over time: learning and good practices do not 'slip' for lack of documentation, adoption and consistency.

3.21 There are several British and international standards for measuring and certifying quality management systems of various types, including the ISO 9000 standard developed by the International Organisation for Standardisation (ISO). Organisations can use the framework to plan or evaluate their own QMS, or can seek third party assessment and accreditation. More importantly, for the purposes of this learning outcome, buyers can set ISO 9000 accreditation as a pre-qualifier for prospective suppliers of strategic items.

3.22 The **ISO 9000 standards** are generic and adaptable to all kinds of organisations. They identify quality management systems as comprising four main processes.

- Management responsibility (management commitment, customer focus, quality policy setting, planning, accountability, communication and review)
- Resource management (provision of resources, human resources, infrastructure and work environment to support quality)
- Product realisation (customer research, product design and/or development, purchasing, production and service operations)
- Measurement, analysis and improvement (monitoring and measurement of performance, control of non-conforming product, analysis of data, and improvement planning).

3.23 The term **total quality management** is used to refer to a radical approach to quality management, as a business philosophy. Total quality management (TQM) is an orientation to quality in which quality values and aspirations are applied to the management of all resources and relationships within the firm – and throughout the supply chain – in order to seek continuous improvement and excellence in all aspects of performance.

3.24 Laurie Mullins (*Management and Organisational Behaviour*) synthesises various definitions of TQM as expressing: 'a way of life for an organisation as a whole, committed to total customer satisfaction through a continuous process of improvement, and the contribution and involvement of people'. A buyer may question suppliers as to their awareness of TQM, and the extent to which they adopt some or all of its key principles, such as: the management of quality across the supply chain; willingness to collaborate on continuous improvement programmes; cross-functional co-operation on quality; aspirations to zero defects ('get it right first time'); and so on.

Environmental, sustainability and CSR performance

3.25 The importance of environmental, ethical and responsibility criteria in selecting suppliers has been highlighted by a number of high-profile cases, in which a buying organisation's reputation and brand have been damaged by the exposure of poor ethical, environmental or labour practice by their first – or even lower – tier suppliers. One example is the reputational damage suffered by social charity Oxfam, as a result of revelations that overseas producers of its 'Make Poverty History' wristbands were exploiting workers. More recently, consumer electronics icon Apple has faced consumer pressure over press reports of long working hours and exploitative terms at the plants of some of its Chinese contractors, in some cases leading to worker suicides.

3.26 A comprehensive definition of the term 'sustainability' embraces economic, environment and social and ethical criteria: sometimes called 'Profit, People and Planet' or 'Economics, Environment and Equity'. Sustainability may therefore be an umbrella term for a number of criteria related to issues such as the supplier's management of environmental impacts; sustainable resource consumption; compliance with environmental protection law and regulation; ethical trading and labour and employment practices; policies for corporate social responsibility and ethical conduct; and reputation management (to avoid the buyer's reputation being put at risk by exposure of the ethical or irresponsible conduct of the supplier).

3.27 **Environmental criteria** might include:

- Location in relation to the buyer and lower tiers of supply (which has implications for transport impacts)
- The use of less and 'greener' (environmentally friendly) materials and packaging
- 'Green' design and innovation capability (eg design for disassembly, recycling or energy efficiency); reverse logistics and recycling capability; and so on

- The development and enforcement of strong environmental policies eg re resource efficiency (managed use of non-renewable and scarce resources), carbon footprint reduction (reduced transport miles and energy use), reduction of waste to land-fill and so on – both within the supplier and throughout its supply chain
- Robust environmental management systems – perhaps including certification under ISO 14001 environmental standards, the Eco-Management and Audit Scheme (EMAS) or equivalents
- Compliance with environmental protection and emissions law/regulation in the country of operation.

3.28 ISO14000 is a series of international standards focusing on environmental management systems (EMS). An EMS gives an organisation a systematic process for assessing and managing its impact on the environment. The standard is designed to help develop such a system, as well as providing a supporting audit and review programme. The major requirements for an EMS under ISO14001 include the following.

- An environmental policy statement, including commitment to prevent pollution, improve environmental performance, and comply with all legal requirements
- Identification of all aspects of the organisation's activities that could impact on the environment
- Performance objectives and targets for environmental performance
- Implementation of an EMS to meet those objectives and targets, including employee training, instructions, procedures etc
- Periodic auditing and review, with corrective and preventive action taken where necessary

3.29 **Social responsibility, ethical criteria and labour standards** might include:

- The development of robust CSR policies and ethical codes
- Location in relation to the buyer (as part of the buyer's policy of support for local suppliers and communities)
- Evidence of responsible and ethical labour policies and practices – including fair terms and conditions or work, provisions for worker health and safety, equal opportunity and diversity
- Compliance with International Labour Organisation standards (eg on supporting worker rights, upholding equality and diversity, and eradicating child and slave labour).
- Evidence of ethical trading policies and practices: supporting diverse suppliers, paying fair prices (particularly in low-cost-labour markets), and not abusing power in supply relationships
- Compliance with Fair Trade standards, or membership of the Ethical Trading Initiative
- Commitment to transparency and improvement, in collaboration with the buyer (eg willingness to undergo monitoring and evaluation of ethical and CSR policies by the buyer; willingness to identify lower-tier suppliers, so the buyer can 'drill down' through the supply chain, and so on).

3.30 Conformance to legislation and regulations, or **compliance**, may be part of a wider assessment of environmental and ethical considerations: the supplier's compliance record (on workplace healthy and safety, product safety and labelling, environmental protection and so on), and its stated policies and values in these areas. A non-compliant supplier may create a risk of non-compliance in the buyer's products, laying it open to product recalls and/or legal action.

The supplier's upstream and downstream supply network

3.31 The prospective supplier's upstream supply chain (ie the supplier's suppliers) should be looked at as:

- A supporting factor in its capacity to produce and its technical capability. Can the supplier dependably access the materials, services, expertise and extra capacity it may require to fulfil the contract, from its own suppliers? How well managed is the supply chain, and the relationships with suppliers: will it support high quality, reliable delivery, flexibility (eg for just in time supply or late customisation) and innovation?
- A supporting factor in its legal, ethical and environmental compliance – and in the management of reputational risk to the buyer. There is increasing pressure for organisations to be aware of (and indirectly responsible for) the practices of their whole supply chains.

3.32 The supplier's downstream supply chain (ie its customer base) will also be relevant for various reasons.

- The buyer may be reassured of the supplier's quality by a customer base including large, reputable and 'blue-chip' clients, particularly if it can approach some of these for references or testimonials about the supplier's performance.
- The supplier's current 'order book' will indicate whether its goods or services are in demand – or whether (for reasons that may need investigating) business is slow.
- The customer base will also indicate whether the supplier's output is relevant to the buyer's industry and requirements, eg if the supplier's customers have similar business processes, technology, products, market position or expenditure budgets to the buyer.
- An additional consideration will be whether the supplier's customer base includes the buyer's direct competitors. If so, there may be a conflict of interests, and at the very least, the buyer will need to check the supplier's policies and practices on the protection of confidential data and intellectual property.

The supplier's organisation culture

3.33 Organisation culture ('the way we do things around here') is a reflection of the shared values, beliefs, assumptions and norms of behaviour that develop in an organisation over time. It is explicitly stated in corporate mission and values statements, but is also visible in the attitudes expressed by managers and staff, in their behaviour, in the 'look' of the premises, the neatness of staff uniforms – and all sorts of other expressions.

3.34 How does the supplier 'feel' about quality and customer service? Is it committed to innovation, creativity, responsibility, ethics and/or the environment? Are employees motivated and quality-conscious, or do they cut corners where possible? How effective is communication within the company? Such things will be an important indicator of the supplier's capability and commitment, and whether constructive working relationships will be possible with the buyer.

3.35 The culture of the supplier may simply be *incompatible* with that of the buyer: their values, or attitudes to quality, or tolerance for risk, say, may simply be too different to allow for collaboration or the management of expectations.

Price and cost factors

3.36 The identified costs of the proposed procurement, or supply contract, will obviously be a key factor in evaluation of a potential supplier – although price may not be directly relevant at the pre-qualification stage. What the buyer will be interested in, however, is:

- How the supplier's costs are structured and allocated, and therefore whether it will be able to offer competitive prices
- Whether the supplier may be willing and able to commit to collaborative cost reduction initiatives
- Whether discounts (eg for bulk purchase or early payment) or extended payment terms may be available
- The total acquisition and ownership costs of the proposed purchase: looking beyond the purchase price of the item, to the costs of after-sales service, warranties, maintenance contracts, spare parts, user training, consumables, waste-products disposal, end-of-life product disposal or recycling and so on.

4   Award criteria

4.1   As we noted in Section 1 of this Chapter, the main reason to distinguish between supplier selection or pre-qualification criteria and contract award criteria is the element of comparison or competition in contract award, in order to ensure competitive supply.

4.2   *Competitive supply* means the extent to which a supply arrangement provides supply which matches or exceeds requirements, at a cost which represents best value in relation to a given supply market. Contract award criteria therefore generally seek to balance:

- **Technical criteria,** which define the supplier's ability to match or exceed specified requirements (as expressed in tender documents and product or service specifications)
- **Commercial criteria,** which define best-value cost (defined either as purchase price or, for more substantial assets, as whole life or lifecycle cost) in relation to the supply market.

Ability to conform to specification

4.3   As we have seen, evaluating and verifying a supplier's technical capability and capacity may involve a complex range of factors, both quantitative and qualitative – especially if the requirement and supply relationship is likely to be ongoing, committed and collaborative. For strategic procurements, therefore, the evaluation of suppliers on technical criteria may require a systematic pre-qualification process, *prior* to a more straightforward negotiation or competitive bidding process (based primarily on commercial criteria) to determine contract award.

4.4   For more routine sourcing exercises, however, technical criteria may be built into contract award criteria, with a more straightforward definition of quality or capability as 'conformance to specification'. In other words, contracts are awarded to:

- The **best solution** to the specified requirement: eg in the case of performance, output or functional specifications, which specify what the product or service must be able to deliver or do – the 'ends' to be achieved, rather than the 'means'
- The **most accurate fulfilment** of the specification: eg in the case of conformance, technical or design specifications, which specify the exact design, composition and methodology to be supplied, within strict tolerances or allowed variations
- The best **package of features or benefits** which meet or exceed the specified requirement – *balanced* with **commercial cost and value considerations**. The best solution or package of benefits is sought – but without incurring unnecessary cost on features or benefits that will not be used, or will not add value (eg if the contract is over-specified, or if the solution over-delivers).

4.5   As you may be aware from your studies for the *Business Need* module, a **specification** is simply a statement of the requirements to be satisfied in the supply of a product or service. The role of a specification is to define and communicate the buyer's requirements, in terms of either:

- *Conformance*: the buyer details exactly what the required product, part or material must consist of, and a 'quality' product is one which conforms to the description provided by the buyer (eg blueprints, designs, chemical composition, identified brands or models or samples and prototypes) – or
- *Performance*: the buyer describes what it expects the supplied item to be able to achieve, in terms of the functions it will perform and the level of performance it should reach. A 'quality' product is one which will satisfy these requirements: the buyer specifies the 'ends' (purpose) and the supplier has relative flexibility about the 'means' of achieving them. This approach offers potential for innovative, collaborative, value-adding solutions. It also widens the potential supply market to include smaller, more innovative suppliers (who might be prevented from competing by prescriptive solutions or standards).

4.6 The specification can then provide a means of evaluating the quality or conformance of a supplier's bids or capabilities – as well as, post-contract, the goods or services supplied, for acceptance (if conforming to specification) or rejection (if non-conforming).

4.7 The use of specification as a basis for contract award raises several issues for buyers.

- Specifications must clearly, comprehensively and unambiguously set out exactly what the buyer's (and other key stakeholders') expectations and requirements are: otherwise, a supplier or bid may conform to specification and *still* not represent 'right quality'.
- Specification may be the best and last opportunity for buyers to build in qualitative, values-based criteria such as social or environmental sustainability or compatibility, which would otherwise be seen as too subjective to be used in the directly competitive stage of contract award.

Reasons for disqualification

4.8 The buyer may exclude suppliers from bidding, or from contract award, if they fail to meet certain basic defined criteria in regard to suitability, financial standing and technical competence. In the public sector, for example, which has strict rules about contract award criteria to protect open, fair and transparent competition, buyers may disqualify suppliers on grounds of:

- **The personal situation of the supplier**: eg bankruptcy, liquidation or similar situations under international laws; conviction of an offence relating to professional ethics or competence, or failure to pay taxes; or false declaration of professional qualifications during the tender process
- **Financial capacity**, based on the estimated level of financial or economic capacity required to fulfil the contract, and the nature of evidence to justify this capacity (eg bank declarations, submission of balance sheets)
- **Technical capacity.** A buyer is permitted to seek information about matters such as: professional qualifications held by the supplier or senior employees; principal services, products or works carried out in the last three years; material and technical equipment used to carry out tasks; methods of assessing the equality of the project; and whether and how the work will be subcontracted
- **Professional qualifications**. A buyer can ask bidders to evidence that their professional qualifications are registered with the appropriate professional body.
- In relation to contract award, only two criteria are allowable: lowest price or 'most economically advantageous tender'. This allows issues such as resource consumption and disposal costs, for example, to be taken into account. Any social or environmental sustainability criteria used must be directly related to the performance of the contract, and appropriately weighted.

Lowest price

4.9 Some measure of price, cost, value or 'economic advantage' is essential to balance technical objectives with *commercial* objectives, such as adding value, reducing costs, contributing to profitability and securing competitive supply. There are also ethical reasons to support the use of quantified commercial criteria: if competitive sourcing methods (such as compared quotations or competitive bidding) are used, the contract should be awarded on the basis of objective, clearly-defined, directly-comparable award criteria.

4.10 Lowest price is perhaps the most obvious, straightforward and easy to apply contract award criterion – once basic technical criteria (or more in-depth pre-qualification criteria) have been met. For routine purchases of goods to standardised technical specifications, lowest price is a simple test of value and competitive supply.

4.11 The initial contract advertisement or invitations to quote should make clear that lowest price will be used as the criterion for contract award, allowing prospective suppliers to pitch their proposals and quotations accordingly. Equally, the contract advertisement should clearly state if the buyer is *not* bound to select the lowest-price bid or solution, so that the buyer retains the freedom to take broader value considerations into account.

Best value or 'most economically advantageous tender' (MEAT)

4.12 If 'best value' or 'economic advantage' criteria are used, the initial contract advertisement or invitations to quote should make this clear, and should explain the criteria that will be used to assess 'value' or 'economic advantage'.

4.13 Value criteria might include: quality, deliverability within target time scales, technical merit, innovation, risk sharing, health and safety or environmental performance. They should be directly relevant to the purpose and performance of the contract, and any specifications provided. For example, the level of performance would be considered directly relevant – whereas the nationality of the supplier's staff would not.

4.14 Such criteria should be listed in all contract notices, and should be meaningfully ranked and weighted so that suppliers know what priority will be given to non-price factors. For example, the buyer's extranet site might list the award criteria for a contract, in order of importance, with weightings to show how important each criterion is (eg price 50%; quality of personnel 30%; implementation 20%).

Best value and total lifecycle cost

4.15 Value for money is not about achieving the lowest purchase price: it has been defined (by the Office of Government Commerce) as *'the optimum combination of whole life costs and quality.'*

4.16 There is a vital difference between the purchase price of an article – particularly a substantial capital asset – and its *total acquisition cost* or *total cost of ownership*. Total acquisition cost includes not just the price of the items being purchased, but also:

- Procurement costs, such as taxes, foreign exchange rate costs and the cost of tendering and drawing up contracts
- Finance costs (if capital has to be borrowed to pay for the asset, say)
- The costs of packaging, transporting and insuring goods for delivery
- Costs of storage and other handling, assembly or finishing required
- Costs of quality management and quality failure (inspection, re-work or rejection, lost sales, compensation of customers etc)
- Costs of installation, maintenance and repair (where relevant, eg for equipment purchases), staff training and so on, over the total lifecycle of the asset
- Costs of de-commissioning, disassembly, recycling or disposal (including a 'negative cost' in the potential to realise the residual value of the asset through re-sale).

4.17 Some or all of these costs may be included in the price quoted by a supplier, and the buyer will need to bear this in mind when comparing two quotations: does a lower price reflect competitive pricing – or a lesser total package of benefits, or 'hidden' lifecycle costs not included in the lower quotation.

4.18 More generally, there is a *trade off* between the purchase price and the total package of benefits. 'It is an obvious fact, yet a commonly ignored one, that a low price may lead to a high total acquisition cost' (Baily *et al*). A lower price may reflect poorer quality, for example, and this will not necessarily be better value for money: the purchase price may be lower, but the total cost of acquisition and ownership may be higher, because of the need for more rigorous quality inspection, the number of rejects and reworks due to poor quality, lost sales through customer disappointment, and so on.

4.19 'Best value' may therefore be defined as the lowest total acquisition cost which meets the purchaser's complex package of requirements (for quality, service, ongoing partnership with the supplier and so on).

Chapter summary

- It is important to distinguish between criteria for supplier selection and criteria for contract award.
- There are various frameworks for supplier selection. Lysons and Farrington provide a framework involving eight perspectives; another framework is provided by Carter's 10Cs; there is also the FACE 2 FACE framework developed by Dawn Dadds.
- Financial appraisal is an important part of pre-qualifying suppliers.
- A potential supplier must also be vetted in terms of technical capability and production capacity.
- Quality control is concerned with the detection and correction of defects; quality assurance is concerned with the prevention of defects.
- Increasingly, potential suppliers are vetted in regard to environmental, sustainability and CSR performance.
- Contract award criteria seek to balance technical criteria against commercial criteria.
- Reasons for disqualifying potential suppliers include the personal situation of the supplier, lack of financial capacity, lack of technical capacity, and lack of professional qualifications.
- Value for money is defined as the optimum combination of whole life costs and quality.

Self-test questions

Numbers in brackets refer to the paragraphs where you can check your answers.

1   List features of the criteria used (a) for supplier selection and (b) for contract award. (1.5, 1.6)

2   What considerations will a buyer take into account when setting criteria for supplier selection? (1.8)

3   List Ray Carter's 10 Cs. (Table 3.2)

4   List checks that a buyer may make to assess a supplier's financial capacity. (3.6)

5   What factors may a buyer be concerned with when evaluating quality? (3.12)

6   Why may it be more difficult to evaluate the quality of a service than the quality of a manufactured item? (3.13)

7   What are the objectives of a quality management system? (3.20)

8   List factors that a buyer may consider when assessing the environmental performance of a potential supplier. (3.27)

9   Distinguish between conformance and performance specifications. (4.5)

10   What value criteria might be assessed under the heading of 'most economically advantageous tender'? (4.13)

11   List cost elements included in total acquisition cost. (4.16)

CHAPTER 4

Supply Chain Perspectives

Assessment criteria and indicative content

1.4 Explain the main consequences on supply chains when sourcing requirements from suppliers

- Sourcing internally
- Sourcing from small and medium-sized enterprises (SMEs)
- Sourcing from third sector organisations
- Ethical sourcing and the fair trade movement
- Supplier tiering and supply chain networks

Section headings

1 The supplier's perspective on sourcing
2 Sourcing from SMEs and the third sector
3 Ethical sourcing
4 Supply chain structures

Introduction

In this chapter we look at the sourcing process, as seen from the perspective of the suppliers or supply chain: the impact on suppliers and supply chain relationships of a buyer's sourcing policies and decisions.

We start by looking briefly at the supplier's perspective on key sourcing processes such as supplier appraisal and selection – just to give you the 'other side' of the viewpoint taken so far in this Course Book. However, this is important for buyer-side decision-making too, in order to develop sourcing approaches which strengthen – rather than undermine – supply market capability and supply chain relationships.

We next go on to explore some of the specific aspects raised by the syllabus.

We start with the special challenges faced by suppliers in the small and medium enterprise (SME) and third sectors, and how buyers can remove barriers to SME and third sector participation in contracts.

We then go on to look at the ways in which buyer sourcing behaviour may impact negatively on suppliers, and how buyers can source more ethically and fairly.

Finally, we look at the consequences of sourcing strategies and policies (such as those discussed in Chapter 2) for the structuring of supply chains and supply chain relationships.

1 The supplier's perspective on sourcing

Access to contracts

1.1 It is important for buyers to consider the supplier identification, appraisal and selection process from the supply market's perspective, in order to help them maximise the benefit of the process.

1.2 One key issue for the supply market in general is the accessibility of contracts and new business – especially to new, small or diverse (eg minority- or women-owned) suppliers.

1.3 In the interests of corporate social responsibility, social sustainability *and* commercial advantage, buyers should consider increasing the accessibility of contracts to a wider supplier base, and – more specifically – removing unnecessary barriers to participation for smaller or less established suppliers who might nevertheless:

- Have the technical capability to fulfil requirements, especially if supported through supplier development
- Be able to add value through qualities such as responsiveness, innovation and entrepreneurship, understanding of consumer segments, and quality of service (due to eagerness to win and retain business).

1.4 We will discuss specific access issues for SMEs and third sector organisations in the following section – together with measures buyers can take to remove unnecessary barriers to participation. In the first instance, however, it is necessary for buyers to:

- Appreciate the value of **widening and developing the supply market** through increasing diversity and participation
- Consider whether **sourcing policies and practices** (such as international sourcing, the use of technical specifications, the aggregation of orders into large contracts to secure economies of scale, or the requirement for high-level quality accreditations) may act as a barrier to participation
- Appreciate the **frustration** of suppliers unable to compete for business, and facilitate access where possible (eg through advance notice of upcoming contracts, information about sourcing processes, or the giving of post-tender feedback)
- Appreciate the **ethical issues** in fair access to contracts. Appraisals, quotations and tenders cost prospective suppliers time, effort and money – and it is unethical to subject them to this cost frivolously or manipulatively: that is, if there is not a genuine, fair and open opportunity for them to win the business.

Supplier attitudes to appraisal and pre-qualification

1.5 Sometimes an appraisal arises because a supplier has asked to be added to an approved supplier list, or has expressed an interest in a selective tender – and in such a case, it may be safe to assume that the supplier is highly motivated to take part in a pre-qualification appraisal process (such as self-assessment questionnaires, site visits and capability surveys).

1.6 However, if the initial approach or request for pre-qualification comes from the buyer, the response from potential suppliers will not necessarily be favourable. There may be reluctance on the part of suppliers for various reasons: Table 4.1.

Table 4.1 *Why suppliers may not welcome an appraisal*

REASON FOR SUPPLIER'S RELUCTANCE	STEPS A BUYER CAN TAKE
A particular supplier may not find the buyer's business attractive.	Estimate the likely attractiveness of the business to potential suppliers, using tools such as the supplier preferencing model (see later).
Suppliers may have bad experiences of previous appraisals, with this or other buyers.	Emphasise that the appraisal process will be carried out fairly and transparently so that suppliers will not just be wasting their time.
Suppliers may be unsure of the selection process, perhaps suspecting that some other supplier has an 'inside track' or that the buyer is not serious.	Provide full information about how the selection process will work, and keep suppliers informed about progress through the various stages.
The timing of the proposed appraisal may be inconvenient.	Ensure that suppliers have adequate time to prepare for the appraisal, and avoid suggesting dates that will obviously coincide with suppliers' busy periods. Be sympathetic if a supplier suggests a different timetable.
Suppliers may believe that the process will be expensive and time-consuming (exacerbated by the fact that it may not lead to profitable business in the end).	Ensure that the exercise is streamlined as far as possible, consistent with obtaining the information required. Consider using trial orders as part of the appraisal.
Suppliers may be wary of sharing confidential information during the appraisal.	Be prepared to sign a confidentiality agreement.

Providing post-appraisal feedback

1.7   Under best practice supplier appraisal and selection procedures, a buyer should provide feedback to each supplier subjected to detailed pre-qualification or assessment. This will happen as a matter of course with the successful supplier, but even unsuccessful suppliers deserve to know how the buyer evaluated them, and what prevented them from achieving approved status or winning a contract.

1.8   A constructive feedback process will:

- Provide the supplier with helpful information to improve its performance and competitiveness for future business development
- Give suppliers some benefit, as a return on their investment in the appraisal process
- Leave suppliers with a positive impression of the buyer's appraisal and selection process, raising confidence and trust for future sourcing exercises or tenders (ie not deterring a potential supplier from bidding for future business for which it may be qualified)
- Help to preserve good relations between the buyer and a future prospective supplier
- Help to preserve the buyer's reputation in the supply market for fair, positive, ethical and transparent sourcing processes.

The supplier preferencing model

1.9   Sourcing can appear to be all about buyers selecting suppliers they want to be part of their supply chain – but this is only half of the story, because suppliers also get to select the customers with whom they will do business! A buyer may want to enter into a relationship with a supplier – but how does the supplier feel about the buyer as a prospective long-term client?

1.10   The supplier preferencing model is an analysis tool, in the form of a matrix, which illustrates how attractive it is to a supplier to deal with a buyer, and the monetary value of the buyer's business to the supplier: Figure 4.1.

Figure 4.1 *The supplier preferencing model*

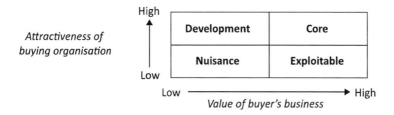

1.11   Looking at each quadrant in turn:

- Nuisance customers are neither attractive nor valuable to do business with. Suppliers practising customer relationship management will regularly review their customer base and downgrade or cease service to unprofitable customers – or raise their prices (in such a way as to turn them into exploitable customers).
- Exploitable customers offer large volumes of business, which compensates for lack of attractiveness. The supplier will fulfil the terms of the supply contract – but will not go out of its way to provide extras (and any extras demanded will be charged at additional cost).
- Development customers are attractive, despite currently low levels of business. The supplier may see potential to grow the account, and may court extra business by 'going the extra mile' in fulfilling contracts: if all goes well, the customer may be converted to 'core' status.
- Core customers are highly desirable and valuable for suppliers, who will want to establish long-term, mutually-profitable relationships with them if possible.

1.12   This is a useful model for sourcing and supplier management, because it suggests strongly that in order to engage the best suppliers – and get the best from suppliers once engaged – a buyer needs to maintain its 'attractive customer' status. There are various factors that might make suppliers keen to do business with a buying organisation, and therefore to present competitive offerings or bids.

- Glamorous or high profile brand: suppliers will want to deal with the organisation in order to enhance their own reputation and attractiveness to customers
- Good reputation and standing in the market eg for environmental or ethical leadership (eg The Body Shop or Marks & Spencer)
- Fair, ethical and professional sourcing and trading practices (eg paying suppliers promptly, not entering into unnecessary disputes, keeping suppliers well informed, not squeezing supplier profit margins excessively)
- Willingness to collaborate and co-invest in capability and performance improvements (eg through supplier training and other forms of supplier development, information-sharing for collaborative cost reduction and continuous improvement programmes etc)
- Willingness to share risks, costs and value gains equitably with supply partners (ie seeking reciprocity or win-win: not making excessive demands and hard bargaining techniques, without offering any benefits or concessions in return)
- Constructive interpersonal relationships with contacts at the buying firm (although these are vulnerable to change, if contacts leave the firm).

2   Sourcing from SMEs and the third sector

Small and medium enterprises (SMEs)

2.1   From your own experience, you will have gathered that organisations vary widely by size: from one-person operations to small businesses to vast global conglomerates. According to a 2005 European Union definition (used for grant-aid purposes):

- A 'micro' enterprise is one which has fewer than 10 employees and annual turnover of less than 2 million euros.
- A 'small' enterprise is one which has 10–49 employees and annual turnover of less than 10 million euros.
- A 'medium-sized' enterprise is one which has 50–249 employees and annual turnover of less than 50 million euros.
- A 'large-scale' enterprise employs more than 250 employees, with annual turnover of more than 50 million euros.

2.2 Particular attention has been given to small and medium enterprises (SMEs) in recent years, because (a) they are a significant contributor to economic activity (by the above definition, some 99% of enterprises in the EU in 2005, providing around 65 million jobs), and (b) because they require financial and guidance support in order to overcome lack of economic strength in competition with larger players.

2.3 SME suppliers may have an advantage over large firms in clearly defined, small markets: it would not be worth large firms entering markets where there is no scope for economies of scale arising from mass production. Such an advantage may apply in a geographically localised market, say, or in a 'niche' market for specialist, customised or premium-quality products. In addition, the entrepreneurial nature and speed of communication in small enterprises makes them particularly well suited to innovation and invention, and they may have an advantage over larger, less flexible firms in fast-changing, high-technology markets.

2.4 On the other hand, SMEs are at a competitive disadvantage in areas such as: raising loan and share capital (because they are a greater risk); managing cashflow (being harder hit by late payment or non-payments); ability to take financial risks (including investment in research and development); and dealing with bureaucratic requirements. They are also unable to take advantages of the economies of scale which are available to larger suppliers, which may affect their ability to price competitively.

Why source from SME suppliers?

2.5 From the above discussion, you may be able to identify particular challenges for a buyer sourcing from SMEs. The buyer will need to take into account issues such as: the supplier's limited capacity to handle large-volume and aggregated contracts; the supplier's potential financial instability (due to cash flow issues and difficulties securing credit); and the ethical and business risk of a small supplier's becoming overly dependent on a large customer.

2.6 In addition, there will be a key sourcing trade-off between:

- The economic advantages of dealing with large suppliers (the ability to aggregate requirements for reduced transaction costs and bulk discounts, and more competitive pricing due to economies of scale)
- The potential for 'better value' arising from dealing with SME suppliers:
  — Access to a wider supply market, potentially enhancing competition (and therefore lower pricing through the market as a whole)
  — Competitive pricing due to lower administrative overheads and management costs
  — Greater responsiveness and flexibility (with shorter decision-making and approval channels)
  — Innovation capability and diversity of business solutions, through the early exploitation of new technology, providing products or services in new or underdeveloped markets, or using innovation capability to differentiate themselves from established market players.
  — Expertise in focused niche markets
  — Willingness and ability to produce small-order, niche, bespoke and customised items (where larger suppliers may have minimum order quantities and standardised offerings)
  — Higher quality specialist products, due to greater skills, originality and commitment (where the market is unattractive to larger enterprises)
  — Higher commitment and levels of service (due to the value of the business to the supplier).

Barriers to access for SME suppliers

2.7   If a buyer wishes to take advantage of these sources of value, for appropriate procurements, it may be able deliberately to prioritise, or give preference to, SME suppliers in its sourcing decisions. In the public sector, however, this is generally not permissible, as it represents a distortion of competition. Instead, attention is given to identifying and removing barriers to participation and competition that might prevent or deter SMEs from accessing contracts.

2.8   Barriers to SME participation include the following.

- Not being able to find out about opportunities. (In the public sector, for example, low-value procurements may not be widely advertised, due to falling below the EU threshold for open tendering.)
- Lacking marketing resources to raise their profile in the supply market
- Believing that the process involved in bidding will be (unnecessarily) complex and costly, and therefore being deterred from participating
- Lacking expertise in areas such as interpreting complex requirements documentation or constructing good-quality proposals or tenders
- Lacking a track record of performance, or several years of financial records, for pre-qualification (since SMEs are more likely to be recent start-ups)
- Lacking the capacity to handle large volume contracts, where the trend (in both public and private sectors) is towards aggregation of demand into fewer, larger contracts; the use of framework contracts; and a reduced supplier base.

2.9   Buyers can support, encourage and facilitate SME participation by measures such as the following.

- Publicising opportunities widely, particularly for small and low-value contracts, using the trade press and services such as Business Links
- Regularly 'refreshing' approved supplier lists, to include SMEs where appropriate
- Using the corporate website to make information available to potential suppliers (including 'Selling to...' or 'Doing business with...' guidance on sourcing procedures, pre-qualification requirements, buyer policies and expectations, and contacts for questions)
- Holding 'Meet the Buyer' events to discuss requirements and sourcing processes with potential suppliers
- Explaining the sourcing process, and what will be required, to suppliers at the outset
- Ensuring that sourcing procedures and pre-qualification requirements are appropriate to the size and complexity of the requirement (ie not unnecessarily onerous for small, routine purchases)
- Keeping tender and specification documents concise and jargon-free – and using outcome or performance specifications where possible (more flexibly focusing on 'what' is to be delivered, rather than 'how')
- Using a pre-qualification questionnaire to minimise the initial administrative burden on small suppliers
- Ensuring that sourcing exercises are based on a sound business case, to avoid wasted effort on procurements that are cancelled or delayed due to lack of authorisation or funding
- Setting realistic timescales for sourcing processes
- Considering dis-aggregating contracts: making smaller contracts available to SME suppliers, eg by separating out specialist elements or new work from the main contract; or dividing large requirements into smaller lots for multi-sourcing
- Encouraging large first-tier or prime contractors to use SMEs as sub-contractors, particularly where they can provide specialist or innovative products
- Publishing the names of prime contractors in upcoming contracts, to help SMEs identify subcontractor opportunities
- Ensuring that the buyer, and its main contractors, pay SME subcontractors on time – or as soon as possible. Other cashflow support may be provided by considering stage or interim payments (linked to progress or work done), or advance payments.

- Being open to consortium bids from groups of SMEs, for large procurements
- Giving constructive feedback to successful and unsuccessful suppliers.

Sourcing from the third sector

2.10 The 'third sector' of an economy comprises non-governmental organisations (NGOs) which are operated on a not-for-profit (NFP) basis, generally reinvesting any 'surplus' from their activities to further social, environmental, cultural or other value-driven objectives. Such organisations include: charities, churches, political parties, museums, clubs and associations, co-operatives, pressure groups, trade unions and professional bodies such as CIPS. In addition, the term 'social enterprises' is given to businesses that trade with a social purpose, using business tools and techniques to achieve primarily social aims (such as employment opportunities, environmental protection or funding for social projects).

2.11 Organisations in the third sector have typically been set up to achieve a defined objective (eg for a charitable or awareness-raising purpose, or to represent the interests of members, or to raise funds for social projects) rather than to maximise profit. NFP organisations usually derive their funding from voluntary donations, legacies (money left to the organisation in someone's will), sponsorships and government grants and subsidies. Social enterprises in particular may also have a profit-seeking trading arm to generate revenue (as in the case of 'charity shops', say).

2.12 Buyers in the public sector are perhaps most like to source requirements from third sector organisations, as they source (or 'commission') the delivery of public services, such as education, health and aged care, leisure and arts services and so on. The OGC booklet *Smaller Supplier: Better Value?* notes that: 'successful social enterprises operate in sectors across a range of public services including waste management, transport, manufacturing, leisure, education and care.' Social and not-for-profit enterprises may therefore provide goods and services of interest to private sector buyers.

2.13 In common with other SMEs, smaller social enterprises can offer cost effective, responsive and innovative solutions to procurement needs. They also undergo many of the challenges faced by small businesses, in terms of cost issues, credit restrictions, resource limitations, lack of capacity and problems in accessing opportunities.

2.14 Here are some possible additional issues in sourcing from some third-sector organisations.

- A lack of capability, skills and professional management, as a result of the need to use volunteer labour (and limited resources for training and supervision)
- A lack of financial stability and cashflow, due to reliance on external funding, from donors and grants
- A focus on resource efficiency (maximising use of, and accountability for, scarce and vulnerable stakeholder funds), values and mission, and the priorities of key stakeholders, rather than a competitive focus on customer satisfaction, product or service quality.

3 Ethical sourcing

3.1 'Ethics' are simply a set of moral principles or values about what constitutes 'right' and 'wrong' behaviour. For individuals, these often reflect the assumptions and beliefs of the families, cultures and educational environment in which their ideas developed. Ethics are also shaped more deliberately by public and professional bodies, in the form of agreed principles and guidelines which are designed to protect society's best interests.

3.2 Ethical issues may affect the sourcing of requirements from suppliers at three levels.

- At the **macro** level, there are the issues of the role of business and capitalism in society: the debate about the impacts of globalisation and global sourcing, the exploitation of labour in low-cost supply markets, the impacts of industrialisation on the environment and so on. This is the sphere addressed by the Ethical Trading Initiative, for example: an alliance of companies, non-governmental organisations and trade unions committed to working together to promote internationally-agreed principles of ethical trade and employment.

- At the **corporate** level, there are the issues which face a buying organisation as it formulates strategies and policies about how it interacts with its various stakeholders. Some of these matters will be covered by legislative and regulatory requirements, and an organisation may have a 'compliance based' approach to ethics which strives merely to uphold these minimal requirements. The sphere generally referred to as 'corporate social responsibility' covers policies which the organisation adopts for the good and wellbeing of stakeholders, taking a more proactive 'integrity based' approach. As we saw in Chapter 3, this includes issues such as environmental protection and sustainability, fair trading and labour standards in the supply chain.

- At the **individual** level, there are the issues which face individuals as they act and interact within the organisation and supply chain: refusing to be party to fraud, say; not discriminating in the award of tenders; or deciding whether to accept gifts or hospitality which might be perceived as an attempt to influence a sourcing decision. This is the sphere which is often covered in a corporate or professional Code of Ethics.

Ethical sourcing policies

3.3 Ethical, sustainable or responsible sourcing policies may cover a range of matters, depending on the ethical risks and issues raised by the organisation's activities and markets. Here are some examples.

- The promotion of fair, open and transparent competition in sourcing (and the avoidance of unfair, fraudulent, manipulative or coercive sourcing practices)

- The use of sourcing policies to promote positive socio-economic goals such as supplier diversity, support for local and SME suppliers, and minimisation of transport miles (to reduce environmental impacts and carbon emissions)

- The specification and sourcing of ethically produced inputs (eg certified as not tested on animals; drawn from sustainably managed or renewable sources; or manufactured under safe working conditions)

- The selection and management of suppliers to promote ethical trading, environmental responsibility and labour standards at all tiers of the supply chain (eg by pre-qualifying suppliers on CSR policies, ethical codes, environmental management systems, reverse-logistics and recycling capabilities, and supply chain management; and incentivising, monitoring and developing supplier ethical performance)

- A commitment to supporting the improvement of working terms and conditions (labour standards) throughout the supply chain, and particularly in low-cost labour countries with comparatively lax regulatory regimes

- A commitment to supporting sustainable profit-taking by suppliers (eg not squeezing supplier profit margins unfairly) and to ensuring that fair prices are paid to suppliers back through the supply chain, particularly where buyers are in a dominant position (eg in developing and low-cost supply markets)

- Adherence to the ethical frameworks and codes of conduct of relevant bodies such as the International Labour Organisation (ILO), Fair Trade Association or Ethical Trading Initiative, the International Standards Organisation guidelines on Corporate Social Responsibility (ISO 26000: 2010), or the Codes of Ethics of relevant professional bodies (such as CIPS)

- A commitment to compliance with all relevant laws and regulations for consumer, supplier and worker protection.

Supply chain ethics management

3.4 It is important to note that, in addition to its own internal guidelines for ethical sourcing, trading and employment, a buying organisation may take responsibility for encouraging (or even insisting on) ethical employment and/or environmental practices in its suppliers.

3.5 Sources of supply may be pre-qualified, for example, on the basis of basic principles such as non-use of child labour or forced labour, the paying of reasonable wages, the provision of adequate working conditions, health and safety, and the protection of workers' rights. Alternatively, suppliers may be pre-qualified on the basis of having robust CSR, environmental and ethical policies – or willingness to develop them, or to adhere to the policies laid down by the buyer as a condition of supplier approval.

3.6 Supplier ethical policies and performance can be monitored by site visits and audits, to verify claims made on pre-qualification questionnaires. Where this is particularly difficult (eg with international or subcontracted suppliers), the buyer may use references, approved supplier or stockist lists and, where available, third party monitoring and certification services.

The Ethical Trading Initiative (ETI)

3.7 The ETI is an alliance of companies, non-governmental organisations (NGOs) and trade union organisations committed to working together to identify and promote internationally-agreed principles of ethical trade and employment, and to monitor and independently verify the observance of ethics code provisions, as standards for ethical sourcing.

3.8 The ETI publishes a code of labour practice (the 'base code') giving guidance on fundamental principles of ethical labour practices, based on international standards.

1   Employment is freely chosen.
2   Freedom of association and the right to collective bargaining are respected.
3   Working conditions are safe and hygienic.
4   Child labour shall not be used.
5   Living wages are paid.
6   Working hours are not excessive.
7   No discrimination is practised.
8   Regular employment is provided.
9   No harsh or inhumane treatment is allowed.

The Fair Trade movement

3.9 'Unfair' trading arises when large buyers exert their bargaining power to force down the prices of small suppliers, to levels that bring economic hardship to producers, exacerbating poor wages and working conditions for their workers, and bringing no economic benefit to their communities. Most commonly, fair trade issues arise in developing economies: the media has recently highlighted the plight of coffee and tea growers, and textile and garment trade workers. The Body Shop is one example of an organisation that has proactively cultivated a fair trade ethos as part of its brand positioning, with a policy of assisting small-scale indigenous communities and supporting small business development by offering fair prices (a policy called 'Trade Not Aid').

3.10 Started over sixty years ago, Fair Trade has developed into a worldwide concept, seeking to ensure decent living and working conditions for small-scale and economically disadvantaged producers and workers in developing countries. It involves an alliance of producers and importers, retailers, labelling and certifying organisations – and, of course, consumers willing to pursue ethical consumption by support for certified Fair Trade products. Meanwhile, the comparatively new discipline of 'fair trade marketing' involves 'the development, promotion and selling of fair trade brands and the positioning of organisations on the basis of a fair trade ethos' (Jobber, 2007).

3.11 Fair Trade products are marketed in two different ways. The traditional or integrated route is where goods are produced, imported and/or distributed by specialised Fair Trade organisations, under standards developed by the International Fair Trade Association (IFAT). The other route to market is through Fair Trade labelling and certification, whereby goods (mainly food products) are certified by an independent third party verification body, to guarantee that their production chains respect the International Fair Trade standards developed by Fair Trade Labelling Organisations International.

3.12 Recent years have seen a significant increase in both consumer awareness and sales of Fair Trade goods, with sales showing annual growth rates of 20% to 30% – and this is likely to provide a strong influence on sustainable sourcing policies.

3.13 The International Fair Trade Association's Fair Trade standards advocate basic ethical sourcing principles, including:

- Creating opportunities for economically disadvantaged producers
- Integrity (transparency and accountability in dealings with trading partners)
- Capability building (developing producers' independence by providing continuity, during which producers can improve their skills and access new markets)
- Fair payment (paying a fair price which covers not only the cost of production but enables production that is just and sound, and takes into account the principle of equal pay for equal work by men and women)
- Working conditions (provision of a safe and healthy working environment for producers)
- Gender equity and children's rights
- The environment (encouraging better environmental practices and the application of responsible methods of production).

Ethical conduct of sourcing processes

3.14 In addition to 'big picture' sourcing and supplier management policies – directed at ensuring that supply chains adhere to basic ethical standards in their conduct and management – a range of ethical issues is raised by the sourcing process itself. Sourcing decisions potentially involve large sums of money, and the use of power to grant or withhold access to business. They are therefore prone to ethical issues such as abuse of power, conflicts of interest, fraud and misuse of funds.

3.15 Let's look at a few key ethical principles, and the ethical issues arising from them in sourcing requirements from external suppliers.

Use of information

3.16 One of the key principles of business ethics is the provision of fair, truthful and accurate (not false or misleading) information. This makes unethical, for example, the practice of deliberately inflating estimates of order sizes in order to obtain a price that would not be offered if the true usage patterns were admitted.

3.17 Another key ethical principle is protecting the confidentiality of information, where appropriate. Confidential information obtained in the course of supplier appraisal, for example, should not be disclosed without proper and specific authority, or unless there is a legal duty to disclose it: for example, if there is suspicion of money laundering or terrorist activity.

Fair dealing

3.18 A particularly important principle in ethical sourcing is what might be called 'fair dealing'. A temptation to unfair dealing may be offered, for example, where:

- A supplier or potential supplier makes an error in a quotation or invoice, in the buyer's favour. (Will it be brought to the supplier's attention? Will the buyer seek to force the supplier to honour the price as quoted?)
- There is potential to pay later than the payment terms agreed (which may be particularly damaging to the cashflow of small suppliers)

- Where quotations or tender bids are sought from suppliers where there is no intention to purchase (eg if the contract has already been earmarked for an existing or preferred supplier)
- Where some vendors are favoured over others in a tender situation (eg by providing them with more information, or allowing post-tender negotiation).

Deception or unfairness in such situations may be perceived as unethical, as well as potentially damaging to ongoing trading relationships.

Inducements and conflicts of interest

3.19   Another key principle in sourcing processes, which is often the subject of procurement ethical codes, is not offering or accepting gifts or **inducements** which may – or may be *perceived* to – influence the recipient's sourcing decisions. A related principle is that individuals should not make sourcing decisions (or divulge confidential information) for personal gain. Such situations create a **conflict of interest**, because the best interests of the firm or internal client (eg contract award on the basis of best value) conflicts with the personal interests of the individual (eg personal gain). Another such situation would be if the buyer stood to gain from promoting a particular supplier because he had a financial or personal interest in the supplying firm: as a shareholder, perhaps, or as someone with a close relationship to the supplier's management.

3.20   The giving of gifts and offers of hospitality are among the common courtesies of business dealings. The problem for procurement professionals is to decide when such practices amount to an attempt to induce a favourable sourcing or contract award decision, information disclosure or other favourable treatment. There are obvious cases where buyer and seller collude to ensure that the seller wins a contract, the buyer in return receiving a reward: this is defined as bribery and corruption – and it is illegal in the UK (with strict legislation covering public bodies, in particular).

3.21   The more difficult cases are those where no explicit link is made between the gift and the award of business. A major difficulty may be the difference in perceptions between buyer and seller. To the seller, a gift may be merely a token of appreciation, of a kind that his organisation virtually expects him to bestow on most or all customers. To the buyer, however, the gift may become a material inducement to favour that supplier. (In international business dealings, this difference in perception may also be a cultural issue.)

3.22   Most organisations have clear rules on the receiving of gifts and hospitality, where this is perceived as an ethical issue. This is also the subject of codes of ethics in the procurement profession. As a general principle, any potential interest or conflict of interest should be *disclosed,* so that proceedings are transparent and open to control.

Procurement codes of ethics

3.23   National and international bodies representing procurement professionals have published ethical codes setting out (usually in fairly broad terms) what moral principles or values are used to steer conduct, and what activities are considered unethical.

3.24   The CIPS Professional Code of Ethics is the ethical standard and disciplinary framework (the basis of best conduct) for procurement professionals in the area of procurement ethics. The code makes it clear that seeking membership of the Institute is in itself an undertaking to abide by ethical standards, and failure to do so may be dealt with according to a defined disciplinary process.

3.25   The guidance emphasises the overriding principle that members should not use a position of authority for personal gain. Equally, members have a responsibility to uphold the standing (dignity and reputation) of the procurement profession and the Institute, by their conduct both inside and outside their employing organisations.

3.26 Specific guidance is also offered in the following areas.

- Members must disclose any personal interest which might impinge on their work activities, or which might appear to do so in the eyes of others.
- Members must respect the confidentiality of information and must not use information received for personal gain. The information they provide should be true and fair.
- Members should avoid any arrangements which might prevent fair competition.
- Except for small-value items, business gifts should not be accepted.
- Only modest hospitality should be accepted. Members should not accept hospitality which might influence a business decision, or which might appear to do so.
- Any doubt on these last two points should be discussed with the individual's superior.

(You should download the CIPS Professional Code of Ethics from the CIPS website, if you have not already done so as part of your studies or work.)

4   Supply chain structures

The concept of supply chains and networks

4.1 The process of sourcing requirements from external suppliers is increasingly considered in relation to 'supply chains': as an issue of developing and managing flows of goods and value towards an end customer – not just as a series of one-to-one transactions or contractual relationships.

4.2 The concept of the 'supply chain' can therefore be defined as follows.

- 'The supply chain encompasses all organisations and activities associated with the flow and transformation of goods from the raw materials stage, through to the end user, as well as the associated information flows. Material and information flows both up and down the supply chain.' (Handfield & Nichols, *Supply Chain Redesign*)
- 'The supply chain includes all those involved in organising and converting materials through the input stages (raw materials), conversion phase (work in progress) and outputs (finished products). The cycle is often repeated several times in the journey from the individual producer to the ultimate customer, as one organisation's finished good is another's input.' (Baily *et al*)

4.3 A supply chain may be very short. As an example, you may have driven past a farm and noticed a sign advertising fresh eggs for sale: the farmer is producing the goods and selling direct to his customers with no intermediaries. In other cases, the supply chain may be very long. For example, if you purchase a washing machine from a department store there will clearly have been many organisations involved in the process (or flow of value) leading to your purchase: to analyse the supply chain you would have to go right back to the extraction of a metallic ore forming the main material of the washing machine.

4.4 The chain metaphor highlights several useful characteristics of the sourcing process and supplier relationships.

- It emphasises 'serial co-operation' (Jespersen & Skjøtt-Larsen) or 'working together in turn': each player contributes value at its stage of the sequence of activities.
- It emphasises mutual dependency and collaboration, because each link in a chain is essential to the completeness and strength of the whole: weak links and breakages (eg an underperforming or failing supplier or distributor) may disrupt the flow of supply.
- It emphasises the importance of 'linkages' or interfaces between members: value is added not just by each element in the chain, but by the quality of the relationships between them.

4.5 This has some clear implications for the sourcing of requirements from suppliers, because it emphasises the need to:

- Co-ordinate activities across the supply chain, in order to maximise the efficient flow of value towards the customer
- Develop appropriate relationships with suppliers, in order to ensure that linkages are maintained
- Structure supply chains effectively, in order to maintain control over their activities (to minimise the risk of supply disruption or reputational damage), while minimising the effort and cost of doing so (eg by dealing primarily with an immediate or 'first-tier' supplier with control over its own supply chain)
- Select, evaluate and develop suppliers in relation to the effectiveness of their *own* supply chain management
- Work collaboratively with supply chain members, to secure added value, cost and quality improvements throughout the supply chain as a whole – to the benefit of all its members.

Supply chain structure

1.6   In Chapter 2 we discussed sourcing strategies such as supply base optimisation, and the trade-offs between (a) the desire to minimise the costs and complexity of managing a large supplier base and (b) the desire to minimise the risks of having a very narrow supplier base. We noted the trend towards aggregating supply, and establishing closer, longer-term partnership relationships with a few trusted, qualified suppliers. At the same time, in this chapter we have noted the benefits of dis-aggregating supply, in order to encourage the participation of SME and third-sector suppliers in smaller contract 'lots'.

4.7   One of the solutions to these trade-offs lies in the way the supply chain is structured: specifically, in the development of supplier tiering.

Supplier tiering

4.8   Suppose that a manufacturer wishes to maximise its own part in the value adding process by taking in only a minimum contribution from outside suppliers. For example, the manufacturer buys in parts from a number of suppliers, and assembles them through a number of stages to produce a finished product. The structure of the supply chain in such a case is as illustrated in Figure 4.2.

Figure 4.2 *All manufacturing performed by top-level purchaser*

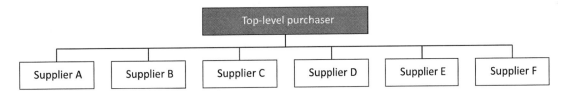

4.9   By contrast, suppose that the manufacturer sees strategic advantage in outsourcing all activities other than the final stages of production. In that case, its direct procurement relationship may be (in simplified terms) with a single supplier or tier of suppliers. Each supplier in the first tier would have an extensive role to fulfil in the manufacture of the final product, making use of 'second tier' suppliers: Figure 4.3.

Figure 4.3 *Top-level purchaser outsources most manufacturing*

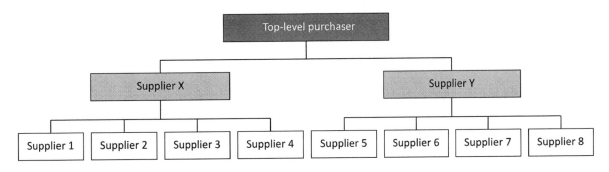

4.10 An organisation might adopt a deliberate policy of tiering its suppliers, so as to reduce the number of first-tier suppliers: the 'vendor/supplier base' with which it has to deal directly. This may be part of a process of supplier rationalisation or supply chain re-structuring, for example. The organisation deals directly only with its first-tier suppliers: second-tier suppliers deal with a first-tier supplier.

4.11 For example, in a manufacturing operation such as an automobile manufacturer, the top-level purchaser is the 'original equipment manufacturer' (OEM) or assembler. It might have 180 different suppliers with which it deals directly. In order to rationalise its commercial relationships, it might reduce its vendor base to, say, 20 first-tier suppliers (specialist manufacturers of subassemblies). These in turn will organise and manage a second tier of suppliers (component manufacturers, metal finishers and so on) from which they can source required items on the OEM's behalf.

4.12 The relationship between an organisation and its first-tier suppliers will obviously be critically important. First-tier suppliers are often expected to collaborate with the top-level purchaser to add value (making improvements and eliminating wastes) throughout the supply chain, and pursue innovation in products and processes. With only a small number of first-tier supplier relationships, the top-level purchaser can focus on developing these as long-term, collaborative supply partnerships.

4.13 The reasons for tiering of suppliers might be any of the following.

- The OEM wants to develop long-term relationships with key suppliers, but only has the time and resources to develop a limited number of such relationships.
- Standardisation of parts and variety reduction has reduced the number of parts required, so that the OEM needs fewer suppliers than in the past.
- There has been consolidation of suppliers within the supply market.

Sourcing implications of supplier tiering

4.14 The impact of supply chain tiering on sourcing and supplier management in the top-level purchasing organisation or OEM may include the following.

- The sourcing, selection and contracting of the first-tier suppliers will be a crucial strategic exercise. It should involve a range of key stakeholders (including senior management, procurement and user functions). Adequate resources and time must be allocated to comprehensive appraisal, selection and negotiation processes. Where competitive sourcing is desirable or necessary (as in the public sector), competition should only be applied as a final stage, following (a) rigorous pre-qualification of shortlisted candidates and (b) negotiation or dialogue to develop collaborative solutions and agreements.
- There will be fewer commercial relationships to source and manage, so the procurement function can direct its attention to managing, developing and improving these key relationships. Indeed, this is essential, since extensive responsibility has been delegated to the first-tier suppliers.
- In order to minimise business and reputational risk, procurement staff will still need to 'drill down' through the tiers in the supply chain: appraising and monitoring policies, systems and performance to ensure that the first-tier supplier's supply chain is being well managed. Priorities for 'drill down' may include risk management; ethical, environmental and labour standards; and quality assurance and compliance.
- The buyer may exercise influence over the first-tier supplier to adopt some of its own existing suppliers as subcontractors or lower-tier suppliers, in order to maintain business relationships and the benefit of relationship-specific investments and adaptations.
- Procurement may be freed up to pursue a more strategic focus and contribution (such as sustainable sourcing, global sourcing or supplier relationship development) with fewer operational tasks and transactions to handle.
- More and better supply chain improvements and innovations may be available from sharing information and collaborating with expert first-tier suppliers.

Supply chain networks

4.15 Even a tiered supply chain model offers a simplified picture. In reality, each organisation in the supply chain has multiple other relationships with its own customers, suppliers, industry contacts, partners and advisers – and even competitors (in trade associations or industry think tanks, say) – any and all of whom may also be connected with each other! Many writers (such as Cox & Lamming, and Christopher) now argue, therefore, that a more appropriate metaphor for the supply process is not a chain, but a network or web – which describes a more complex set of interrelated relationships and transactions.

4.16 Seeing the supply chain as a network is helpful for a number of reasons.

- It is a more strategic model for mapping and analysing supply chain relationships, and therefore for seeking to exploit synergies and improve performance in innovative ways.
- It raises the possibility of a wider range of collaborations (eg buyer or supplier associations or consortia) which may offer mutual advantages – and perhaps alter the balance of power in supply relationships (eg increasing the buying power of small buyers by participation in a buying consortium, or increasing the capacity of small suppliers by collaboration in a consortium bid).
- It recognises the potential of 'extended enterprises' and virtual organisations: extending the strategic capability of the firm through the collective resources and performance of network contributors – and extending the strategic importance of sourcing activities as a way of accessing those contributions.
- It recognises that extended enterprises may overlap (with particular suppliers or customers in common), creating complex patterns of relationship, competition and potential risk (eg to information and intellectual property).

Sourcing internally

4.17 This caption (taken from Unit Content 1.4) raises issues of:

- Intra-company trading (see Section 3 of Chapter 2)
- The choice between making/doing internally or sourcing from outside (see Section 4 of Chapter 2)

Chapter summary

- Corporate social responsibility dictates that buyers should make contracts accessible to a wide range of potential suppliers.
- Best practice for buyers includes giving appropriate post-appraisal feedback to potential suppliers.
- The supplier preferencing model suggests that suppliers prefer customers who are inherently attractive to deal with and valuable in terms of volume business.
- SMEs are a huge contributor to total economic activity. There are sound reasons why buyers should encourage suppliers from this sector.
- Sourcing from third sector organisation is typically a public sector practice, but private sector buyers should not neglect this source of supply.
- Modern thinking emphasises the importance of ethical sourcing.
- The Ethical Trading Initiative is one example of a code promoting ethical sourcing. It publishes nine fundamental principles of ethical labour practices. Another source of ethical principles in buying is the International Fair Trade Association.
- It is important for buyers to beware of potential conflicts of interest.
- An important strategic consideration for buyers is the structure of their supply chain. Modern supply chains are often based on a tiered structure.

Self-test questions

Numbers in brackets refer to the paragraphs where you can check your answers.

1   Why may suppliers not welcome an appraisal by the buyer? (1.6, Table 4.1)

2   List elements of a constructive feedback process following supplier appraisal. (1.8)

3   Sketch the supplier preferencing model. (Figure 4.1)

4   Describe the advantages and disadvantages attached to SMEs in comparison with larger potential suppliers. (2.3, 2.4)

5   List barriers faced by SMEs in accessing potential supply contracts. (2.8)

6   List measures that buyers can take to support SMEs. (2.9)

7   Describe the three levels at which ethical issues may affect sourcing decisions. (3.2)

8   List possible policies designed to promote ethical sourcing. (3.3)

9   What are the nine fundamental principles of labour practices laid down by the ETI? (3.8)

10 Explain how buyers may be subject to a conflict of interest. (3.19)

11 Define 'supply chain'. (4.2)

12 List implications for buyers of the supply chain metaphor. (4.4, 4.5)

13 Describe what is meant by 'supplier tiering'. (4.8)

14 What are the sourcing implications of supplier tiering? (4.14)

CHAPTER 5

Financial Appraisal of Suppliers

Assessment criteria and indicative content

3.1 Identify the main sources of information on potential suppliers' financial performance

- Financial reports
- The role of credit rating agencies
- Secondary data on markets and suppliers

3.2 Calculate measures of liquidity, profitability, gearing, investment from relevant financial data on potential suppliers

- Financial statements such as the profit and loss, balance sheet and cashflow statements

Section headings

1 Why appraise suppliers' financial position?
2 Sources of financial information on suppliers
3 The balance sheet
4 The profit and loss account
5 Cashflow statements

Introduction

In this chapter and the next, we cover the learning outcome which requires you to 'understand how to assess the financial stability of suppliers'. We have split the coverage across two chapters, to give students unfamiliar with finance and accounting concepts the opportunity to work through the topic in manageable segments.

In this chapter we look at some basic principles and terminology for the financial appraisal of suppliers, and introduce the key financial statements which form the basis of analysis. In Chapter 6 we will go on to look at how financial information can be analysed – using a technique called 'ratio analysis' – to evaluate suppliers on key measures of financial health, including profitability, liquidity or solvency, gearing (debt) and investment.

Try not to get bogged down in the financial concepts and terminology, if they are unfamiliar at this stage. This is not a module for financial accountants or investment analysts! Remember *why* this material is in the syllabus: to help buyers to manage sourcing risk, by *evaluating the financial health and stability of prospective suppliers and existing vendors*.

1 Why appraise suppliers' financial position?

1.1 The assessment of a supplier's financial position is often a very straightforward exercise, and should therefore be undertaken at an early stage in the sourcing process. If there are any doubts about financial stability or health, the supplier can then be eliminated from consideration without the need for more elaborate appraisal.

1.2 Buyers need to appraise the financial position of their suppliers for two main reasons.

- They want to deal with suppliers who are financially *stable:* whose financial position is healthy. A supplier in financial difficulties cannot be counted on to fulfil a major supply contract – let alone maintain a continuous, secure stream of supply within a long-term supply partnership. It may lack liquid funds (cash) to pay its own suppliers or staff, as required to fulfil the contract – or it may be forced to cease trading altogether (supplier failure).
- Buyers should seek to obtain prices which are fair to their own organisations and also fair to their suppliers. Negotiation of fair prices will revolve around the *costs* that a supplier must incur in providing the goods required – and its need to secure a reasonable *profit margin* to reinvest in the business (or return to shareholders, in order to maintain investment).

1.3   The importance of financial stability should be fairly clear. Dobler and Burt cite three nightmare scenarios that can arise if dealing with a financially weak supplier.

- You need to insist on maintaining quality, but the supplier is forced to cut costs.
- You have a financial claim against the supplier, but it does not have sufficient working capital to meet it.
- You need to insist on speedy delivery to meet a promised delivery date, but the supplier cannot afford to pay overtime.

What kinds of information are you looking for?

1.4   A variety of financial tools are available for analysing the financial stability and strength of suppliers (in order to minimise the risk of their unexpectedly going bust and disrupting supply) and competitors (in order to identify their ability to invest in competitive pricing, innovation and promotion). Information for this analysis is available in the published financial statements of public, private and not-for-profit organisations.

1.5   Examples of the kind of thing you might be looking for include signs that an organisation:

- Is not making much profit, is experiencing falling profit margins, or is making a loss, which suggests that it is operating inefficiently (revenue is too low or costs are too high) – and that it may run out of finance to continue or develop the business
- Is not managing its cashflow (the balance and timing of cash coming in and going out), or is experiencing a strong cash 'drain' from the business, making it difficult to meet its short-term debts and expenses
- Has more loan capital (borrowed from lenders) than share capital (invested by owners), incurring high finance costs (interest payments) and the obligation to repay the loan. This is known as 'high gearing'.

1.6   An article in *Supply Management* (6 February, 2006) identified the following additional signs of financial difficulty (other than poor financial ratios or posted losses).

- Rapid deterioration in delivery and quality performance
- Senior managers leaving the business within a short period of time
- Changes in the auditors and bankers of the firm
- Adverse press reports
- Very slow responses to requests for information
- Problems in the supply chain (and/or changes in subcontractors)
- Chasing payment before it is due.

1.7   Any of these signs may suggest a risk of financial instability in a supplier, or a weakness in a competitor. The opposite signals (high profits, plenty of liquid assets to cover debts, 'low' gearing) would suggest a strong and financially stable organisation.

1.8   In Chapter 3, we mentioned UK government guidelines which recommend a range of financial checks for sourcing suppliers and evaluating tenders, including:

- The assessed turnover (total revenue) of the supplier enterprise, over a three-year period
- The profitability of the enterprise, and the relationship between its gross and net profits (highlighting cost efficiency), over a three-year period
- The value of capital assets, return on capital assets and return on capital employed (indicating the efficiency with which the enterprise utilises its assets and capital resources)
- The scale of the supplier's borrowings, and the ratio of debts to assets (indicating areas of risk and cost associated with debt finance)
- The possibility of a takeover or merger, which might affect the supplier's continuing ability to supply (eg if the business will be broken up, or if it is acquired by a competitor of the buying organisation)
- The firm's dependency on a small number of major customers (indicating a risk that if one or more withdrew their business, the supplier might face financial difficulties)
- Whether or not the organisation has sufficient resources and capacity to fulfil the order.

1.9 **Ratio analysis** examines the relationship between sets of financial factors, expressed as a ratio or percentage. It defines performance indicators for organisations which can be *measured* using available financial data, and *compared* with performance in previous years (to highlight trends) or with other organisations (to highlight competitive strengths and weaknesses).

- Profitability ratios (including the gross and net profit percentage) measure the extent to which a firm has traded profitably.
- Liquidity ratios (including the current ratio, acid test ratio and gearing ratio) measure the extent to which a firm is able to meet its liabilities or debts, both in the short term and in the medium-to-long term.
- Efficiency ratios (such as the asset ratios and stock turnover ratios) measure the efficiency with which a firm utilises its assets.
- Investment ratios (such as earnings per share) measure the attractiveness of a firm to potential investors.

1.10 We will look at ratio analysis in detail in Chapter 6.

2 Sources of financial information on suppliers

2.1 Financial information about suppliers can be obtained from various sources.

- Their published financial statements and accounts: balance sheet, profit and loss account and cashflow statements (described in the following sections of this chapter)
- Secondary data on markets and suppliers: for example, analysis of financial statements and results in the business or trade press (and their websites); or published or bespoke financial reports by research agencies such as Dun & Bradstreet or DataMonitor
- Credit rating companies, which, for a fee, will provide information on the credit status of a supplier. Such information is available via a number of websites, eg www.experian.com, or www.dnb.com (the website of Dun & Bradstreet). The financial director of the firm may be able to access such reports on behalf of the procurement function.
- Networking with other buyers who use the same suppliers.
- Inviting the supplier's financial director to make a presentation on its current and predicted financial position to procurement and finance managers. This may only be worth doing for major or strategic suppliers – and a prospective (or current) strategic supplier should not decline the invitation!

2.2 The most accessible source of information on a supplier is its published financial accounts. This is not a textbook on financial accounting, but you should know enough to realise the importance of factors such as financial gearing (ie the extent to which the supplier relies on loan capital), working capital levels (ie the extent to which the supplier has assets in the form of cash and debtor balances, rather than tied up in long-term and inaccessible assets), and of course profitability.

2.3   A supplier's financial accounts present only historical data, but supplemented by financial forecasting techniques (where appropriate) and comparison with the accounts of similar companies, they are a most useful source of information to the buyer.

2.4   Credit reporting and risk management agencies may offer a menu of services to businesses wishing to access credit and financial information about other businesses (such as suppliers). Dun and Bradstreet, for example, offer:

- Business Information Reports on a named company, giving a comprehensive business credit check, including: a business summary, payment history and organisation chart; industry trends and public report/return filings; financial statements; and a credit limit recommendation (on the basis of credit worthiness) and D&B credit rating
- Comprehensive Insights Reports on a named company, for a complete business credit check and financial insights, including: business summary payment history and organisation chart; public report/ return filings; industry comparisons; financial statements; credit limit recommmentation; D&B credit rating; and commercial credit and financial stress scores
- Credit Evaluator Reports on a named company: a summary credit report, usually used to support business credit decisions, including report monitoring, credit limit recommendation and industry payment benchmarks.

Financial statements

2.5   Let's start by looking at the two main financial accounting statements of a company.

- The *balance sheet* is a statement of assets and liabilities at a point in time (the balance sheet date).
- The *profit and loss account* is a summary of income earned and expenditure incurred over a period of time.

2.6   First of all, here is some basic terminology.

- An *asset* is something which is owned by the business and used in achieving business objectives.
  - *Fixed assets* will be used in running the business for a long period of time (more than a single accounting year) and are of high value: they include intangible assets (such as goodwill and brands) and tangible assets (such as land and buildings, plant and machinery, office furniture, and vehicles).
  - *Current assets* move in and out of the business quite quickly. They include stocks of goods and materials, money owed by customers, money in the bank and so on.
- A *liability* is a sum owed by the business to outsiders (eg amounts owing to trade creditors and outstanding loans, overdrafts, tax and wages).
  - *Current liabilities* are those liabilities which are payable within twelve months of the balance sheet date.
  - Some businesses might also have *long-term liabilities*, ie liabilities payable more than one year after the balance sheet date (perhaps a long-term bank loan, for example).
- *Income* or *revenue* is amounts *earned* by the organisation eg from sales (sales revenue or turnover), interest on deposits, and dividends on investments.
- *Expenditure* is amounts spent by the organisation. Capital expenditure is spending on items of long-term benefit (fixed assets) and operating expenditure is spending on items of short-term benefit (current assets, maintenance of fixed assets, expenses of running the business).
- If income or revenue exceeds expenditure there is a *profit* for the accounting period (or a 'surplus', in a not-for-profit organisation); if expenditure exceeds income there is a *loss* (or a 'deficit').
- In order to survive, a business must have sufficient *cash* to pay its immediate liabilities (eg to maintain the flow of supplies to its operations). Being *profitable* does not necessarily mean that the business has sufficient cash resources available to pay debts when they fall due. Firms need to ensure that they time incoming and outgoing cashflows, so that at any given time they have sufficient cash resources to maintain operations: the process of *cashflow management*.

- *Working capital* is the company's net total of stock, debtors (amounts owed to it) and cash, *less* creditors (amounts owed by it). In the course of business, stock is sold to customers, who owe the company money (as debtors). When they pay what they owe, debtors are converted into cash. Cash can be used to pay off creditors (such as suppliers) – who in turn supply more goods into stock. The circulation of working capital is thus a continuous cycle.

3   The balance sheet

3.1   The following is a basic summary of the balance sheets for a company: X plc.

X PLC – *SUMMARISED BALANCE SHEETS AT 30 JUNE 20X3*

	20X3		20X2	
	£m	£m	£m	£m
Fixed assets		130		139
Current assets				
Stock	42		45	
Debtors (money owed to the business)	29		27	
Bank (balance on the current account)	3		5	
	74		77	
Current liabilities				
Trade creditors (amounts owed, within 1 year)	36		55	
Taxation owing	10		10	
	46		65	
Net current assets		28		12
Total assets less current liabilities		158		151
Long-term liabilities (amounts due after more 1 year)				
5% secured loan		40		40
		118		111
Capital and reserves				
Ordinary share capital (50p shares)		35		35
Retained profits		83		76
		118		111

3.2   This illustration is not as difficult as it looks! Let's consider step by step what information the balance sheet conveys.

- Note that all figures in the balance sheet are expressed in millions of pounds (£m). And note also that the corresponding figures from the previous year are also displayed by way of comparison.
- The assets used in the business amount to £204m. This consists of fixed assets (£130m) plus current assets (£74m). The least liquid assets are dealt with first, followed by more liquid assets. 'Liquid assets' are cash and assets which can readily be converted into cash.
- Fixed assets (such as land, buildings and office equipment) are, by definition, retained for the use of the company, rather than being resold and converted into cash – so these are the least liquid assets.
- Stock (eg goods held for resale or conversion into products) are next, because when the goods are eventually sold, the business will receive cash in exchange.
- If the goods are not paid for immediately (ie if the company grants credit to its customers) there will be an asset described as 'debtors': amounts owing from customers which will eventually result in the receipt of cash.
- The bank balance refers to the balance on the company's current account at the bank.
- X plc's current liabilities include trade creditors (amounts owing to suppliers) and taxation owing to the tax authorities.

- Its long-term liabilities comprise £40m in the form of a 5% secured loan, repayable more than twelve months after the balance sheet date.
- Total current liabilities are deducted from total current assets to arrive at a subtotal referred to as 'net current assets'. It is important that current assets exceed current liabilities: this means that the company has sufficient available (liquid) assets to pay its creditors. If current liabilities exceeded current assets (a position of 'net current liabilities') the company might be in difficulties: it would not have enough liquid assets to pay its bills.
- The top half of the balance sheet shows the net assets of the company, ie its total assets (fixed and current), less its liabilities. In this case the net assets total £118m: this is the balance sheet value of the business to its shareholders.
- The shareholders provide the finance that pays for these net assets, as shown in the bottom half of the balance sheet: the shareholders have injected £35m into the company as payment for the shares they own.
- The remaining finance (£83m) is provided by retained profits. 'Retained profits' are accumulated profits which have been ploughed back into the business, rather than given to shareholders in the form of dividends (returns on their investment).

3.3   In summary, the balance sheet shows the position of the business at one point in time – in this case at close of business on 30 June 20X3. At that point, the shareholders' investment in the company stands at £118m, and this investment is represented by the net assets listed in the top half of the balance sheet.

4   The profit and loss account

4.1   We have stated that X plc has earned retained profits over the years of £83m. Some of this will have arisen in the current year, while the remainder will have been accumulated and brought forward from earlier years. The profit and loss account shows this in more detail.

4.2   A sample summarised profit and loss (P & L) account for X plc is shown as follows: it summarises the trading activities of the business over the 12 month period.

X PLC – *SUMMARISED PROFIT AND LOSS ACCOUNT FOR THE YEAR ENDED 30 JUNE*

	20X3		20X2	
	£m	£m	£m	£m
Turnover (sales revenue)		209		196
Cost of sales (costs of production)		157		151
Gross profit		52		45
Administration expenses	11		11	
Sales and distribution expenses	14		11	
		25		22
Operating profit (profit before interest and taxation)		27		23
Interest payable (on 5% loan)		2		2
Profit before taxation		25		21
Taxation payable		10		10
Profit after taxation		15		11
Dividends (payable to shareholders)		8		7
Retained profit for the year		7		4
Retained profits from previous years		76		72
Retained profits carried forward		83		76

4.3   Once again, don't panic: this isn't as bad as it may look if you're not an accountant!

- Of the £83m retained profits at the end of 20X3, there is £7m retained from this year's profits, added to £76m accumulated in earlier years.
- The figure for turnover (ie sales revenue) relates to goods sold during the year, whether or not the cash was actually received during the year.

- To get a figure for *gross profit*, we take the figure for the sales value of the goods sold (turnover) and *deduct* the cost of buying or producing those goods (the cost of sales). In this case, £209m minus £157m gives a gross profit of £52m.
- To get a figure for *operating profit* (profit before interest and taxation), we deduct the various expenses incurred by the business from gross profit: in this case, grouped under the two headings of administration expenses, and sales and distribution expenses. The net operating profit in this case is £27m.
- To get a figure for *profit after interest and taxation*, we deduct amounts paid in loan interest and corporation tax (payable on the company's profits). X plc has a net profit of £15m. This can theoretically be paid out to the shareholders, as a return on their investment, as all expenses have now been covered.
- In practice, however, the directors of the company have decided to pay out only £8m to shareholders, in the form of dividends, and to retain the rest of the year's profit within the business. Added to retained profits from previous years, the company has a total figure of retained profits at 30 June 20X3 of £83m. This ties in with the balance sheet presented earlier. The total amount of retained profits is sometimes known as the 'profit and loss reserve'.

4.4   Retained profits are a useful figure to look at, because they reflect the supplier's financial success and management skills. They also suggest commitment to reinvesting in the business (which may bode well for development of future capability).

Other statements contained in the published accounts

4.5   The financial accounts published by a limited company are usually a bulky document. Apart from the balance sheet and profit and loss account they will typically contain a number of other statements relating to the company's financial position. Here are some examples.

- A **cashflow statement**. This is designed to identify the sources of cash coming into the business and the ways in which it has been spent. The statement ends by showing the overall cash surplus or deficit at the beginning of the year, during the year, and at the end of the year.
- A **five-year summary**. This shows key accounting statistics and ratios from the current year and from the four previous years. The idea is to highlight trends in the company's financial performance.
- A **chairman's statement**. This is a high-level overview of key developments during the year, presented mostly in narrative format rather than tables of numbers.

5   Cashflow statements

5.1   We have already remarked on the fact that earning profits does not necessarily guarantee a healthy cash position. This is a limitation of the profit and loss account: a business showing a healthy profit may still be financially unstable if the cash position is weak.

5.2   To overcome this shortcoming in the profit and loss account, company accounts include a further statement: the cashflow statement. This is designed to identify the sources of cash coming into the business and the ways in which it has been spent. The statement ends by showing the overall cash surplus or deficit at the beginning of the year, during the year, and at the end of the year.

5.3   An example is shown below.

SENTINI LIMITED – *CASHFLOW STATEMENT FOR THE YEAR ENDED 31 DECEMBER 20X3*

	£000	£000
Net cash flows from operating activities		540
Returns on investment and servicing of finance		
Interest paid		(28)
Taxation		
Corporation tax paid		(108)
Capital expenditure		
Payments to acquire tangible fixed assets	(90)	
Receipts from sales of tangible fixed assets	12	
Net cash outflow from capital expenditure		(78)
		326
Equity dividends paid		(66)
		260
Financing		
Issues of share capital	32	
Long-term loans repaid	(300)	
Net cash outflow from financing		(268)
Decrease in cash		(8)
Cash at beginning of the year		92
Cash at end of the year		84
Reconciliation of operating profit to net cash inflow		£000
Operating profit		420
Depreciation charges		136
Increase in stocks		(4)
Increase in debtors		(18)
Increase in creditors		6
Net cash inflow from operating activities		540

5.4   What does this statement tell us about Sentini Limited?

- The company's day-to-day trading is a healthy generator of cash: 'operating activities' during the year generated a cash surplus of £540,000. (This might not be apparent from the profit and loss account, since operating profit might suffer from the deduction of large non-cash outgoings such as depreciation – significantly understating the amount of cash generated.)
- There were three substantial cash outgoings during the year: £28,000 in interest payments, £108,000 in taxation, and £78,000 in net expenditure on new fixed assets (eg equipment). All of this reduces the cash surplus to £326,000.
- Of this disposable surplus, the company has elected to pay out £66,000 in dividends to its shareholders, leaving a surplus of £260,000.
- By issuing new share capital, the company has raised further cash of £32,000, but this is more than offset by the company's repayment of a £300,000 long-term loan. Both of these are movements in the company's long-term capital funding, which is why they are shown together.
- The net effect of all this is that over the year the company's cash position has worsened by £8,000 (from £92,000 in the black at the beginning of the year, to £84,000 in the black at the end of the year).

Chapter summary

- A buyer appraises the financial situation of a potential supplier because he wants to ensure the supplier is stable and because he wants to verify that prices are 'fair'.
- Ratio analysis is a tool for appraising an organisation's financial situation.
- Buyers can access a wide range of information sources to evaluate a supplier's financial situation (published accounts, credit rating companies etc).
- Important statements included in a supplier's financial accounts are the balance sheet, the profit and loss account and the cashflow statement.
- The balance sheet shows the supplier's assets and liabilities at a moment in time.
- The profit and loss account shows the suppliers revenue, expenditure and profit or loss over a period of time (usually one year).
- The cashflow statement shows the amount of cash coming in from various sources, the amount of cash expended for various purposes, and the net change in the supplier's cash holdings over a period of time (usually one year).

Self-test questions

Numbers in brackets refer to the paragraphs where you can check your answers.

1   What signs of a financially weak supplier might a buyer find? (1.5, 1.6)

2   List possible financial checks that a buyer might carry out on a potential supplier. (1.8)

3   List possible sources of financial information on a supplier. (2.1)

4   Define asset, liability, income and expenditure in terms of financial accounts. (2.6)

5   Distinguish between fixed and current assets in a balance sheet. (3.2)

6   What is meant by 'net current assets'? (3.2)

7   What is meant by 'turnover' in a profit and loss account? (4.3)

8   What information is provided by a cashflow statement? (5.2)

CHAPTER 6

Ratio Analysis

Assessment criteria and indicative content

3.2 Calculate measures of liquidity, profitability, gearing, investment from relevant financial data on potential suppliers

- Measures and ratios of profitability, liquidity, gearing and investment

3.3 Evaluate the financial performance of potential suppliers using relevent financial data

- Ratio analysis to make conclusions on profitability, liquidity, gearing and investment
- The limitations of ratio analysis

Section headings

1. Key measures of supplier financial stability
2. Profitability ratios
3. Liquidity and gearing ratios
4. Efficiency and working capital ratios
5. Investment ratios

Introduction

As we saw in Chapter 5, financial stability is a key criterion in the pre-qualification and selection of suppliers – as well as a key consideration in the management of ongoing supplier risk. Much of the information for assessing suppliers' financial stability will be gathered by surveying financial statements (and other available sources), and calculating *financial ratios*, which are used as measures of profitability, liquidity, gearing and investment.

As quantified measures, ratios give buyers a 'snapshot' of a supplier's financial position, and also facilitate comparison of the supplier's financial performance with:

- performance in previous years (is it improving or deteriorating?)
- budgeted or planned performance in the current year (is it meeting its objectives?)
- the performance of similar businesses (is it 'normal' for its industry? Is it competitive?)

In this chapter we show how the main accounting ratios are calculated from financial statements, and how they can be interpreted to give buyers useful information about suppliers. We will be using the data provided in the specimen balance sheet and profit & loss account of X plc from Chapter 5: we recommend that you identify (or photocopy) those pages, so that you can review them side by side with the ratio calculations here.

1 Key measures of supplier financial stability

1.1 As we saw in Chapter 5, a buyer should have ready access to the published financial information of potential suppliers and current vendors. This data can be used to analyse suppliers' financial standing, strength and stability (or vulnerability), using measures such as profitability, liquidity, gearing and investment.

Profitability

1.2 Profit is the amount earned by a company once it has covered its costs of doing business: in a public or third sector organisation, we might speak of a 'surplus'.

1.3 Both buyers and suppliers seek to make a profit for a number of reasons.

- Profit means that the business has covered its costs and is not 'bleeding' money in losses. This is important for the business to survive in the long term.
- Profit belongs to the owners or shareholders of the business, as a return on their investment: a share of profits is paid to them in the form of a 'dividend' on their shares. Strong and consistent profits are therefore important to encourage shareholders to continue to invest in the company, and to maintain the share capital of the company through a high share price (reflecting market demand for the shares).
- Profits which are not paid to shareholders ('retained profits') are available for reinvestment in the development of the business, enabling it to acquire assets, meet long-term borrowings, update plant and equipment, and build up reserves for future contingencies – without the cost and risk of borrowing funds for these purposes.

1.4 If a supplier is making a loss, or only minimal profits, the buyer may conclude that it is operating inefficiently (revenue is too low or costs are too high). There may be a risk that the supplier will run out of finance to continue or develop the business: a risk of supplier insolvency or supplier failure.

1.5 On the other hand, if the supplier is making very high profits, the buyer may conclude that its profit margins may be unnecessarily high. Further analysis of the supplier's costs, cost structures and future commitments (eg plans which require high profits to be re-invested in the business) may be required – but the supplier may have room for negotiation on price, to the buyer's advantage.

1.6 It is important for buyers to understand that suppliers are entitled to make a profit: that is, they are entitled to set or quote prices on goods which allow them to cover their costs and make a reasonable profit margin. This is important:

- To protect the security of supply (not creating financial instability for suppliers)
- To protect the quality of supply (allowing suppliers to maintain standards and develop their business)
- In the interests of corporate social responsibility (supporting sustainable supply chains).

Liquidity

1.7 As we emphasised in Chapter 5, being *profitable* does not necessarily mean that the business has sufficient cash resources available to meet its financial obligations when they fall due. For example, the profits may have been used to purchase 'non-liquid' assets (eg buildings, plant and machinery) which cannot easily be converted into cash at need. Or they may have been committed to shareholders, in the form of dividend payments.

1.8 The key point is that:

- A supplier must have sufficient *cash or 'liquid assets'* (assets, such as stock and debtors, which can be relatively quickly turned into cash) to meet its short-term debts and expenses (eg to pay its own suppliers) and thus to maintain its operations and the flow of supply to its customers.
- A supplier must also demonstrate sound *cashflow management*: ensuring that it consistently times incoming and outgoing cashflows, so that at any given time it has sufficient cash resources to meet its immediate obligations.

1.9 'Liquidity' is a measure of the extent to which a supplier is able to meet its liabilities or debts, both in the short term and in the medium-to-long term. It therefore impacts on key issues such as the stability and ongoing viability of the business; its exposure to financial risk; its costs of capital (if it has to borrow to cover its liabilities); and its potential to invest in growth and development – as well as its ability to pay its debts.

1.10 These issues will be of interest to various external stakeholders.

- Customers and buyers (particularly for strategic supplies, or in partnership relations with the business) will seek warning that their source of supply may be at risk due to the threat of insolvency.
- Financers of the business will be interested in its ability to meet debt repayment obligations (such as the interest on loans).
- Suppliers of the business will be interested in its ability to pay for goods and services supplied, whether on one-off purchases or ongoing contracts. Payment in full and on time is important for suppliers' own cashflow position, as well as avoiding the costs and relational damage of debt collection and disputes.
- Shareholders will have an interest in both short- and long-term liquidity, as it impacts on the value (and risk exposure) of their shareholding and investment returns.

Gearing

1.11 Gearing is a measure of the proportion of a business's long-term funding that is represented by long-term debt or loans – as opposed to share or equity capital (shareholder capital and reserves, which also belong to the ordinary shareholders). A business is said to be 'highly geared' if a high proportion of its funding comes from long-term debt.

1.12 Gearing is relevant to the long-term liquidity (or solvency) and stability of a business.

- High gearing means that there is a lot of fixed-return capital in the overall financial structure of the company, which may be a risk factor in the long term: having to meet the regular interest costs of fixed-return loans may place strain on a company if times become lean (as they are at the moment in most global markets), so it is generally advisable to restrict the proportion of such finance in the mix.
- Low gearing means that the company is relying mainly on equity capital (with no expectations of fixed returns), and should therefore have less difficulty in weathering difficult years.

Investment

1.13 Investment, in this context, is a measure of how attractive a business is to potential investors (buyers of shares, financiers or lenders), based on the financial strength of the company and the likely return on investment that can be expected.

1.14 In some ways, this may be a less relevant measure for a buyer looking to appraise a supplier, because it mainly appraises the business from the point of view of returns for potential investors. However, it may be relevant in suggesting:

- The general financial and managerial strength of the supplier, as reflected in the confidence of investors
- The attractiveness of the supplier to investors, which may encourage investment – leading to stronger solvency, lower gearing and costs of capital, investment in business and capability development, and so on
- The commitment of the supplier to paying investor dividends (reducing the share of profits available for price negotiation with buyers).

Ratio analysis

1.15 A key tool in the analysis of all the above measures is the use of financial ratios. Ratios fall into several groups, the relevance of particular ratios depending on the purpose for which they are required. The ratios specified in the syllabus fall into three main groups:

- Profitability ratios – measuring the extent to which the business has traded profitably
- Liquidity and gearing ratios – measuring the extent to which the business has liquid assets sufficient to meet its short-term and long-term liabilities
- Investment ratios – measuring the strength and consistency of returns on investment delivered to shareholders and other investors.

1.16 The sheer number of ratios that can be calculated may lead to confusion. Try to organise your thoughts in this area by mentally dividing ratios into the categories above. This will help you to give structure to the solutions you write in the examination – and remind you of the purpose and meaning of the various ratios you are discussing.

1.17 Remember above all that the ratios are not an end in themselves. Examiners are interested in your ability to interpret and draw sourcing-related conclusions from information about prospective or current suppliers. Calculating a ratio is not the same as drawing a conclusion, but it can point you towards a conclusion.

Limitations of ratio analysis

1.18 Ratios may highlight significant trends, but they do not in themselves provide reasons for the trends. To do this effectively, the interested party may need more information and a deeper insight into the affairs of the business. Often this may be difficult to obtain, because the amount of information available is limited unless the user is a manager within the organisation.

1.19 Another problem is the date at which the accounts are drawn up. Accurate information can only be obtained with any degree of certainty from up-to-date figures. Furthermore, seasonal variations in the particular trade should be taken into account.

1.20 Finally, accounting is not an exact science! Despite efforts by the accountancy profession to standardise accounting practice there is still room for a variety of methods in particular cases. This may affect the comparability of different accounts.

Before we get started on ratios . . .

1.21 Try not to get bogged down in the detail of ratio calculations. Remember *why* you are doing them, and what they *mean* for supplier financial appraisal. Ratio analysis may be particularly helpful in highlighting:

- Significant comparisons **between suppliers** (eg as to profit margins or financial security, measured by liquidity and gearing)
- Significant **year-on-year trends** (eg if a supplier's financial position is getting better or worse).
- Significant **sources of supplier risk** (eg if a supplier lacks profitability or liquidity).

1.22 We will use the accounts of X plc displayed in Chapter 5: again, we recommend that you 'tag' those pages – or photocopy them – so that you can view them together with our ratio calculations, and see where we get our figures from.

2   Profitability ratios

2.1 *Profitability ratios* measure the extent to which a business has traded profitably. Every business needs to generate sufficient sales revenue (turnover) to cover its costs *and* pay a dividend to its shareholders (as a return on their investment in the business) *and* retain some profit as a reserve.

2.2 If a supplier is not showing consistent profits, the business may be in trouble, posing a supply risk. On the other hand, if the supplier is making large or increasing profits, a buyer may question whether he might be able to reduce costs by squeezing the supplier's profit margins a little.

Gross profit percentage

2.3 Many ratios are expressed as a relation between a particular item and the level of sales turnover. Placing items in the context of turnover is a useful technique, because turnover tends to be a good guide to the overall size of a business.

2.4 The first ratio we look at is the gross profit percentage. This expresses the gross profit as a percentage of turnover. The ratio is in very common use, and is calculated as follows.

$$\frac{\text{Gross profit}}{\text{Sales}} \times 100$$

2.5 Using our example of X plc (see Chapter 5), the ratios for the two years are as follows.

20X3: $\frac{52}{209} \times 100 = 24.9\%$

20X2: $\frac{45}{196} \times 100 = 23.0\%$

2.6 X plc's gross profit percentage has improved but it is not known why. Nor is it obvious whether these figures are better or worse than those which would be expected in a similar type of business. Before coming to definite conclusions one would need further information.

2.7 For example, most businesses sell a wide range of products, usually with different gross profit percentages (or profit margins). It may be that in 20X3 the sales mix changed and that a larger proportion of items with a high profit percentage were sold, thus increasing the overall gross profit percentage of the business.

Net profit percentage

2.8 As the name suggests, this ratio relates the amount of *net profit* to the amount of sales turnover. It is calculated as:

$$\frac{\text{Profit before tax}}{\text{Sales}} \times 100$$

2.9 In the example of X plc (see Chapter 5), the ratios for the two years are as follows.

20X3: $\frac{25}{209} \times 100 = 12.0\%$

20X2: $\frac{21}{196} \times 100 = 10.7\%$

2.10 A business might also use the figure for *operating profit* (profit before *interest and taxation*), if it has substantial loans or 'gearing'. The difference between the net profit percentage and the operating profit percentage will show the effect of gearing on the company's profits. For, example for X plc, the operating profit percentage for 20X2 would be 11.7%, while for 20X3 it would be 12.9%.

2.11 Profit figures are meaningful in themselves: is the supplier profitable (indicating efficiency and stability) or struggling (posing the risk of supplier failure)? Is it 'excessively' profitable (indicating potential to squeeze its profit margins in price negotiation)? However, it will also be useful to analyse year on year improvements and deteriorations: is the supplier's situation, or management, getting stronger or weaker?

2.12 So what conclusions can be drawn from X plc's apparent improvement in profitability between 20X2 and 20X3? In fact, not many, since so many variables are unknown from this analysis alone.

2.13 Since operating profit equals gross profit less expenses, it would be useful to tabulate the various expenses for each of the two years, and to express them as a percentage of sales. (These are known as **costs to sales ratios**.) A suitable tabulation might be as follows.

	20X3		20X2	
	£m	%	£m	%
Sales	209	100.0	196	100.0
Cost of sales	157	75.1	151	77.0
Gross profit	52	24.9	45	23.0
Administration expenses	(11)	(5.3)	(11)	(5.6)
Sales and distribution expenses	(14)	(6.7)	(11)	(5.6)
Operating profit	27	12.9	23	11.8

2.14 Given a detailed trading and profit and loss account, the above type of summary could be very useful. Care must be taken in interpreting the results, however, particularly since sales (£) are used as the denominator. An increase in sales (£) could be due to a combination of price and quantity effects.

Return on capital employed (ROCE)

2.15 ROCE is also known as the 'primary ratio': it is a particularly important ratio, as it describes profit as a percentage of the capital (long-term finance) employed in the business, as follows:

$$\frac{\text{Profit before interest and tax}}{\text{Average capital employed}} \times 100$$

2.16 Average capital employed is calculated by averaging the capital employed in the opening and closing balance sheets (adding the two totals and dividing by two). It includes long-term finance but does not include short-term finance such as bank overdrafts. (The interest referred to is the interest payable on long-term liabilities: any interest on short-term liabilities is deducted from *profit*.)

2.17 In the case of X plc (see Chapter 5) for 20X3, we have:

$$\text{ROCE} = \frac{27}{(158 + 151)/2} \times 100 = 17.5\%$$

2.18 Long-term finance for a business (from shareholders and suppliers of long-term debt capital) comes at a cost. Loan finance requires the payment of interest, and shareholder finance requires the payment of dividends. So it is important for the company to maximise the profits per £ of capital employed.

Return on assets

2.19 While ROCE focuses on the return the company makes on the amounts invested in it (by shareholders and the suppliers of debt capital), 'return on assets' looks at how well the *total assets* of the company are being used.

2.20 The calculation is:

$$\frac{\text{Profit before interest and tax (operating profit)}}{\text{Total assets (fixed assets + current assets)}} \times 100$$

In the case of X plc:

$$20X3: \quad \frac{27}{130 + 74} \times 100 = 13.2\%$$

$$20X2: \quad \frac{23}{139 + 77} \times 100 = 10.6\%$$

2.21 This ratio highlights the fact that X plc is successfully making an increased profit out of the same level of assets from 20X2 to 20X3.

3 Liquidity and gearing ratios

3.1 Liquidity ratios measure the extent to which a business has the liquid assets sufficient to meet its short-term and long-term liabilities. (Liquid assets include cash plus other assets that can quickly be converted into cash, for example amounts owing from debtors or stocks of finished goods which can be sold.) In order to survive, a business must ensure that it has plenty of cash and other liquid assets, so that it can meet its obligations.

Short-term liquidity (or stability) ratios

3.2 Two main ratios relate to *short-term* liquidity, measuring the relationship between the organisation's liquid assets and its current liabilities.

- The **current ratio** (also called the **working capital ratio**):

$$\frac{\text{Current assets}}{\text{Current liabilities}} \quad \text{In the case of X plc for 20X3: } \frac{74}{46} = 1.61$$

   This ratio indicates whether or not the business has sufficient current assets to cover its current liabilities. The 'ideal' ratio is sometimes said to be 2, so X plc isn't doing too badly.

- The **quick ratio** (also called the **acid test ratio** or **liquidity ratio**):

$$\frac{\text{Current assets} - \text{stock}}{\text{Current liabilities}} \quad \text{In the case of X plc for 20X3: } \frac{32}{46} = 0.7$$

   This ratio focuses only on the most liquid assets (cash, debtors), which can quickly be used to pay off liabilities (unlike stock, which has to be sold and paid for, which may take time). If the ratio is low, debts payable in the near future (creditors) may not be fully covered: the 'ideal' ratio is sometimes said to be 1.

3.3 Year on year improvements or deteriorations will again be significant. X plc's current ratio and quick ratio in 20X2 were 1.2 and 0.49, so both of these ratios show a strengthening from 20X2 to 20X3. The extent of the change between the two years seems surprising and would require further investigation. It would also be useful to know how these ratios compare with those of a similar business, since typical ratios for supermarkets, say, are quite different from those for heavy engineering firms.

3.4 What can be said is that in 20X3 X's current liabilities were well covered by current assets. Liabilities payable in the near future (creditors), however, are only partly covered by cash and debtors.

Medium- and long-term solvency (gearing) ratios

3.5 Gearing is relevant to the long-term liquidity and stability of a business. It refers to the proportion of a business's long-term funding that is represented by debt or loans – as opposed to shareholder capital and reserves (which also belong to the ordinary shareholders). A business is said to be 'highly geared' if a high proportion of its funding comes from long-term debt.

3.6 There are different ways of calculating a gearing ratio, but the idea is to consider the relationship between fixed-return capital (debt capital or long-term loans, on which fixed interest payments are owed) and shareholders' funds (equity capital and reserves, for which shareholders have no fixed expectations in regard to dividend returns).

3.7 A simple gearing ratio can be expressed as:

$$\frac{\text{Fixed return capital (long-term loans)}}{\text{Ordinary share capital and reserves (net worth)}} \times 100$$

For X plc in 20X3, the gearing ratio is:

$$\frac{40}{118} \times 100 = 33.9\%$$

In 20X2, the figure was 36.0%, so the company's position is improving.

3.8 A high gearing ratio means that there is a lot of fixed-return capital in the overall financial structure of the company, which may be a risk factor in the long term: having to meet the regular interest costs of fixed-return loans may place strain on a company if times become lean, so it is generally advisable to restrict the proportion of such finance in the mix.

3.9 A low ratio means that the company is relying mainly on equity capital, and should have less difficulty in weathering difficult years.

Interest cover

3.10 Interest on loans (debentures) must be paid whether or not the company makes a profit. The interest cover ratio emphasises the cover (or security) for the interest by relating profit before interest and tax (operating profit) to interest paid. In other words, it indicates the extent to which profits are sufficient to meet interest payments.

3.11 A high interest cover ratio means that profits are more than sufficient to cover the interest that must be paid. A low interest cover ratio is a danger signal: it suggests that the company is only just able to meet its interest payments.

3.12 The ratio is calculated simply by dividing the relevant profit figure by the amount of interest. The relevant profit figure is profit *before* deduction of interest and *before* deducting tax and dividends. For X plc in 20X3 the interest cover is therefore as follows.

$$\frac{27}{2} = 13.5 \text{ times}$$

3.13 This indicates that the company is earning enough profit to meet its interest payments more than 13 times over, a comfortable position. From the point of view of medium- and long-term solvency, the company is in a strong position as regards the payment of interest. Profit would have to drop considerably before any problem of paying interest arose.

4 Efficiency and working capital ratios

4.1 Efficiency ratios measure the efficiency with which a business is managing its assets. We will look at asset turnover in general, and then at two asset classes in particular: stock and debtors. Since 'stock *plus* cash *plus* debtors *minus* creditors' is often referred to as the 'working capital' of a business, these ratios are known as 'working capital ratios'.

Asset turnover

4.2 Asset turnover is a measure of how well the assets of a business are being used to generate sales. A business that 'turns over' its assets frequently is getting good value from them, so high turnover ratios suggest efficient management, though there are dangers in taking this idea too far.

4.3 Looking at all of the operating assets within a business, asset turnover is calculated as follows.

$$\frac{\text{Sales}}{\text{Operating assets}} = \text{Times per year}$$

4.4 Operating assets can be defined in various ways but the most sensible approach is to use the same amount as computed for capital employed. In the case of X plc this was £154,500, the average of the 20X2 and 20X3 figures. Asset turnover for 20X3 is then computed as follows.

$$\frac{209}{154.5} = 1.35$$

4.5 The meaning of the ratio may now be clearer: for every £1 of assets employed in the business X plc is generating £1.35 in sales revenue. Clearly it is desirable to generate as much sales revenue as possible for as little investment as possible, so a higher ratio is preferable to a lower one. A ratio of 1.35 does not seem particularly impressive.

Stock turnover

4.0 Companies have to strike a balance between being able to satisfy customers' requirements out of stock (which suggests a need for high stock levels) and the cost of having too much capital tied up in stock (which suggests that stock levels should be kept low). By calculating a stock turnover ratio, and monitoring it from one period to the next, buyers can assess how successfully suppliers are balancing these conflicting needs. In addition, a low turnover of stock may indicate that the supplier's capacity is under-utilised: there may be a risk of stock deterioration or obsolescence (creating quality risks), or an implication that the supplier's order book is low (raising questions about quality, reliability or competitiveness).

4.7 The **stock turnover ratio** measures the number of times stock is turned over in a year:

$$\frac{\text{Cost of sales}}{\text{Average stock value}} = \text{Times per year}$$

In the example of X plc the calculation for 20X3, based on average stock value, is as follows.

$$\frac{157}{(45 + 42)/2} = 3.6 \text{ times per year (or turnover roughly every 100 days)}$$

This seems a fairly high level of stock, but of course this will depend on the nature and norms of the business. A jeweller would stock items that might well remain in stock for 100 days, or even much longer. At the other extreme, you would hope that a fishmonger's stocks would turn over much more quickly!

Debt collection period

4.8 The debt collection period measures how long after purchase customers pay the supplier for their goods. This is important, because failure to send out invoices on time or to follow up late payers will have an adverse effect on the cashflow of the business. The debt collection period relates closing trade debtors to the average daily credit sales, to indicate how many days' sales are represented by the debtors figure – in other words, how many days worth of sales the supplier (or whatever organisation is being examined) has not been paid for. The quickest form of the calculation is:

$$\frac{\text{Closing trade debtors}}{\text{Credit sales for the year}} \times 365$$

For X plc in 20X3 (assuming that all sales were credit sales):

$$\frac{29m}{209m} \times 365 = 50.6 \text{ days}$$

4.9 This indicates that X plc's customers pay for goods about 51 days after purchasing them. This should be compared with:

- The credit period offered by X plc. If the company usually offers 60 days credit, then collecting debts within 50 days on average is very efficient; on the other hand if the usual credit period offered is 30 days, then most customers appear to be taking more credit than they are entitled to

- The similar ratio for the previous year, to indicate whether matters are improving or worsening.

Creditors payment period

4.10 The debt collection period is sometimes referred to as the 'credit period' ratio, though that term is more often applied to the opposite side of the debt collection coin. It refers to how long after purchase the supplier (or other organisation being examined) pays for the goods it has *bought* on credit from its suppliers.

$$\frac{\text{Closing trade creditors}}{\text{Credit purchases for the year}} \times 365$$

If this is greater than the requested payment period, the suppliers' trade creditors (those to whom it owes money) are effectively contributing to its working capital! However, there is a risk in consistently paying late: lost discounts for prompt payment, loss of good customer status, broken supply chain relationships, disputes and so on.

5 Investment ratios

5.1 In this final section of the chapter, we consider the position of a potential investor wondering whether to purchase shares or lend money to a company. How can such an investor assess the financial position of the company and the likely return to be expected from investment in it? (Similar questions might be asked by an investment analyst whose job is to advise clients on suitable companies to put their money into.)

5.2 A number of ratios have a bearing on the decisions of potential investors, including:

- Dividend per share
- Dividend yield
- Earnings per share
- Dividend cover
- Price earnings ratio
- Return on shareholders' funds

Dividend per share

5.3 A key consideration in the mind of a potential shareholder is the amount of dividend income he can expect: it is therefore common for companies to quote in their published accounts an amount of 'dividend per share'. An investor holding 1,000 shares can then simply multiply by 1,000 to calculate how much he will receive.

5.4 However, just in case you need to calculate dividend per share yourself, the following methodology can be used. We will assume, for this syllabus, that dividend per ordinary share is required (ignoring the more complex case of preference shares).

- First, we find the total amount of the ordinary dividend for the year. This is shown in the profit and loss account. In the case of X plc in 20X3: £8m.
- Next, we need to find the number of ordinary shares in issue. The figure for ordinary share capital in X plc's balance sheet in 20X3 is £35m – and we are told that the ordinary shares have a nominal value of 50p each. So there must be 70m ordinary shares in issue.
- We can now calculate the amount of ordinary dividend per share:

$$\frac{£8,000,000}{70,000,000} = 11.4\text{p per share, approximately}$$

5.5 A holder of, say, 2,000 shares could expect to receive about £228 in dividend income. Of course, this information relates to the year just ended, so it is only a starting point for making predictions for the future.

Dividend yield

5.6 By itself, the figure of dividend per share does not help the potential investor very much. Knowing that he may earn about £228 per year on a holding of 2,000 shares is only part of the story: he also needs to know how much that investment will *cost* – which depends on the price of the shares.

5.7 Remember that the price of a share depends on market conditions: in particular, on the market's assessment of the value of X plc and its future prospects. It has no connection at all with the 'nominal value' of the share, which is an arbitrary amount probably determined when the company was first formed.

5.8 The reason why this is important is that our investor wishes to compare his likely return from different potential investments. If banks are paying 4% interest per annum on deposit accounts, the investor knows that placing £5,700 on deposit will earn £228 per year – and this is a risk-free investment. Buying shares in X plc is a much riskier investment, and will not be attractive to the investor unless he can buy 2,000 shares for significantly less than £5,700.

5.9 The *yield* from the bank deposit account is known: it is 4 per cent per annum, or £4 for every £100 invested. The potential investor needs to do a similar calculation for shares in X plc, comparing the price to be paid with the dividends to be expected. This is called the *dividend yield*.

5.10 In simple terms, the dividend yield is calculated as follows:

$$\frac{\text{Amount of dividend per share}}{\text{Price of one share}}$$

5.11 In the case of X plc we have already calculated the dividend per share in 20X3: 11.4p per share. Suppose that a share in X plc is currently priced on the share market at £2.35. We calculate the dividend yield as:

$$\frac{11.4p}{235p} = 4.9\%$$

This is slightly better than our (fictional) yield of 4 per cent from bank deposits, but perhaps not enough to compensate for the additional risk from this kind of investment.

Earnings per share

5.12 Earnings per share (EPS) is a key ratio in investment analysis. It is calculated just like dividend per share, except that 'earnings' are usually not exactly equal in amount to 'dividends'.

5.13 *Earnings* are the profits available (after the payment of tax and dividends to preference shareholders) to benefit ordinary shareholders. But companies rarely pay out *all* of their earnings in the form of dividends: some earnings will be retained in the business. For example, a company with earnings of £50,000 may decide to pay dividends of only £20,000, retaining £30,000 for use in the business.

5.14 In the case of X plc the profit after tax for 20X3 was £15m. We know that there are 70m ordinary shares in issue, so the earnings per share is:

$$\frac{£15,000,000}{70,000,000} = 21.4p$$

Dividend cover

5.15 The ordinary shareholders may need to know how 'safe' the dividend payment was, ie how many times the current year's earnings could have covered the dividend payment. If the dividend cover falls to very low levels, ordinary shareholders may not be able to rely on the current level of dividends being maintained in the future.

$$\text{Ordinary dividend cover} = \frac{\text{Earnings (profits after interest, tax and preference dividends)}}{\text{Ordinary dividend for the year}}$$

Note that 'earnings' is effectively the amount of the current year's profit that the directors had available to pay out as ordinary dividend if they had wished.

For 20X3 the dividend cover is:

$$\frac{£15,000,000}{£8,000,000} = 1.9 \text{ times}$$

Price earnings ratio (P/E ratio)

5.16 Again, this is a vital ratio in investment analysis. It is calculated exactly as its name suggests: divide the price of a share by the earnings relating to the share.

For X plc in 20X3 we know that the price of an ordinary share is £2.35. We have just calculated the earnings per share as 21.4p. The P/E ratio is simply price divided by earnings:

$$\frac{235p}{21.4p} = 11.0$$

5.17 In effect, this indicates that investors buying shares in X plc are prepared to wait 11 years before they get their money back. If a similar company has a price ratio of, say, 6.5, investors are only prepared to pay an amount which will return to them within 6.5 years: in other words, they are less impressed with this company than with X plc.

5.18 A high P/E ratio is therefore an indication that the market is impressed with the potential of a company – and this may be the most useful thing for a buyer to know, in appraising the financial stability and future prospects of a supplier.

5.19 However, P/E ratios vary enormously between different industry sectors. You would not expect a publishing company to have a similar ratio to a heavy manufacturer. But by looking at the P/E ratios of companies of similar size, and operating in a similar industry sector, useful comparisons can be made.

Return on shareholders' funds

5.20 It could be argued that this ratio belongs with the profitability ratios in Section 2 of this chapter. However we have included it here as an investment ratio since, like the other ratios in this section, it focuses on the returns generated for ordinary shareholders. Return on shareholders' funds (ROSF) is calculated as follows.

$$\frac{\text{Earnings (profits after interest, tax and preference dividends)}}{\text{Ordinary share capital plus reserves}} \times 100$$

For X plc in 20X3, ROSF is:

$$\frac{£15,000,000}{£118,000,000} \times 100 = 12.7\%$$

In 20X3 the company generated a return of 12.7 per cent on shareholders' funds invested.

5.21 The formula we have used above calculates net ROSF, ie after taxation. Some analysts calculate gross ROSF, ie based on profit before taxation. If you are required to calculate ROSF in an examination you should use the formula shown above, but state that you are aware that the calculation may also be based on profit before taxation.

Chapter summary

- Ratios are a useful method of assessing the performance of a business, especially when used in comparison with similar ratios from other businesses or from earlier years.
- Profitability ratios measure the extent to which the business has traded profitably. They include gross profit percentage, net profit percentage and return on capital employed (ROCE), the primary accounting ratio.
- Liquidity ratios measure the extent to which the business has liquid assets sufficient to meet its short-term and long-term liabilities. They include current ratio, quick ratio, gearing ratio and interest cover.
- Efficiency ratios measure the efficiency with which the business is managing its assets. They include operating assets turnover, stock turnover, debtors collection period and creditors payment period.
- Investment ratios measure the attractiveness of a business to potential investors. They include dividend per share, dividend yield, earnings per share, dividend cover and price earnings ratio.

Self-test questions

Numbers in brackets refer to the paragraphs where your answers can be checked.

1   How are (a) profitability and (b) liquidity relevant to the decision-making of a buyer when appraising the financial position of a supplier? (1.4–1.8)

2   List some limitations of ratio analysis as a means of assessing business performance. (1.18–1.20)

3   How is gross profit percentage calculated? (2.4)

4   What is meant by the term 'costs to sales ratios'? (2.13)

5   How is ROCE calculated? (2.15–2.18)

6   What is the difference between the working capital ratio and the acid test ratio? (3.2)

7   What items are included in the term 'fixed-return capital'? (3.6)

8   How is dividend per share calculated? (5.4)

9   What is meant by the dividend yield? (5.9)

10   What is meant by 'earnings' in the context of company accounts? (5.13)

CHAPTER 7

Surveying the Supply Market

Assessment criteria and indicative content

 Assess commonly used sources of information on market data that can impact on the sourcing of requirements from external suppliers

- The importance of analysing markets
- Compiling data on expenditure of suppliers
- Indices that measure economic data
- Secondary data on markets and suppliers
- Commodity pricing
- Analysing potential sales

Section headings

1   Purchasing research
2   Demand analysis
3   Sources of market and supplier data
4   Supply market analysis

Introduction

In Chapter 1 we looked briefly at some of the sources of information buyers could use to research the supply market, specifically in order to identify and appraise potential sources of supply. 'Surveying the market' means identifying or locating suppliers that may potentially be able to supply the requirement. Buyers will constantly be monitoring the supply market(s) relevant to their organisation's requirements, as well as the performance of the existing supplier base – and may also carry out formal supply market research for a given requirement.

In this chapter we look at the broader process of gathering information on the supply market, which can be used to support decisions on the sourcing of requirements from external suppliers. This process is sometimes known by the umbrella term 'purchasing research'. It embraces key disciplines such as: demand analysis (estimating potential sales of the buyer's product, and its implications for its input requirements); vendor analysis (appraising the existing supplier base and potential suppliers, as discussed in Chapter 1); and market analysis (gathering data on market structure, prices, trends and risks).

1   Purchasing research

1.1   To achieve its sourcing objectives, it is clearly essential for the procurement function to understand its supply markets.

1.2   **Purchasing research** is 'the systematic study of all relevant factors which may affect the acquisition of goods and services, for the purpose of securing current and future requirements in such a way that the competitive position of the company is enhanced' (van Weele).

1.3   In relation to a particular sourcing exercise or cycle, or for a particular material or category of materials, the focus of purchasing research should include three basic aspects.

- **Demand analysis**. Standard procedures (such as Pareto analysis) should be operated to ensure that particular attention is paid to accurate demand forecasting for high-value, high-usage, high-risk materials. The objective is to estimate likely usage in the period ahead. We will look at demand analysis and forecasting in Section 2 of this Chapter.
- **Vendor analysis**. Buyers must evaluate the performance of current suppliers, as well as identifying, appraising and pre-qualifying potential suppliers not currently being used. We covered this process broadly in Chapter 1.
- **Supply market analysis**. Buyers must appraise general supply conditions in the market, in relation to factors such as: likely availability and the risk of shortages or disruptions; market prices, price fluctuations and trends; and environmental factors affecting supply or demand. We will look at various aspects of the market analysis process, and sources of market analysis data, in Sections 3 and 4 of this chapter.

1.4   Here are some of the questions purchasing research seeks to answer, to support sourcing decisions.

- What is the likely future demand level and usage rate of the item (which may or may not be linked to demand for the product in which it is incorporated)?
- How many suppliers are there in the supply market? Where are they based? Of what type and size are they?
- What new products, processes and technologies are developing in the market? What sustainability- or innovation-supporting capabilities are available or emerging?
- What determines 'market price' for a given input; how much price variation is there between suppliers; how much price fluctuation is there over time (linear, cyclical or seasonal, or chaotic); and what price trends can be identified to support cost estimation?
- What threats and opportunities are presented by any or all of the above data?

1.5   The research into supply markets conducted by procurement departments is generally of an ongoing nature – involving constant market scanning and analysis – although there is sometimes cause for a defined project of research to supplement this (eg in the case of new procurements or identified risk factors). Its objectives are as follows.

- To provide information on which the organisation can plan to adapt to changes in the supply environment (ideally, earlier and better than its competitors) – whether to take advantage of new opportunities or to take defensive action in the light of perceived threats
- To secure competitive advantage by means of early information on innovations in supply markets.

1.6   To begin with, procurement staff must define the scope of the research work. If they identify trends with a potential to impact on the organisation a sensible next step might be to conduct a limited research project, perhaps by means of consultation with suppliers. The aim is to obtain early warning of anything that could have a serious impact, for good or bad, on the organisation's supply chain activities.

1.7   Of course, consultations with suppliers are not the only sources of information. For example, a buyer interested in the possibility of price changes in a certain material may be guided by any or all of the following factors.

- Historical trends
- Published price indices for the relevant industry or commodity
- Economic models (eg extrapolating historical trends, modelling the effect of changes in variables such as supply and demand, taking into account macro-economic indices such as inflation and growth)
- Information from specialist price analysis and forecasting agencies.

We will look at such sources of data – both primary and secondary – in Section 4.

The importance of purchasing research

1.8 Basic supplier and supply market data – eg on supply factors and risks, supplier capabilities and performance, market prices, and supply market structure and competition – can be used to support sourcing decisions:

- At a strategic level: eg in relation to make-do or buy, local or international sourcing, supply base optimisation or partnering decisions
- At a tactical level: eg in relation to supplier appraisal criteria, sourcing policies and methods, price targets, risk management or inventory policy
- At an operational level: eg in relation to negotiating strategies; the conduct of price negotiations, auctions and tenders; and supplier appraisal.

1.9 However, a procurement function may also need to respond to a wide range of factors in the external purchasing environment.

- Emerging economic opportunities and threats, such as the opening up of new supply markets, falling or rising prices for critical supplies, or competitors tying up the best sources of supply
- Changes in social values, preferences and expectations, which may give rise to demand for new or modified products (eg using recyclable materials) or business processes (eg e-commerce) or higher expectations on the part of suppliers and other stakeholders (eg for 'fair trade' dealings or sustainable sourcing)
- Technological developments: supporting new products, materials and sourcing approaches (such as e-sourcing), while rendering others obsolete
- The trend towards globalised supply markets, changing sourcing and supply chain strategies
- Constant amendments and additions to the law and regulation of business activities by the EU, national governments and other agencies. One major example is the 2006 revision of EU regulations on public sector procurement – but much of the law affecting purchasing is also constantly altered by decisions made in the courts.

2   Demand analysis

2.1 Demand analysis provides essential data to enable buyers to source the 'right quantity' of items to meet the organisation's requirements. If you receive a requisition from the operations manager to replace one worn lathe, say, the 'right quantity' is one. If a bill of materials for a customer order specifies 2,000 subassemblies, the 'right quantity' is 2,000 subassemblies.

2.2 But what if your company manufactures cars? In this case, the question is: what will be the demand for its cars in a given period – or how many cars does it think will sell? This information influences a wide range of sourcing decisions, starting with how many cars the organisation will seek to produce; how many components or subassemblies it will need to produce them; how much oil will it need to lubricate its assembly line (among other consumables); and even how much toilet paper will be needed for the number of workers required to maintain such a level of production.

2.3 Lysons & Farrington suggest that the most important factors determining the size of the requirement to be sourced in a given situation are as follows.

- *Demand for the final product* into which the purchased materials and components are incorporated. This is identified as *'dependent demand'*, because the quantity of inputs required relates directly to the quantity of outputs planned. Obviously, the more cars you anticipate selling, the more wheels you are going to have to buy – and if you are planning on producing 1,000 cars in a given period, you will need 4,000 wheels in the same period. The key data for estimating requirements of dependent demand items are therefore estimated sales of the final product, and therefore estimated production volumes.

- *Demand for purchased finished items*, such as office equipment and supplies, computer hardware and software or maintenance services. This is identified as *'independent demand',* because the quantity of such items required is *not* directly related to the volume of production. Estimates of demand must instead be based on data such as past and average usage and replacement rates. If your office gets through an average of 60 reams of paper per month, for example, you will probably plan to purchase a similar quantity on a monthly basis.
- *The inventory policy of the organisation*: whether its main aim is to secure service levels by holding stocks (as a 'buffer' against unforeseen demand or supply difficulties) – or to minimise or eliminate stocks, to avoid the costs and risks associated with holding stock
- *The service level required*: whether an item must be available in full on demand 100% of the time (eg for critical production items or hospital supplies) or only 90–95% of the time (eg for routine supplies)
- *Market conditions*, affecting the price and security of supply, which dictate whether requirements must be 'stockpiled' to secure supply or take advantage of low prices, or can be bought on an *ad hoc* or opportunistic basis
- *Supply-side factors*, such as minimum order quantities and values, or price incentives for bulk purchases.

Forecasting dependent and independent demand

2.4 Many externally sourced items are subject to *dependent demand*: that is, demand for the item (eg components or subassemblies) depends on the specification and production volume of a larger item (finished product) of which it forms a part. Demand can thus be accurately measured on the basis of production schedules and materials requirements: if 1,000 units are due to be manufactured, and each unit requires five sub-modules, then an order will need to be placed for 5,000 sub-modules.

2.5 But what informs the decision about the volume of production: that is, the number of finished products to be made? In order to avoid wasted costs of production, and operating losses, the organisation will want to produce a volume of outputs that is as close as possible to the volume it will be able to sell to customers. Ideally, it would only produce goods in response to actual demand, in the form of customer orders – and in some contexts (eg the production of bespoke items or the final assembly of late-customised goods) such a 'pull' system may be possible.

2.6 More often, however, the volume of production must be based on forecasts of market demand, or estimates of potential sales.

2.7 Other stock items will be subject to *independent demand*: not linked to production of another finished item. The amount of oil required to keep a machine in working order does not depend on which products are being processed on that machine: it should simply be possible to identify that a certain (average) amount of oil is used each day, week or month. The same may be true of purchases such as office equipment and supplies, computer hardware and software, motor vehicles, marketing services, maintenance services and so on.

2.8 In the case of independent demand, forecasting will be based on estimating usage (and therefore replacement) rates.

Forecasting techniques

2.9 A key function of marketing, as an organisational discipline, is forecasting (or 'predicting') what products customers will want, and in what volumes. However, this information is also important for procurement, so that it can source the right inputs, in the right quantities, to support the organisation in satisfying customer demand efficiently and competitively.

2.10 The accuracy of demand forecasting is vital – but difficult to achieve. Forecasts are effective in certain areas, such as predicting stable demand, tracking sales trends, dealing with predictable seasonality, and projecting the effects of cyclical changes. They are not so effective in dynamic environments where demand and/or supply is erratic or chaotic.

2.11 Predictions are generally made by using the following sources of information.

- Historical data (eg on sales, or usage)
- Current data and information (such as that available from sales and production records, and suppliers)
- Market research and environmental monitoring, to identify 'what is happening' within the product market (affecting demand) and the supply market (affecting supply).

2.12 If product prices are falling in the market, demand may increase – whereas if product prices are rising, demand may fall. Rising demand may lead to supply shortage problems – whereas falling demand may lead to slow moving and obsolete stocks. All forecasts require constant monitoring and revision in order to maximise and maintain their accuracy.

2.13 It is fairly easy to predict the pattern of demand for some items. For example, if a product is obsolete, demand will almost certainly decline over time. If a special promotional campaign is planned, demand should rise. Demand for seasonal items (such as air conditioning or heating units or Christmas decorations) will fluctuate on a predictable cyclical basis. Very often, however, the position is not so obvious, and statistical techniques may be required to establish trends or patterns in the available data, which can be projected to give a statistically 'probable' forecast of future demand.

2.14 Various statistical techniques can be used to forecast market demand (sales) and/or independent demand (usage rates): Table 7.1.

2.15 Statistical methods are unlikely to be able to take into account all the various environmental factors which may cause fluctuations in demand. A number of more subjective or 'qualitative' methods may therefore be used, based on the knowledge, experience and judgement of expert buyers, suppliers, consultants or other stakeholders.

- **Marketing and/or customer research** can be used to ascertain potential interest and demand, particularly in new products, or to help identify trends in sales and customer buying preferences, and the reasons behind them. This is generally the preserve of the marketing function in an organisation, rather than the focus of purchasing research.
- **Expert opinion** is the gathering of views, judgements and opinions from people regarded as knowledgeable and experienced in relevant business areas, markets and disciplines (such as consumer behaviour).
- **The Delphi method** (named after an ancient Greek oracle) seeks to add some objectivity and statistical rigour to the gathering of expert opinion. Under this method, expert opinions are gathered using postal or email questionnaires and follow-up questions. This removes the risk – common in expert opinion panels – of people being influenced too early by each other's ideas, creating bias or distorted group positions. The Delphi method has proved useful in answering specific, single-dimension questions. There is less support for its use to determine more complex forecasts that involve multiple factors.

Table 7.1 *Statistical forecasting techniques*

Simple moving average	This technique assumes that demand for a coming period will be 'average', that is an average of the demand recorded in recent past periods. So if sales (or usage) of a given item from January to June ran at 450, 190, 600, 600, 420 and 380 units respectively, we might anticipate that July's sales (or usage) would be an average of these six months: 2,640/6 = 440 units. The reason this is called a moving average is that each month we move along by one step: in forecasting August's demand, for example, we would take an average of sales/usage in February to July; in forecasting September's demand, an average of sales/usage in March to August. This isn't a very accurate method, as it doesn't take into account the fluctuations hidden by the average: in our example, actual monthly demand could be anywhere from 190 to 600 units.
Weighted average (or exponential smoothing)	This technique recognises that older data is generally less reliable as a guide to the future than more recent data, and therefore gives extra weight to more recent data in calculating the average. This adds some sophistication and accuracy by reflecting more recent trends, such as sales growth due to increasing customer awareness, promotional campaigns or competitor failure, or sales decline due to product obsolescence, say. Continuing our earlier example, we might base an estimate of sales/usage for July on just the four previous months (March to June). We could recognise the higher importance of recent months by giving a weighting of 0.4 to the June figure, 0.3 to May, 0.2 to April and 0.1 to March (or whatever appropriate weightings will give a total weighting of 1). The estimate for July would therefore be calculated as: $(0.4 \times 380) + (0.3 \times 420) + (0.2 \times 600) + (0.1 \times 600) = 458$ units.
Time series (trend) analysis	This method works by examining past data in chronological order, identifying underlying trends (consistent upward or downward movements over time) and projecting or 'extrapolating' these trends into the future. This is a more subjective, broad-brush approach. Historical data may show: *A steady trend*: an increase or decline in demand, moving with a predictable pace that can easily be forecast *A fluctuating trend*: rises or falls in demand are volatile or unstable, and reliable predictions are hard to achieve It may be possible to identify repeated seasonal variations (eg peak demand periods at certain times of year) and cyclical variations (eg peaks and troughs of demand in industry performance over time), which can be taken into account in forecasting. However, there may also be irregular fluctuations, due to one off events or environmental factors: no statistical analysis can account accurately for every variation in demand patterns.
Regression analysis	This method works by identifying connections or 'correlations' between certain measured variables (such as advertising spend, or price increases, and sales levels) and predicting the effect of changes in one variable (eg increasing advertising or lowering prices) on the other (hopefully, increased sales). This may involve complex modelling, and is often done using computerised spreadsheet or scenario analysis programmes.

3 Sources of market and supplier data

3.1 Supply market research is an essential process for gathering, analysing and evaluating data relating to businesses, markets and suppliers. The purpose of gathering such information is to achieve an optimal supply base to support developing business needs related to key performance factors such as cost, quality, delivery responsiveness etc.

3.2 Supply market research can be considered from both macro and micro perspectives. Obtaining market macro data and developing intelligence of the wider trends and opportunities is vital to ensure purchasing understand the relevance of these developments. Equally, the micro analysis that subsequently identifies specific suppliers and opportunities is essential to develop alternative business proposals.

3.3 Supply market research is expensive and time-consuming. It should therefore be focused on the areas that are most strategically critical to the business, which can be identified using risk assessment and prioritisation tools such as the Kraljic matrix (discussed in Chapter 1).

3.4 As we saw in Chapter 1, a number of sources of data may be consulted to identify and research potential suppliers, and to gather information on supply market structure, risks, prices, demand-and-supply trends and so on.

Primary data

3.5 Primary data are data collected especially for a particular purpose, directly from the relevant source: the 'horse's mouth', whoever that may be eg customers, supply chain partners or industry analysts. Primary research is usually 'field research', involving surveys, interviews, questionnaires, observation or experiments – although with the development of ICT-enabled communication (eg via the internet), it may nowadays overlap with 'desk research'.

3.6 Here are some primary sources of data on suppliers and the supply market.

- *Communication with suppliers*: eg via Requests for Information; 'Meet the Buyer' events; online supplier and buyer forums; networking at trade conferences and exhibitions; non-negotiatory dialogues (with existing or prospective suppliers) to discuss requirements and supply market issues; and so on. This is particularly valuable in **compiling supplier spend data** which is difficult to obtain from the supplier himself.
- The buyer's *database of suppliers and market data,* including records of supplier offerings and performance evaluations; market risk assessments; price movements; demand forecasts and data. Organisations should carry out – and capture data from – their own environmental scanning, monitoring, risk assessments, PESTLE or STEEPLE and SWOT analysis, competitor and industry analysis, benchmarking, pricing and price trends analysis and so on.
- The *marketing communications* of suppliers: advertising, direct mail, brochures and catalogues, visits from sales representatives, websites and so on. Catalogues (and their electronic equivalents) may be particularly helpful, with detailed product descriptions, trading terms, price lists and so on.
- *Online market exchanges*, auction sites and supplier/buyer forums, which may also allow the posting of requests for quotation and other exchanges
- *Advisory and information services,* including relevant professional institutions (such as CIPS)
- *Commissioned reports and analyses* from specialist purchasing consultancies (such as the Purchasing Research Service: http://www.touchbriefings.com) and other sourcing service agencies
- *Trade fairs, exhibitions and conferences,* which may provide opportunities for visitors to view competing products and prototypes, meet supplier representatives and contacts, discuss supplier offerings and buyer requirements, gather relevant literature for the catalogue file, and hear expert industry analysis and reports.
- *Informal networking* and information exchange with colleagues, other purchasing professionals, suppliers and other stakeholders.

Secondary data

3.7 Secondary data are data which have already been gathered and assembled for other purposes, general reference or publication. They are generally accessed by 'desk research', which can literally be carried out from the researcher's desk (given appropriate reference sources).

3.8 Here are some secondary sources of data on suppliers and the supply market.

- *Websites* including business directories and listings and searchable databases designed to promote trade or exports
- *Published listings* of suppliers and stockists: general directories (eg the Yellow Pages) and specialist trade/industry directories and registers. Trade directories (eg Dun & Bradstreet, Kompass or Kelly's Directory) provide information about suppliers' products or services and may also include analysis or rating of the firm's capabilities or financial profile.
- *Financial and trade/industry press* (newspapers, magazines, journals and bulletins) and specialist procurement journals (such as *Supply Management* or *Procurement Professional)* which may carry news and feature articles, market analysis, statistical digests and so on.
- *Published economic indices* such as the consumer price index (CPI), the labour market index, the FTSE 500 index and various commodity price indices (discussed further below)

- *Published and online industry and market analysis,* in the form of searchable databases and reports eg provided by organisations like Gallup, MORI, Euromonitor and Mintel. Euromonitor's website, for example, makes available (at cost) detailed profiles of countries and markets: summaries can be viewed free, and links to further information sources are provided. If you are interested, see: http://www.euromonitor.com.

- *Published statistical surveys and reports* from the government, which is a major source of economic, industrial and demographic information. Here are examples of government publications.
  - *Social Trends* (annual)
  - *Economic & Labour Market Review* (monthly)
  - *Census of Production* (annual, providing data about production by firms in each industry in the UK)
  - *British Business* (published weekly by the DTI, giving data on industrial and commercial trends both domestically and overseas)
  - *Business Monitor (*published by the Office for National Statistics, giving detailed information about various industries)

  If you are interested, you might like to browse National Statistics Online, at http://www.statistics.gov.uk. Official statistics are also published by the European Union, the United Nations and local authorities.

- *Organisations promoting trade,* such as trade associations, embassies, Chambers of Commerce, export associations and professional institutes – and their websites

- Price-*listing and price comparison websites,* which allow the gauging of market prices. In some cases (eg for commodities) market prices will be directly quoted on market exchanges such as The London Stock Exchange

- Specialist *libraries,* such as the City Business Library in London, which collect published information from a variety of sources

3.9   Much of the above-listed secondary published materials is accessible and inexpensive to gather – although it may need processing and analysis (discussed in the following section of this chapter) in order to produce sufficiently targeted and meaningful information to support sourcing decisions. Tailor-made information is also available, if the organisation commissions or undertakes primary research – but this is a costly exercise.

3.10 A middle course may be to buy in reports prepared by third parties, whether as commissioned primary research for another organisation (and then syndicated or released) or as a commercial service to industry data users.

Third party research organisations

3.11 There are some very specialist areas of research that most organisations will not have the necessary knowledge and experience to conduct effectively – or cost-effectively. For example, obtaining global supply information is now a common requirement for many organisations, and although the internet has revolutionised information management, specialist local intelligence may be required to develop informed business options.

3.12 A wide range of specialist organisations are engaged in providing market research and intelligence. Research industry associations and professional bodies sponsor a range of reliable websites to assist organisations in obtaining market research intelligence. These sites are useful sources of knowledge as they often contain searchable directories, advice on setting up a research programme, commissioning research etc. Here are some examples.

- The Market Research Portal (http://www.marketresearchworld.net). This site gives guidance on market research topics such as commissioning and conducting research, an explanation of the research process, basic introductions to areas such as sampling and data analysis, articles on market research etc.

- The Market Research Society, which offers free online access to its annual Research Buyers Guide (http://www.rbg.org.uk/). The Research Buyer's Guide is a directory of organisations in the UK and Republic of Ireland offering market research and related services.
- ESOMAR: the European Society for Opinion and Marketing Research (http://www.esomar.org/), which provides search facilities by country, sector, and by research methods or techniques used.

Economic indices

3.13 In economics, an 'index' (plural: 'indices') is a statistical measure of changes in a group of data. Economic indices are designed to track a nation's, or supply market's, stability and health, from a number of perspectives. For example:

- Stock market indices track the performance of selected companies in different stock marekts, in order to evaluate and predict economic and industry trends. Examples include the FTSE 100 (UK), the Nikkei 225 (Japan), the SENSEX (India), and S&P (Standard & Poor) Global 100.
- Specialised indices exist to track the performance of specific sectors of the market: for example, the Morgan Stanley Biotech Index (36 US firms in the biotechnology sector).
- Some indices have multiple versions, according to how the index components or stock performance is calculated and weighted (eg price weighted, market-value weighted, or market-share weighted).
- Specialist indices also exist for other performance management criteria, such as sustainability, environmental responsibility, CSR and ethics. Examples include the FTSE4Good Index and the Dow Jones Sustainability Index.
- Specialist agencies such as Thomson Reuters have developed indices for a range of decision-support applications: analysing the impact on markets of global news events (eg natural disasters, sovereign debt or political unrest); the sectors most likely to be affected by environmental changes, threats and opportunities; and market volatility (trading signal indices)
- The Small Business Lending Index (SBLI) by Thomson Reuters/PayNet, is an indicator of economic trends and market 'signals', because small businesses gnerally respond to changes in economic conditions more sensitively and rapidly than larger businesses.
- Commodities indices, or commodity price indices, track the weighted average of selected commodity prices, and are designed to be representative of a broad commodity asset class or a subset of commodities (such as energy, metals or agriculture). Examples include the World Bank Commodity Price Index, the Goldman Sachs Commodity Index, the Thomson Reuters/Jefferies CRB Index, the S&P Commodity Index; and the Merrill Lynch Commodity Index eXtra (MLCX).
- The Consumer Price Index (CPI) tracks variations in prices for a range of consumer goods and services over time, in a particular geographic location. This acts as an indicator for the calculation of inflation rates, and related issues such as salary and pension adjustments and tax thresholds.

Commodity pricing

3.14 Primary commodities are items that occur in nature and provide raw materials for businesses to incorporate in their products. They include crops such as cotton, coffee, tea, wheat and soya; and also minerals such as coal, iron ore and bauxite. Because commodity trading often involves complex international transactions, a range of dedicated commodity markets or exchanges has been developed to support trade, and determine prices.

3.15 The main markets in which commodities are traded are in the United States. They include the market for precious metals (Comex) in New York, the New York Mineral Exchange (Nymex) and the Chicago Board of Trade, where grain, rice and soya are traded. Major markets in the UK include the London Metal Exchange, with dealings in metals such as copper, zinc, tin and aluminium, and the International Petroleum Exchange.

3.16 Four groups participate in these markets: producers, buyers, traders, and speculators.

- Producers (eg farmers with a crop to sell) are interested in securing a good price for their produce.

- Buyers are interested in guaranteeing the price they will pay for commodities to be used in their businesses.
- Traders make the wheels go round. They are both buyers and sellers, and make a small commission on trades in either direction.
- Speculators are also both buyers and sellers, but their aim is usually to make a substantial profit from their expertise in forecasting price movements. Speculators play a valuable role in that they foster the liquidity of the market by, in effect, introducing a greater number of both buyers and sellers.

3.17 From a sourcing viewpoint, the main challenges of commodities are that:

- They are unequally distributed, geographically: often, involving procurement in international sourcing – which brings a complex set of costs and risks (including currency exchange risk, transport risk, differences in legal jurisdictions, language and cultural barriers and so on).
- They are subject to significant and unexpected fluctuations in price. For example, if production is damaged by weather conditions or industrial action (or supply is disrupted because of war, civil unrest or government policy), the commodity will be scarce on the world markets, and prices will rise for the limited supplies that are available. These effects are exacerbated by the difficulty of taking compensating measures: if a rubber crop fails, say, a planter might increase planting to make up the deficit – but it will be years before newly-planted trees are productive, and in the meantime the price may remain unusually high.

3.18 It is important for buyers continuously to monitor:

- Relevant factors in commodity supply. Factors which may cause price rises (by lowering or disrupting supply) include: weather conditions, natural disasters (such as drought, flood, fire or crop diseases), political or industrial instability, export quotas and a range of other risks. Factors which may cause price reductions or collapses (by raising supply or causing a 'glut' or oversupply) include: bumper yields, low incidence of risk events, removal of production or export quotas; and so on.
- Trends and fluctuations in commodity prices, eg as flagged by Commodity Price Indices (tracking the weighted average of selected commodity prices) and listed prices on the commodities markets.

3.19 Buyers must try to minimise the effects of commodity price fluctuations – minimising the risk and cost of price rises, and seizing opportunities presented by price reductions. One solution may be to adopt a policy of forward buying, which means that buyers deliberately overstock or stockpile, in order to take advantage of a low price. If prices then rise, the existing stocks make it unnecessary to purchase until conditions become more favourable again. Of course, the benefits of this policy must be weighed against the costs of storing and insuring the additional stock.

3.20 Commodity markets also offer a number of methods to dampen price fluctuations and enable sensible forecasting and budgeting, notably 'futures contracts'. A futures contract is essentially the right to purchase or sell a specified quantity of a commodity in the market. Any price fluctuation that is bad for a *buyer* (ie the price has gone up) will equally *benefit* him as a *seller:* 'hedging' the contract by making sure that the movement in price has a self-cancelling or off-setting effect on his financial position.

3.21 To illustrate this, suppose a buyer *purchases* 5,000 bushels of wheat on 1 January, when the price stands at £3 per bushel, for incorporation in products for sale on 1 March. If by 1 March the price of wheat has fallen to £2 per bushel, the buyer may be forced to sell those products to customers for £5,000 less than expected: bad news.

However, our buyer could enter a futures contract on 1 January, under which he agrees to *sell* 5,000 bushels of wheat on 1 March. He can purchase 5,000 bushels of wheat at the March price of £2 per bushel, knowing that he has a guaranteed customer for this quantity at a price of £3. (The 'forward price' of wheat for delivery in two months time will not in practice be exactly the same as the 'spot price' at the time, but we are illustrating the perfect hedge.) By gaining £5,000 on the futures contract, he offsets his loss on the physical purchase of wheat.

3.22 This is a complex area of procurement, and the detail is beyond the scope of this syllabus, but the point about price volatility in commodity procurement is worth bearing in mind.

4 Supply market analysis

4.1 The collection and presentation of raw data is of limited value without any subsequent analysis and evaluation. It is the added processes of analysis and evaluation that differentiates 'market intelligence' from mere 'market data'.

The structure of supply markets

4.2 A useful starting point in the analysis of supply markets is to examine the main structural features that can be discerned. These are features that a buyer is unable to influence – the market has just developed in that way – but which may be an important influence on sourcing strategies and outcomes. Examples of these include:

- The number of buyers in the market
- The number of suppliers in the market
- Methods of pricing in the market
- The degree of product differentiation in the market (are there many closely similar products or just a single product on which all buyers are dependent?)
- Technological developments in the market.

4.3 A market may range from a state of **pure competition** (where many buyers and suppliers are active, and no one player is big enough to influence market prices by its actions) to a state of **monopoly** (a single supplier, who has a captive market and can effectively dictate a price to maximise its profits) or **monopsony** (a single buyer, who can effectively dictate the price it is willing to pay suppliers).

4.4 A buyer must be aware of these characteristics in its supply market, because they influence the strength of its negotiating position. For example, a buyer facing a monopoly supplier, in a market with little product differentiation and few substitute products, is in a weak negotiating position, with few options for influencing – or switching – suppliers. If there are many suppliers, and many products of comparable quality, the situation is very different: the buyer's position is strong, because it can easily switch to the most competitive supplier.

Stable and unstable supply markets

4.5 Market analysis is particularly important for procurements which are subject to instability. Purchasers of commodities such as metals or agricultural products (wheat, vegetable oils, cotton), for example, have to contend with severe fluctuations in price and availability, compared to purchasers of standard manufactured industrial supplies.

4.6 The analysis of a particular supply market as stable or unstable has an impact on sourcing strategies and tactics (eg the timing of purchases). In stable markets, for example, the timing of purchases is usually not a critical matter – but in unstable markets, where prices are fluctuating rapidly, the timing of purchases can have a dramatic effect on the total price paid.

4.7 If the supply market for a particular material is analysed as stable, a buyer may well decide, in effect, to ignore market conditions (since they are generally unchanging). If the supply market is unstable, there will be a much stronger emphasis on purchasing research, environmental monitoring, risk assessment and forecasting.

7

Supply market analysis tools

4.8 Supply market monitoring and analysis may include various forms of environmental scanning, strategic information gathering and analysis, including:

- Environmental audits and PESTLE analysis: classification of external environmental factors affecting the market, under the headings Political, Economic, Socio-cultural, Technical, Legal and Environmental factors.
- Industry analysis: examining the structure of the industry, its key players, and the nature and intensity of competition in the industry. One commonly used model for this kind of analysis is Porter's Five Forces model.
- Strengths, Weaknesses, Opportunities and Threats (SWOT) analysis and/or risk (likelihood and impact) analysis, to identify the implications of supply market factors for the organisation.
- Competitor analysis: monitoring and analysing the actions, strengths and weaknesses of key competitors and their supply chains
- Critical success factor analysis: examining what objectives must be achieved in order to secure competitive advantage for a supply chain in a given market
- Supply, demand and capacity forecasting: eg using statistical analysis or expert opinion gathering to estimate future sourcing requirements
- Vendor analysis: evaluating the performance of current suppliers, and the capability and suitability of potential suppliers
- Market analysis: appraising general supply conditions in the market, in regard to supply factors, risks, pricing and pricing trends.

4.9 We will highlight some of the most useful tools for supply market analysis here.

PESTLE analysis

4.10 Buyers may gather and classify information on critical factors, changes and trends in a supply market, using the PESTLE framework – and then consider their implications for sourcing and other procurement decisions. A broad example of the kind of analysis that can be conducted is shown in Table 7.2. Obviously, more specific factors or changes would raise more specific questions.

Table 7.2 *PESTLE analysis*

FACTOR	DESCRIPTION	ANALYSIS
Political	Government policy and influence on the industry/supply market	What are the likely implications of a change in government or EU policy?
Economic	Growth trends; patterns of employment, income, interest/exchange/tax rates etc.	How might changes affect future demand for your products/services, and future supply and cost of inputs?
Socio-cultural	Changing demographics, attitudes, values, consumption patterns and education of the population	How might changes affect the demands and expectations of customers, suppliers and other stakeholders, or skill availability?
Technological	Changing tools for design/manufacturing, information and communications etc.	Are there opportunities for development – or risks of obsolescence? Are competitors adapting more quickly?
Legal	Law and regulation affecting the supply market	How will the organisation need to adapt policies and practices in order to comply with forthcoming measures?
Ecological	Resources, sustainability, pollution/impact management, weather, 'green' pressures	Which factors may cause supply or logistical problems, compliance issues, market pressure or risk to reputation?

Risk assessment

4.11   A simple risk or impact assessment can be performed by using a matrix on which supply market factors, changes or events can be plotted according to (a) the likelihood of their happening and (b) the seriousness of their effect if they do happen: Figure 7.1.

Figure 7.1 *Risk assessment grid*

Impact/effect on organisation

		Low	High
Likelihood of occurrence	Low	A	C
	High	B	D

4.12   Taking the segments of the grid one by one:

- Segment A will contain events which are not likely to happen and would have little effect if they did: say, a power failure at all suppliers' factories at once, when they all have emergency back-up generators. Given the low level of impact, the organisation can safely *ignore* such factors as low-priority.
- Segment B will contain events which are relatively likely to occur, but will not have a major effect: say, an exchange rate fluctuation, if the organisation is not heavily exposed by international sourcing outside the EU. The appropriate response is to *monitor* such factors, in case the situation changes and the impact may be greater than expected.
- Segment C will contain events which are not likely to happen, but will have a big impact if they do: say, failure of suppliers of critical requirements. The appropriate response is to draw up a *contingency plan* to minimise the impact, in case the event occurs: perhaps having a back-up source of supply, and insurance.
- Segment D will contain events which are both likely to happen and serious in their impact: say, the emergence of a new technology that will alter the supply market. The appropriate response is to *respond* to the perceived threat or opportunity, including it in strategic analysis and planning.

Porter's Five Forces Model

4.13   According to competition guru Michael Porter (*Competitive Advantage*), 'competition in an industry is rooted in its underlying economics'. Porter developed a framework which argues that the extent of competition in an industry or supply market depends on the interaction of five forces in the environment: Figure 7.2.

Figure 7.2 *Porter's five forces model*

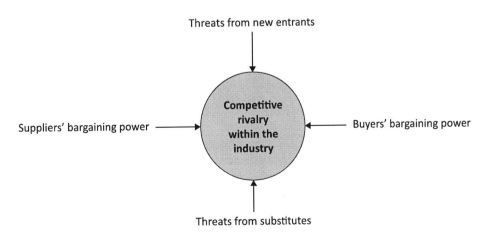

4.14 Taking each of the five forces in turn:

- **Potential new entrants** to a supply market may make it more competitive by: expanding supply (without increasing market demand); and striving to penetrate the market by innovating or competing aggressively. The likelihood of new entrants will depend on the strength of 'barriers to entry', such as high investment costs; reliance on protected designs and patents; strong brand loyalty; or existing players' control over sources of supply and distribution channels.

- **Substitute products** are alternative products that serve the same purpose, making it easy for buyers to switch, and therefore limiting the price that a supplier can charge for its products.

- **Buyer power** may make a supply market more competitive by enabling buyers to: force down prices; bargain for higher quality or improved services; or play competing providers against each other. Buyers are particularly powerful if they are limited in number and/or large in size, relative to supplying firms; represent a high proportion of suppliers' revenue; can easily switch suppliers (eg if products and services are undifferentiated or there are substitute products).

- **Supplier power** in a supply market is generally exercised to raise prices, squeezing buyers' profits (especially if they are unable to recover their cost increases by raising their own prices). Suppliers are particularly powerful if they are limited in number and/or large in size, relative to buying firms; their product or service is important to buyers' business; or it is hard or costly for buyers to switch suppliers (eg because products and services are highly differentiated or there are no substitute products).

- The **intensity of rivalry** among current competitors may range from collusion between competitors (in order to maintain and share the profits available in the industry) to the other extreme of aggressive competitive strategies such as price wars. Rivalry is likely to be more intense where there are equally-balanced competitors; a slow rate of industry growth (so that sales growth can only come from market share); and there is a lack of product or service differentiation.

Chapter summary

- Purchasing research includes three basic aspects: demand analysis; vendor analysis; and supply market analysis.
- Data on suppliers and supply markets can be used to support sourcing decisions at strategic, tactical and operational levels.
- Demand analysis enables buyers to source the appropriate quantity of goods to meet the organisation's requirements.
- In terms of forecasting demand, it is important to distinguish between items subject to dependent demand and those subject to independent demand.
- Forecasting techniques include simple moving average, weighted average, time series analysis, and regression analysis.
- Primary data are collected especially for a particular purpose. Secondary data have already been gathered for some purpose other than the buyer's immediate interest.
- Third party research organisations are an important source of data.
- The structure of a supply market reflects a number of factors, such as the number of buyers and suppliers in the market, methods of pricing, the degree of product differentiation, and technological developments.
- PESTLE analysis is an important tool in supply market analysis. Other tools include risk analysis and Porter's Five Forces Model.

 ## Self-test questions

Numbers in brackets refer to the paragraphs where you can check your answers.

1   List three main elements of purchasing research. (1.3)

2   What are the objectives of purchasing research? (1.5)

3   Distinguish between dependent and independent demand. (2.4, 2.7)

4   What are the usual sources of information used by a buyer in forecasting demand? (2.11)

5   What is meant by the Delphi method? (2.15)

6   List possible statistical forecasting techniques. (Table 7.1)

7   What is meant by 'primary data'? (3.5)

8   List secondary sources of data on suppliers and the supply market. (3.8)

9   Give examples of economic indices useful to a buyer in analysing the supply market. (3.13)

10   List four groups of participators in commodity supply markets. (3.16)

11   List important factors determining the structure of a supply market. (4.2)

12   List tools that can help a buyer in supply market monitoring and analysis. (4.8)

13   What are the five forces in Michael Porter's model of competitive advantage? (4.14)

CHAPTER 8

Quotations and Tenders

Assessment criteria and indicative content

4.2 Explain the main processes used for obtaining quotations and tenders

- Advertising requirements
- Requests for information or quotations
- The operation of tendering
- Formalised arrangements for tendering

4.3 Evaluate the criteria that can be commonly applied to the assessment of quotations or tenders

- Assessment of suppliers' proposals
- The use of weighted points systems for assessment
- Recommending sources of supply

Section headings

1 Enquiries and quotations
2 The tendering process
3 Assessment of suppliers' proposals
4 Recommending sources of supply

Introduction

In Chapter 2 we mentioned tendering as one approach to the sourcing of requirements, particularly for large contracts which might benefit from open competition between suppliers – and therefore competitive pricing and supply solutions.

In this chapter we look at the basic sourcing processes and procedures used to place contracts on a competitive basis. For comparatively simple or low-value requirements, or re-buys, this may mean obtaining and comparing quotations from different suppliers, in order to ensure that prices and offerings are broadly competitive. New purchases of high value and high risk, however, may justify the operation of a structured competitive bidding or tendering exercise.

We will look at the principles of quotations and tendering here. In Chapter 10, we will look at the more specific requirements for tendering in the context of public sector procurement, which is subject to EU Public Procurement Directives on tendering procedures.

1 Enquiries and quotations

1.1 A requirement can be signalled to prospective, pre-qualified or approved suppliers in various ways, depending on the sourcing policies of the organisation for particular types of purchase (as discussed in Chapter 2). For routine, low-value purchases or re-buys, there may be framework agreements or call-off contracts in place. Or the buyer may simply be able to refer to approved suppliers' catalogues or price lists. For more modified, new, non-standard or high-value requirements, the buyer may have to initiate negotiations with, or solicit proposals from, one or more suppliers.

1.2   As we mentioned in Chapter 2, an organisation may have different procedures in place for orders of different volume or value.

- For order values under £100, say, there may be no formal requirement for supplier selection.
- For orders between £100 and £5,000, there may be a negotiation process, or a minimum of three suppliers may be requested to provide quotations, to ensure competitive pricing and value for money.
- For orders over £5,000 in value, a full competitive bidding or tendering process may be required.

Request for quotation

1.3   One approach is to send an enquiry, 'request for information', 'request for quotation' (RFQ) or 'request for proposal' (RFP) to one or more suppliers. Unsolicited proposals or quotations may also be sent in by suppliers, for standard items, or if the buyer's requirements are known (eg from market exchanges or directories).

1.4   Whether or not a formal tendering procedure is being used, it is common for a buyer to contact a number of suppliers in search of quotations. Often the buyer's enquiry will be on a pre-printed form. This makes life simpler for the buyer, ensures that important points of concern are not overlooked, and makes it easier to compare quotations from suppliers when they are eventually received.

1.5   A standard enquiry or RFQ form will typically set out the details of the requirement.

- The contact details of the purchaser
- A reference number to use in reply, and date by which to reply
- The quantity and description of goods or services required
- The required place and date of delivery
- The buyer's standard (and any special) terms and conditions of purchase
- Terms of payment

1.6   It will then invite the supplier(s) to submit a proposal and price (a 'quotation') for the contract. Quotations may be evaluated:

- On a comparative or 'competitive bidding' basis: eg the best value bid or quotation 'wins' the contract (as in competitive bidding or tendering)
- As a basis for negotiation with a preferred supplier eg if a preferred or approved supplier is asked to present a quotation as the basis for negotiation to refine contract terms
- As a way of 'testing the market': checking the current market price for requirements coming up for contract renewal.

1.7   It is worth noting that there are ethical issues in the use of requests for quotation, which may be the subject of procurement ethical codes. It is not ethical practice to solicit quotations if there is no intention to purchase; or to solicit quotations from multiple suppliers if you have already decided where the contract will be awarded (eg to check the competitiveness of a current supplier, to 'motivate' a preferred supplier or to provide leverage in negotiation with a preferred supplier). Potential suppliers are being misled by an illusory hope of work, and the preparation of quotations costs them time and resources.

1.8   Where the request for information is being used in anticipation of price negotiations with one or more suppliers, the buyer may also request appropriate cost data in support of the price proposal. If the buyer requires right of access to the supplier's cost records, this must also be established during the enquiry phase of the procurement, when potential suppliers believe that there is active competition for the job.

1.9   Suppliers will usually respond to the enquiry by supplying a quotation, representing their best price for supplying the buyer's stated requirements. This will usually be regarded, in terms of the formation of a valid contract, as constituting an 'offer' which the buyer may or may not wish to accept.

Evaluating quotations

1.10 Once the suppliers' quotations have been received, the buyer will need to analyse them to see which one provides the best value. If the buyer's requirement is very simple or standardised (eg the provision of goods specified by sample, brand or market grade), there will be little difference between the various quotations except in price. Subject to reasonable undertakings on delivery and quality, the buyer will most likely choose the supplier offering the lowest price.

1.11 You may be asked to analyse and compare supplier quotations in an exam, and to recommend the best value source of supply.

1.12 In addition to the direct comparison of prices between different suppliers, you might consider the following underlying questions.

- Have all suppliers calculated their costs in the same way?
- Are all costs known – or is more information required (to avoid potentially costly price variations, if the contract is not to be a fixed price agreement)?
- What is included in the different costings?
- The implications of low pricing: is the supplier being competitive – or might the price imply (or force the supplier into) some compromise on quality?
- Is there a difference in credit period or payment terms that would add to the value of the bid?

1.13 Even then, not all selection decisions will be as simple as a direct price competition. For example, suppose the buyer is aiming to buy 20 laptop computers for use by senior managers in the organisation.

- There will be differences in the specifications of the machines offered by different suppliers. Presumably all the offerings will at least match the minimum requirements laid down by the buyer, but some machines will exceed that specification. How valuable, if at all, are the additional features?
- There will be differences in the level of support offered by the suppliers (for example, some may offer a one-year warranty at an additional cost, while others may include a three-year warranty in the basic quoted price). How valuable, if at all, is the extra support?
- There may be differences between the buyer's standard terms and conditions and those quoted by the supplier. How amenable is the supplier likely to be in negotiating terms, and how important are the differences anyway?

1.14 As we saw in Chapter 3, there will be a range of factors (other than basic price) for the buyer to consider in evaluating the supplier quotations. Examples include:

- Previous performance of the supplier (including financial stability, reliability etc)
- Delivery lead time
- Add-on costs (freight, insurance, installation and training), running costs (including energy efficiency), and residual value and disposal costs (for capital assets)
- Warranty terms
- Availability of spares and maintenance cover
- Risk of obsolescence, and ability to upgrade to higher specification
- Payment terms
- In the case of overseas suppliers, exchange rates, taxes and import duties.

1.15 One other issue may be borne in mind, when evaluating quotations. Suppliers will, as we have said, typically quote their best price for supplying what the buyer wants. However, in exceptional cases, there may be a supplier 'cartel': collusion between suppliers, whereby they agree among themselves not to compete on price, keeping prices uncompetitively high.

1.16 Such an agreement, being anti-competitive in nature, is illegal under EU and UK competition law. However, buyers need to be aware of the possibility of illegal collusion. Possible signs of this include the following.

- All the prices offered by suppliers are higher than expected.
- One or more suppliers are reluctant to negotiate.
- One or more suppliers have declined to quote.
- The lowest price offered is significantly lower than all the rest (suggesting that all the other prices have been pitched artificially high).

2 The tendering process

2.1 The organisation may prefer to use a more formalised *competitive bidding* or tendering procedure, in which pre-qualified suppliers are issued with an invitation to tender (ITT), or an invitation to bid for a contract, with the buyer intending to choose the supplier submitting the best proposal or the lowest price.

2.2 Lysons & Farrington define tendering as 'a purchasing procedure whereby potential suppliers are invited to make a firm and unequivocal offer of the price and terms on which they will supply specified goods or services which, on acceptance, shall be the basis of the subsequent contract'.

2.3 A full competitive bidding or tendering process may typically be required for contracts over a certain value threshold, in order to ensure the competitiveness of supply. We discussed other circumstances in which tendering should – and should not – be used (compared to direct negotiation with suppliers) in Chapter 2: review Section 2 of that chapter, if you need to refresh your memory.

Types of tendering

2.4 Tendering, at its simplest, is the process by which suppliers are invited to put themselves forward (or 'bid') for a contract. There are several approaches to this (as we saw in Chapter 2).

- **Open tendering**, in which the invitation to tender is widely advertised and open to any potential bidder (eg in an open reverse e-auction).
- **Selective tendering**, in which potential suppliers are pre-qualified (eg on the basis of their technical competence and financial standing) and 3–10 suppliers are shortlisted for invitation to tender.
- **Restricted open tenders**, in which prospective suppliers are invited to compete for a contract, but are partly pre-qualified by advertising of the tender being restricted (eg to appropriate technical journals)

2.5 Where the buyer has a choice, *selective* tendering will often be used, because it:

- Is less time-consuming and costly for both buyer and suppliers
- Is less likely to present later problems with technical capability or capacity, since special consideration is given to pre-qualification (non-price) criteria
- Is less frustrating for non-pre-qualified suppliers who may incur the trouble and expense of tendering without having a realistic chance of succeeding.

2.6 Pre-qualification of potential bidders on defined criteria provides a systematic means of eliminating suppliers that should not advance to the tendering stage because they:

- Lack recent experience in the relevant kind of work
- Lack secure financial or economic resources to complete the work
- Lack personnel or managerial resources to complete the work successfully
- Lack required technology, facilities or capabilities (eg design capability, quality or risk management systems, reverse logistics arrangements)
- Rely heavily on subcontracting, and lack adequate controls to manage the supply chain effectively
- Represent a high risk (eg if they have convictions for fraud or a history of unethical dealings, say).

2.7 However, supplier appraisal and pre-qualification adds an extra layer of time and cost to the tender process and may not be required for standard, low-risk, low-value requirements. As with so many procurement decisions, it will be helpful for buyers to use segmentation, prioritisation and risk analysis tools (such as the Kraljic matrix or Pareto analysis) to determine which procurements are sufficiently high-value or high-risk to warrant the extra effort.

Formalised arrangements for the operation of tendering

2.8   A best-practice tender procedure would have the following steps.

- Preparation of detailed specifications and draft contract documents, setting out the requirement in detail: this is important in providing tender information to potential bidders, so that bids can be (a) accurately costed and (b) directly compared. Once the tender procedure is in motion, there is little room for re-negotiation and adjustment of specifications. Attention must be given to accurate specification of the requirement, including non-price criteria (eg quality measures or sustainability standards), so that the buyer's task will later be simply to (a) check that tenders received comply with the requirements, and (b) choose the lowest price (or best value) bid.

- Decision on whether to use open or selective/restricted tendering (where not already determined by regulation or company policy)

- Determination of a realistic timetable for the tender process, allowing reasonable time for responses at each stage.

- Advertisement of the requirement, tender procedures to be followed, and timetables for expression of interest (in a selective tender) or submission of bids (in an open tender)

- Sending out of Pre-Qualification Questionnaires (in a selective tender) in response to expressions of interest, with timescales for these to be returned. Follow-up information or clarification may be sought as part of the pre-qualification or appraisal process.

- Issue of invitation to tender (ITT) and tender documentation to those responding to the advertisement or invitation to tender within the prescribed time frame. Tender documents would normally include: an invitation to tender (ITT) and instructions to tenderers; a pricing document and/or form of tender; the specification; contract conditions or conditions of purchase; deadlines for submission; and pre-addressed tender return label.

- Specifications, and other tender documents (eg criteria for contract award) should be issued to each potential supplier in identical terms and by the same date. It should also be made clear to all tenderers that they are to comply strictly with the timetable for submission of bids.

- Submission of completed tenders or bids by potential suppliers, within the deadline specified

- Opening of tenders on the appointed date, in the presence of appointed officers (generally from the procurement department and an external department such as finance). Tenders received after this date should be returned un-opened. No tenders should be opened early.

- Logging of received tenders, with the main details of each listed on an analysis sheet or spreadsheet for ease of comparison. Tender details should be kept strictly confidential, with access confined to authorised procurement staff or evaluation teams.

- Analysis of each tender, according to the stated criteria, with a view to selecting the 'best offer'. This will usually be on a lowest-price or best value basis, but other criteria (such as environmental or social sustainability or innovation) may be taken into account, as long as they have been clearly notified in the invitation to tender, together with the weightings to be allocated to those criteria (see below).

- Post-tender clarification, verification of supplier information, and/or negotiation, where required. Again, if this is to happen, the invitation to tender must state clearly that the buyer will not be bound to accept the lowest price quoted, and that post-tender negotiation may be entered into, if necessary to qualify or clarify tenders, or to discuss potential improvements or adjustments to suppliers' offers. In general, any fine-tuning or clarification of the winning tender should not alter the basics of the offer – as this would inject a new element, on which other bidders did not have an opportunity to compete.

- Award of the contract, and advertisement or notification of the award

- 'De-briefing': the giving of feedback, on request, to unsuccessful tenderers, to enable them to improve the competitiveness of future bids, to develop the market – and to help the procurement function to improve future tender processes.

3 Assessment of suppliers' proposals

3.1 Tenders should be evaluated against the specific, objective award criteria set out in the initial invitation to tender (particularly if the contract is subject to statutory control).

3.2 The general principle is that the successful tender will be the one with the lowest price or the 'most economically advantageous tender' (defined on the basis of whatever value criteria have been specified). However, there is more to it than this.

- The evaluation team may need to analyse whether and how effectively each bid meets the requirements of the specification, especially if performance, outcome or 'functional' specifications are used. Such specifications define the requirement in terms of performance, functionality or outcomes – without prescribing how these will be achieved. They are specifically designed to allow maximum flexibility for suppliers in coming up with value-adding, innovative solutions to the requirement.
- There may be considerable variety in the total solution 'package' being offered by bids: one may be more attractive (innovative, environmentally friendly, risk-reducing, value-adding) than another – even if price tells against it. Non-price criteria will have to be reviewed with particular care (and more details sought, if required), especially if suppliers have not been pre-qualified on these criteria.

3.3 It will be important, therefore, for any invitation to tender to state clearly that:

- The buyer will *not* be bound to accept the lowest price quoted (especially in the case of open tenders, where there has been no pre-qualification of suppliers)
- Post-tender negotiation may be entered into, if necessary to qualify or clarify tenders, or to discuss potential improvements or adjustments to suppliers' offers.

3.4 The following guidelines summarise the main points to take account of in analysing tenders: Table 8.1.

Table 8.1 *A checklist for analysing tenders*

1.	Establish a routine for receiving and opening tenders, ensuring security
2.	Set out clearly the responsibilities of the departments involved
3.	Establish objective award criteria, as set out in the initial invitation to tender
4.	Establish a cross-functional team for the appraisal of each tender
5.	Establish a standardised format for logging and reporting on tenders
6.	Check that the tenders received comply with the award criteria. Non-price criteria will need to be carefully reviewed (and more details sought, if required).
7.	Check the arithmetical accuracy of each tender.
8.	Eliminate suppliers whose total quoted price is above the lowest two or three quotes by a specified percentage (say 20%).
9.	Evaluate the tenders in accordance with predetermined checklists for technical, contractual and financial details.
10.	Prepare a report on each tender for submission to the project or procurement manager (and as a basis for feedback to unsuccessful bidders, where relevant).

The use of weighted points systems

3.5 As a result of the comparison of bids which are amenable to fairly simple award criteria (eg based on conformance or technical specifications, where the supplier either can or cannot supply the materials as supplied, and the only remaining question is availability and price), it may be apparent that one prospective supplier clearly offers superior value.

3.6 However as we have suggested, the choice may not be so clear, and a numerical weighted-factor rating system may help to quantify complex evaluations to support fair and objective decision-making. It breaks a complex decision down into its key components, so that each can be analysed separately – while recognising that some aspects are more important in the contract award decision than others. If the factors and weightings are also supplied to potential suppliers, as part of the invitation to tender, both buyers and suppliers have a very clear awareness of how the contract award decision will be made.

3.7 A weighted points system involves:

- The development of selection criteria (factors) and 'weights' (maximum ratings for each factor, as a proportion of the total decision). This is typically done by a cross-functional tender team, comprising relevant stakeholders in the sourcing decision (eg representatives of design, operations, procurement and finance).
- The assignment of numerical ratings or 'points' to each competing supplier, on each factor, based on the collective judgements of the tender evaluation team.

3.8 Dobler *et al* supply the following example, by way of illustration: Figure 8.1.

Figure 8.1 *Weighted points system for tender evaluation*

Factors	Maximum rating (weight)	Supplier A	Supplier B	Supplier C
Technical:				
Understanding of problem	10	9	9	7
Technical approach	20	19	16	16
Production facilities	5	4	5	3
Operator requirements	3	2	3	2
Maintenance requirements	2	2	2	2
Totals	40	36	35	30
Ability to meet schedule	20	20	16	15
Price	20	16	20	15
Managerial, financial and technical capability	10	10	8	8
Quality management processes	10	9	8	9
RATING TOTAL	100	91	87	77

Post-tender negotiation (PTN)

3.9 Sometimes, as we have suggested, it is not advisable to accept a supplier's tender without qualification or clarification. It may also be advantageous to find out, post-tender, whether there is the possibility of improvement in the supplier's offer – provided that this does not distort competition (eg by enabling a preferred supplier to better a losing offer, in order to beat out the competition and win the contract). The possibility of post-tender negotiations should be clearly flagged in the invitation to tender.

3.10 CIPS defines post-tender negotiation as: 'negotiation after the receipt of formal tenders and before the letting of contract(s) with the suppliers(s)/contractor(s) submitting the lowest acceptable tender(s), with a view to obtaining an improvement in price, delivery or content in circumstances which do not put other tenderers at a disadvantage or affect their confidence or trust in the competitive tendering system.'

3.11 Such negotiations must be carried out by a trained buyer. Post-tender negotiations are generally not permitted for tenders let under EU Public Procurement Directives in the public sector: however, this does not prevent clarification and fine-tuning of tenders.

3.12 If post-tender negotiation proves unsuccessful on important terms of the tender, it may be necessary to abandon the first choice supplier and move on to the second choice. The first supplier must have irreversibly been eliminated from the process before any negotiations can commence with the second supplier: the purpose is *not* to permit a drawn-out post-tender bidding war, or unethical leverage and manipulation of suppliers.

3.13 Typically, buyers will put forward suggestions as to how the tenderer may offer better value for money. The tenderer is not obliged to accept these suggestions – but doing so may enable it to meet the buyer's requirements more effectively.

3.14 CIPS offers certain guidelines for buyers in this area.

- Post-tender negotiation meetings should be conducted by at least two members of the purchasing organisation, to ensure transparency and accountability.
- The negotiators from the purchasing organisation should have cleared their proposed negotiating strategy with relevant managers before entering the meeting. Equally, they should have pre-determined criteria as to what terms are acceptable from the supplier.
- Notes of the meeting should be taken to ensure that a record is kept of the negotiations and conclusions. It is good practice to show the notes to the supplier at the end of the meeting so that it can agree they are a fair summary – or suggest amendments.
- Buyers should (needless to say, we hope) conduct the negotiation in a professional and ethical manner.

Contract award

3.15 The contract should now be formally recognised by issuing the relevant contract documentation. Typically, the components for the actual contract will be the invitation to tender, the supplier's written proposal, plus any modifications (as may have been agreed at a bid presentation or in the post-tender negotiation). The contract should be issued in duplicate and signed by both parties, with each party retaining an original copy.

3.16 Where practical, all contract papers should be bound together in date order, and a duplicate issued for the supplier's retention, so that both parties can be satisfied as to the completeness of contract documentation. Any subsequent contract variations can be attached to all the copies, as and when they are authorised and issued (in accordance with contract variation protocols).

Contract transition arrangements

3.17 Where supply is switched from one supplier to another, or an existing contract is not renewed, successful tenderers should formally be asked to produce a plan showing how they propose to take over smoothly from existing suppliers. Similarly, it is important to make sure that any future transition to a new supplier, whether at the end of the current contract or sooner (eg in the event of termination), is planned to minimise disruption. It is good practice to cover these requirements as part of the tender.

3.18 The invitation to tender might, for example, require tenderers to produce, for agreement with the buyer, a transition plan for handing over to a different supplier at the end of the contract. This might deal with the handover of documentation, data and other assets used in the course of the contract; guarantees of confidentiality and intellectual property protection; and so on.

4 Recommending sources of supply

4.1 The outcome of a competitive quotation or tender process may be a report from the procurement or tender evaluation team, recommending the supplier or bid which the team believes should be awarded the contract – and justifying the decision with reference to the selected contract award criteria (eg defining 'most economically advantageous tender', and demonstrating how the selected bid meets this criterion).

4.2 In less clear cut situations, where there has not been a formalised competitive procedure, the procurement team may be required to:

- Submit a report, outlining and justifying the supplier appraisal and selection process, and recommending a shortlist of sources of supply, or a preferred supplier, for contract award.
- Present a business case for recommendation of a given supply approach, strategy or market (eg international or local sources, single or multiple sourcing, outsourcing or subcontracting and so on) for procurement policy makers

- Approve, prefer, confirm or certify suppliers for use by non-procurement buyers.
  — Preferred suppliers are a small number of suppliers with whom the buyer has a supply agreement
  — Approved suppliers have been pre-qualified as satisfactory suppliers for one or more products or services
  — Confirmed suppliers have been specifically requested by a user (eg design or production) and accepted by the procurement function (on the basis that there is no preferred or approved supplier listed for the requirement).

4.3 In an exam situation, you are perhaps most likely to be asked to justify a sourcing or supply approach, strategy or market for a case study organisation, on the basis of information given – and/or to conduct an evaluation and comparison of two or more suppliers (or supplier quotations) in order to recommend which supplier should be chosen for contract award or further negotiation.

4.4 Quotation and bid evaluation lends itself well to case study questions. You may be given basic data about two or three suppliers, their proposals and bids or quotations – either in narrative or descriptive form ('Supplier X has a good reputation for quality and is able to supply roughly half the company's monthly requirements at a competitive price') or in tables of comparative data (as if quotations or bids have already been put in an analysis sheet for comparison). Such data will generally correspond to key selection criteria, such as price, quality, delivery, accreditations (such as quality or environmental standards) and so on.

4.5 If asked to compare and evaluate quotations or offers, and to recommend a source of supply, a generic framework for doing so might include the following.

- A heading or memo-style header, identifying: the compiler of the report (you, in whatever role the case study requires you to adopt); the intended recipient of the report; and the date
- Requirement: a brief introductory paragraph identifying the requirement being sourced
- Background: a brief paragraph identifying the methods used (if any) to engage the market; pre-qualification processes used (if any); and the suppliers invited to quote or bid
- Evaluation and comparison of the suppliers' quotations or bids. Examiners usually prefer not to see answers in 'bullet point' form, where this leads to poor writing and insubstantial answers. However, in an exercise such as this, evaluation and selection is facilitated (as it would be in a real-life bid evaluation context) by formatting the available data for ease of comparison: for example, in a 'spread sheet' or tabular format.
- Brief commentary or analysis on each supplier in turn, focusing on key strengths and weaknesses, and key risks (eg weaknesses on areas such as financial stability or quality management systems) *OR*
- Brief commentary or analysis on each key criterion in turn, (a) highlighting its importance to the selection decision, and (b) focusing on key points of comparison between the suppliers on each criterion (eg best and worst supplier)
- Recommendation and justification: naming the supplier, quote or offer which represents best value – and explaining *why* this supplier, quote or offer has been chosen. Justification may require a brief explanation of:
  — Which criteria were considered most important in the decision (or given the highest weighting) and why (eg their potential to add value or manage risk)
  — Why the chosen supplier appears superior across key criteria
  — Why other suppliers were ruled out (on grounds of risk, under-performance, logistical constraints or other difficulties)
  — How any weaknesses of the chosen supplier are outweighed by benefits, and/or how they can be managed or mitigated to improve the bid further.
- Qualifying remarks (if any) such as:
  — Whether more information might be required, or quoted information needs verifying, before the recommendation is confirmed or the selection decision made
  — Whether 'close second' suppliers might be retained as secondary or back-up sources of supply (in the event of supply risk attached to single sourcing from the chosen supplier).

8

4.6   When formatting case study data about suppliers and their quotations for ease of comparison, bear in mind that you don't have unlimited time – and there are limited marks available just for format and presentation. We recommend a simple approach.

- Pros and cons for each supplier – an accepted decision-making tool for *evaluating* suppliers, quotations and bids: Figure 8.2.
- A table or 'spreadsheet', tabulating data on all suppliers for all key criteria: Figure 8.3.

Figure 8.2 *Basic supplier evaluation format*

SUPPLIER A

Pros (plus points)	Cons (points against)
Lowest price	Poor On-Time-In-Full record
Strong environmental policy	Doesn't monitor supply chain performance
Etc	Etc

SUPPLIER B

Pros (plus points)	Cons (points against)
Second lowest price	New supplier: unknown track record
Low whole life costs	Some quality defects in process sampling
Etc	Etc

Figure 8.3 *Basic supplier/quotation comparison format*

Criteria	Supplier A	Supplier B	Supplier C
Price	£6,000	£6,600	£8,250
Whole life costs	High maintenance/ spares costs	Unknown	High residual value
Quality	No ISO 9000		
	Poor results on process sampling	ISO 9000 certified	IOS 9000 certified
			EFQM quality award 200X
Capacity	10,000 units	8,000 units	7,000 units
CSR/sustainability	No policy depth	Strong CSR policy and supply chain monitoring	Strong sustainability policy; recyclable options
EDI/extranet capability	Yes	No	Yes
Etc	Etc	Etc	Etc

Supplier SWOT analysis

4.7   A SWOT analysis (Strengths, Weaknesses, Opportunities and Threats) is a strategic tool designed to appraise the overall state of an organisation and indicate areas for concern and areas for improvement. In the normal situation we are looking at our own organisation to identify our own strengths etc. In the present context, we are using the tool as a method of evaluating and comparing prospective suppliers, quotations or bids.

4.8   A simple format for a SWOT analysis has been recommended by various CIPS examiners: see the two-by-two grid in Figure 8.4.

Figure 8.4 *A basic SWOT matrix*

INTERNAL	**Strengths** Distinctive competencies or resources which help achieve objectives	**Weaknesses** Factors which may constrain or hinder achievement of objectives
EXTERNAL	**Opportunities** External aspects creating positive potential to achieve objectives	**Threats** External aspects that may hinder achievement of objectives

4.9   Here are some of the questions you might pose, depending on the information available.

Figure 8.5 *Populating the SWOT matrix*

Strengths:	**Weaknesses:**
• What are the strengths of the supplier (and/or this bid) compared with competitors? • What unique resources and competencies can the supplier draw on? • What resources are available to the supplier at lower cost than to other suppliers?	• What aspects of the supplier's performance could be improved? • What managerial, operational, technological or financial limitations constrain the activities of the supplier? • Where is the supplier's bid weak, compared to competing bids?
Opportunities:	**Threats:**
• Is this contract a significant opportunity for the supplier? • What trends (eg technology development) is the supplier exploiting, or could the supplier exploit, in order to improve performance? • How might this supplier contribute to opportunities for the whole supply chain?	• What external trends or internal weaknesses expose the supplier (and supply chain) to risk? • How well placed is the supplier to cope with technological, legal or other changes? • Does the supplier have any significant financial problems or instabilities?

8

Chapter summary

- There are various ways by which a buyer may signal a requirement to suppliers (eg he can send a request for quotation, RFQ).
- Once quotations are received, the buyer must evaluate them in terms of best value. This involves factors going beyond basic price.
- Alternatively, the buyer may use a formal tendering process. In the public sector, this is mandatory if the value of the contract exceeds a defined threshold.
- A tendering exercise may be based on open tendering, selective tendering, or restricted open tenders.
- Once tenders are received, they should be evaluated against the specific award criteria set out in the original invitation to tender.
- Often the buyer will use a weighted points system to evaluate tenders.
- It is sometimes appropriate to undertake post-tender negotiation, though this will usually not be permitted in public sector tendering exercises.
- The outcome of a tendering process may be a recommendation from the procurement team as to which supplier should be selected.
- A supplier SWOT analysis is one tool that may be used in the evaluation process.

Self-test questions

Numbers in brackets refer to the paragraphs where you can check your answers.

1   List details typically included on an RFQ form. (1.5)

2   Describe the ethical issues involved in issuing an RFQ. (1.7)

3   List factors, other than price, that a buyer will need to evaluate once quotations have been received. (1.14)

4   List different categories of tendering procedure. (2.4)

5   What pre-qualification criteria might justify eliminating a supplier from a tendering exercise? (2.6)

6   List steps in a best practice tendering procedure. (2.8)

7   Explain why the lowest price is not necessarily the only consideration in evaluating tenders. (3.2)

8   List steps to take in analysing tenders. (Table 8.1)

9   Describe the workings of a weighted points system for evaluating tenders. (3.5ff)

10 What guidelines does CIPS offer in relation to post-tender negotiation? (3.14)

11 Suggest possible questions that might appear in each quadrant of a supplier SWOT analysis. (4.9)

CHAPTER 9

E-Sourcing Tools

Assessment criteria and indicative content

 4.4 Explain how electronic systems can be used to help the sourcing of requirements from external suppliers

- E-requisitioning and purchase ordering systems
- E-catalogues on intranets and the internet
- The use of e-auctions
- E-tendering systems

Section headings

1 E-procurement and e-sourcing
2 Engaging the market
3 E-requisitioning and e-ordering
4 E-catalogues
5 E-auctions
6 E-tendering

Introduction

In our discussion of best practice sourcing processes so far, we have frequently noted that there were 'electronic equivalents' to many of the actions and documentation involved. In this chapter we look in more detail at some of the electronic systems that can be applied to various stages of the sourcing process, and at their impact on the efficiency and effectiveness of those processes.

1 E-procurement and e-sourcing

The impact of information and communications technology (ICT)

1.1 Broadly speaking, developments in ICT have radically changed the way people do business.

- Dramatically increasing the speed of communication and information processing. This also supports more genuine interactivity in information-gathering and transaction processing. Real-time answers to enquiries, updating of information, processing of transactions and conversations can be conducted via a computer network or the internet.
- Offering wider access to knowledge and information, especially from global sources. The internet offers unrestricted, constant access to formal information resources via websites, databases, libraries, expert agencies etc. In addition, the internet allows access to many informal information sources in the form of network contacts, forums etc.
- Facilitating 24-hour, 7-day, global business. The internet and email allow companies to offer service and maintain communication across office hours, international time zones and geographical distances.
- Supporting paperless communications (eg electronic mail messages), business transactions (eg electronic ordering and payment) and service delivery (eg web-based information and education services).
- Creating 'virtual' relationships, teams and organisations, by making location irrelevant to the process

of data-sharing, communication and collaboration. This is particularly important when developing and supporting global buyer-supplier relationships and supply chains.

The internet and e-commerce

1.2   The internet is a worldwide computer network allowing computers to communicate via telecommunications links. The network can also be accessed from laptop computers and personal hand-held devices such as tablet and palm computers and 'smart' mobile phones.

1.3   The term 'e-commerce' (short for electronic commerce) refers to business transactions carried out online via ICT – usually the internet. E-commerce has facilitated direct marketing, linking customers directly with suppliers across the whole value chain. It is a means of automating business transactions and workflows – and also streamlining and improving them.

1.4   Some websites exist only to provide information about products, services or other matters. They might provide contact details for would-be customers to make direct enquiries or orders, or to find a local retail outlet or distributor. A transaction-supporting website, however, can be a 'virtual' retail outlet, warehouse, supermarket, auction room or market exchange – enabling buyers to investigate suppliers, post requirements, receive offers, and conduct a range of P2P functions (from ordering to track-and-trace to payment).

1.5   For sourcing functions, the internet offers particular benefits.

- Wider choice of suppliers, including global and small suppliers, via the internet. (Procurement professionals still have to make strategic and tactical sourcing choices: ICT merely provides better-quality information for doing this.)
- Savings in sourcing costs, through paperless communication, greater accuracy of information, and the automation of routine sourcing processes. (In a research project in 1997, management consultants McKinsey noted that the biggest effect of the internet for business overall is the huge saving in transaction and interaction costs – the costs of 'the searching, coordinating and monitoring that people and companies do when they exchange goods, services or ideas'.)
- Support for low inventory and efficient stock turnover (as in just in time systems), due to the speed or responsiveness of the sourcing system
- Improved supply chain relationships and coordination, arising from better data-sharing. These in turn facilitate collaboration and improved customer service (by streamlining and integrating supply chain processes).

E-procurement and e-sourcing

1.6   CIPS defines e-purchasing as 'the combined use of information and communication technology through electronic means to enhance external and internal purchasing and supply management processes.' The term 'e-procurement' is often used in this context. In CIPS terminology, however, e-procurement specifically addresses the 'purchase-to-pay' stage of the purchasing cycle: the stage from when a purchase has been approved to the receipt of the product, and then (often, but not always) the payment for the product.

1.7   'E-sourcing' is defined by CIPS as 'using the internet to make decisions and form strategies regarding how and where services or products are obtained': in other words, using electronic tools for the sourcing process: Figure 9.1.

Figure 9.1 *The e-purchasing process (as depicted in the CIPS white paper on e-sourcing)*

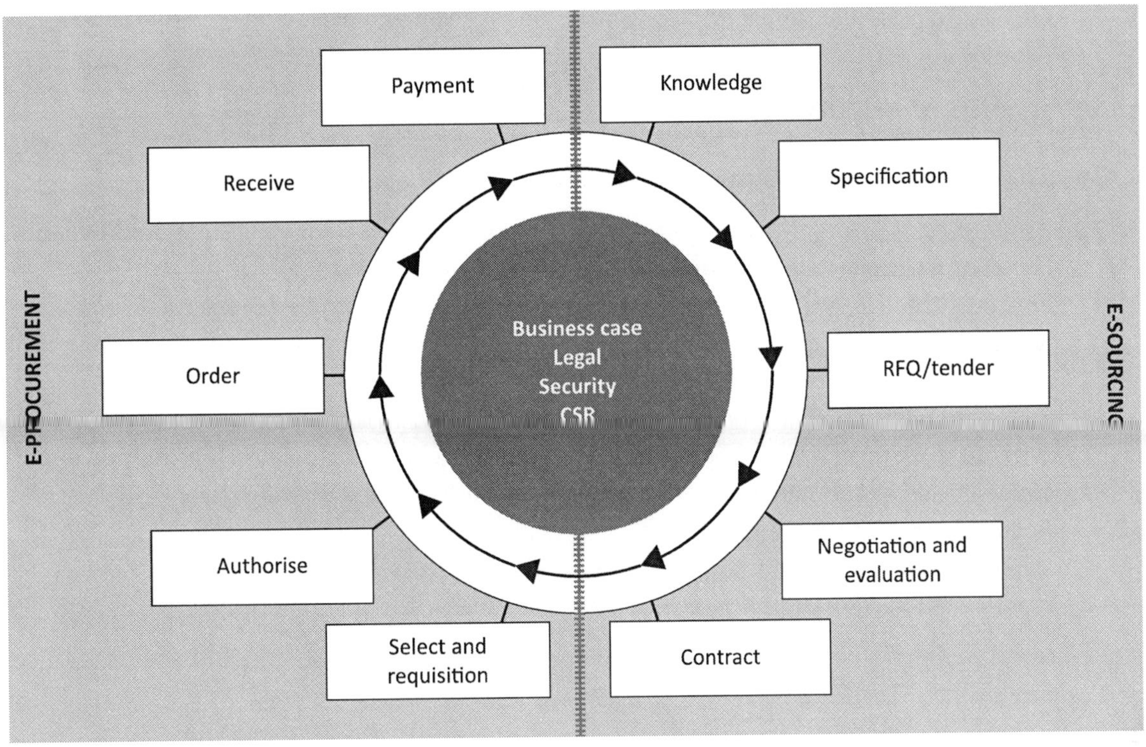

E-sourcing tools

1.8   A comprehensive e-sourcing system allows procurement staff to perform the following tasks (some of which we will go on to explore in more detail in later sections of this chapter): Table 9.1.

Table 9.1 *E-procurement tools*

STAGE OF THE SOURCING PROCESS	E-FUNCTIONS AND TOOLS
Identifying and defining needs	• Check real time inventory, and issue requisitions as required • Access spend analysis, trend analysis and investment analysis tools to support sourcing decisions • Create e-specifications and e-contracts
Sourcing the market	• Access to supply market intelligence tools • Access to supplier e-catalogues, and other supplier performance dataLocate, appraise and pre-qualify suppliers and verify price information • Issue invitations to tender or requests for quotation, and receive and evaluate tender submissions • Participate in auctions or run reverse auctions • Issue call-off orders from partners (under framework or systems contracts) Allow supply partners to control stock and deliveries (vendor managed inventory) for low-value purchases • Access supplier and supply market data for negotiation planning • Generate and transmit purchase orders or contracts (with automatic updating of the contract management database and Purchase-to-Pay systems)

1.9   Major types of e-sourcing tools include the following.

- **E-catalogues:** suppliers exhibit their products in electronic catalogues, which can be viewed online or downloaded by potential purchasers
- **Supplier portals and market exchanges**: sites where multiple buyers and sellers share information about requirements and offerings
- **Online supplier evaluation data**: third party reports, customer feedback, benchmarking reports, market intelligence tools and so on.

- **E-auctions**, conducted online using the buyer's or seller's website, or third party auction sites.
- **E-tendering**, using e-RFQs (electronic requests for quotation) and specifications posted online or emailed to potential suppliers. Bids can also be received and evaluated electronically against pre-set criteria.

Potential benefits of e-sourcing

1.10   The potential benefits of developing e-sourcing in general are as follows.

- Reduced costs through increased process efficiencies, reduced sourcing costs, improvements in contract performance management etc.
- Best practice development: consistent, transparent use of controlled procedures, enabling non-procurement staff (eg user department buyers) to participate in sourcing without compromise of good practice or sound procurement disciplines.
- Enhanced quality and capability, because the total sourcing and management process is transparent. Without e-sourcing it is often difficult for buyers to evaluate fragmented information about potential suppliers and to compare one with another in order to make a final decision.
- Reduced sourcing cycle times
- Improved training and efficiency: e-sourcing applications can be used as offline training tools to give employees hands-on experience with the application without jeopardising the company's actual data.

1.11   The website of the Office of Government Commerce (OGC) claims a number of benefits for e-sourcing in the public sector: Table 9.2.

Table 9.2 *Advantages of e-sourcing in the public sector*

BENEFIT	EXPLANATION
Process efficiencies	Reducing time and effort spent on tendering and contract management; reduced paperwork; fewer human errors
Compliance	Eg with the provisions of the Efficiency Review and the National Procurement Strategy for Local Government
Cost savings	Reducing the direct costs of tendering (for both buyer and suppliers); more efficient comparison, supporting savings through competition
Collaboration	Making it easier for purchasers to work together on common sourcing projects across different departments and regions: creating 'virtual buying organisations' to increase bargaining power
Strategic focus	Allowing purchasing professionals to focus on value-added and strategic procurement activity (such as supplier screening, supply base development and relationship management), rather than administration

1.12   To gain maximum benefits, e-sourcing must be part of an overall procurement strategy. Whilst e-sourcing systems have the potential to achieve many business benefits, they should not be perceived as replacing proven best sourcing practices. E-sourcing is merely designed to *enhance* sound sourcing practices and disciplines, to allow buyers both the time and visibility to make more effective and efficient sourcing decisions.

2   Engaging the market

The internet

2.1   The internet is now one of the most-used sources of information on supply markets. The advantages and disadvantages of using it to identify potential suppliers can be summarized as follows: Table 9.3.

Table 9.3 *Using the internet to identify potential suppliers*

ADVANTAGES	DISADVANTAGES
Global, 24/7 available source of data	Excess volume of information
Low-cost, fast, convenient info search	Information may be unreliable or outdated
Information generally frequently up-dated	Difficulty verifying data, source credibility
Access to small, niche, global suppliers	Limited ability to 'sample' product or service
Access to customer feedback, reports, ratings, certification data etc	Supports global sourcing – creating logistical challenges, risks etc
Some ability to 'sample' product or service (eg virtual tours, digital samples)	May discriminate against developing country suppliers
Facilities for direct contact (eg via email)	

Intranets

2.2 The internet and the world wide web are an accepted framework for implementing and delivering information system applications. The internet is a global collection of telecommunications-linked computer networks, which has revolutionised global communication and commerce through tools such as email, and interactive, transaction-enabled websites. However, the same network protocols can be used more locally as a tool for internal and external supply chain communication.

2.3 An intranet is a set of networked and/or internet-linked computers. This private network is usually only accessible to registered users, within the same organisation or work group. Access is restricted by passwords and user group accounts, for example.

2.4 Intranets are used in internal supply chain and employee communication: only authorised internal users are able to access relevant web pages and dedicated email facilities (as well as having access to the wider internet).

2.5 Intranets offer significant advantages for integrating internal supply chain communications. They support multi-directional communication and data-sharing; link remote sites and workers in 'virtual' teams; allow authorised access to shared database and e-procurement platforms; give employees wider access to corporate information; encourage more frequent use of reference sources (such as procurement manuals, standing orders and policies) and updating of information; and save on the costs of producing and distributing the equivalent printed documents and messages.

Extranets

2.6 An **extranet** is an intranet that has been extended to give selected external partners (such as suppliers) authorised access to particular areas or levels of the organisation's website or information network, for exchanging data and applications, and sharing information. Examples you might be familiar with include the registered-user-only pages of corporate websites, and the member-only pages of professional bodies' websites (like the CIPS website's student/member areas).

2.7 Supplier access to a buyer's extranet system is generally protected, requiring defined verification of identity (eg via a user ID), supplier codes and passwords.

2.8 Extranets are particularly useful tools for relationship management, inter-organisational partnerships and direct e-procurement transactions (which might have previously been carried out by EDI protocols). An extranet may be used to publish news updates and technical briefings which may be of use to supply chain partners; publish requirements and/or conduct e-tenders or e-auctions (via a market exchange portal); exchange transaction data for electronic P2P processes (orders, payments, delivery tracking and so on); share training and development resources (eg as part of collaborative quality or sustainability management); and so on.

2.9 Procurement-focused extranets usually provide suppliers with:

- Real-time access to inventory and demand information, enabling them to proactively manage the buyer's needs, rather than merely reacting to spot orders
- Authorised report information eg their vendor rating analysis – enabling them to be proactive in managing and improving their performance and competitiveness.

2.10 Extranet systems provide potential for removing process costs and increasing supply chain communication, real-time information-sharing, co-ordination and responsiveness (eg for improved demand management and just in time supply). They support the automation of routine procurement tasks (as seen in Chapter 6), and therefore support the increasing focus of procurement professionals on strategic value-adding roles rather than transactional and communication tasks. Suppliers can similarly become more focused on developing innovative, competitive and continuously improving supply solutions.

2.11 Business Link lists the following potential benefits that can be gained from using extranet systems.

- Assists in achieving improved supply chain integration via the use of online ordering, order tracking and inventory management
- Reduces operational costs, for example by making manuals and technical documentation available online. This reduces cost and increases the speed of inter-business communication.
- Improved collaboration and relationship potential by enabling involved parties to work online using common documentation; again this accelerates the business process as well as saving cost by reducing the need to hold expensive meetings.
- Suppliers can directly access authorised business information which often enables them to resolve their own queries.
- Provides a single user interface between business partners.
- Improved security of communications since exchanges take place under a controlled and secure environment.

2.12 However, integrating supply chain processes via extranets still poses challenges and risks. In recent years, the corporate landscape has become littered with extranet initiatives that failed to deliver tangible value. Research indicates that common reasons for failure can be identified as: inadequate planning and preparation; unrealistic expectations; and lack of a clear business case for how the extranet will support organisational objectives. It is easy for extranets to become nothing more than glorified chat groups. It is therefore important that the extranets provide tangible benefits. For best value, such benefits should be aligned to support and achieve overall business and supply chain objectives.

2.13 Extranet security is another critical design consideration. Hackers increasingly probe connected computers for weaknesses in their security, and data corruption, loss or theft – eg through the use of 'malware' (as discussed in Chapter 6) – is a key issue for risk management.

3 E-requisitioning and e-ordering

Electronic requisition

3.1 Electronic requisitioning is designed to simplify the process whereby the procurement function captures requisitions from users, and provides information about both the requisitioner and the requirement.

3.2 The database contains records of all materials and parts, code numbers, descriptions, usage records and current balance – as well as prices of recent acquisitions and supplier details. Stock levels are automatically updated as items are received into, or issued from, inventory, and re-orders are generated automatically when a pre-determined level is reached, or when a master production schedule (or bill of materials) dictates. Where the economic order quantity (EOQ) model is used for stock replenishment, the system can compute and requisition the appropriate re-order quantity.

Requirement planning systems

3.3 Examples of requirement planning and specification tools include:

- Integrated systems for resource planning, such as materials requirements planning (MRP), manufacturing resources planning (MRP II) and enterprise resource planning (ERP) systems. These systems encompass a set of logically related procedures, decision rules and records for managing dependent demand items (eg raw materials, components and subassemblies for manufacturing operations). They are designed to translate a master production schedule (MPS) and a bill of materials (BOM: a breakdown of all the materials and components required for production) into time-phased 'net requirements' (taking into account existing stock levels) which automatically trigger requisitions at the appropriate times.
- Design and development systems (eg computer aided design and manufacture – CAD/CAM), which may similarly generate requisitions and specifications for materials and components included in new product designs.

3.4 In both cases, detailed 'bills of materials' (lists of requirements) are created automatically from production plans, project work breakdown structures (WBS) or design specifications.

Electronic point of sale (EPOS) systems

3.5 Point of sale devices involve the use of barcoding and radio frequency identification (RFID) tagging to record sales at point-of-sale terminals, which are linked to IT systems. Electronic point of sale (EPOS) systems can be connected to inventory management systems, to trigger automatic stock requisition and replenishment.

3.6 In such a system, data on the cost structure and current stock status of each product is stored on a centralised database. When a product sale is processed at the point of sale (using EPOS), the transactional adjustment is made to the product stock status. This enables a real time update of all stock status or inventory records, which can be used to trigger electronic requisitions. When stocks fall to a pre-determined re-order point, the EPOS system generates a replenishment report. In the case of a supermarket branch store, for example, this information would be transmitted to the central distribution centre to arrange delivery of the relevant products.

3.7 EPOS can also be used to track product sales, stock availability and location, and the location of deliveries (using global positioning systems or GPS technology). It can be connected to point-of-sale payment systems (via electronic funds transfer) and management information systems (for sales analysis, demand forecasting and inventory). In marketing contexts, it also supports the use of loyalty cards, as a way of incentivising customer loyalty and gathering customer data.

3.8 The main benefits of an EPOS system are as follows.

- Efficient and accurate processing of customer transactions, reducing queuing time
- Stock management: the real-time nature of the EPOS database enables automatic creation of replenishment orders
- Rapid communication of supply and demand information throughout the supply chain, to support demand forecasting, production planning and responsive replenishment (particularly useful for retailers of fast moving consumer goods, where product shelf-life is a key business factor)
- Access to data on wastage, profit margins, sales trends, consumer purchasing patterns and so on, to support procurement and operations decision making.

E-ordering

3.9 Once an e-requisition has been confirmed, the buyer may specify the selected supplier (where relevant) and the system generates documentation for procurement, accounts, acknowledgement, receiving and inspection.

3.10 Desk-top procurement systems generally also allow users to place electronic call-off orders with approved suppliers, within the framework of a supply contract already set up by the procurement function: for example, a framework agreement or a systems or call-off contract, or e-catalogue ordering (for amounts up to certain pre-approved value thresholds) from approved supplier catalogues.

3.11 Orders or re-orders (stock replenishment) may be *automatically* generated, without human intervention, in the case of requisitions triggered by MRP, ERP, EPOS or electronic inventory management systems, where framework or systems contracts have already been placed with approved suppliers. Nissan UK, for example, operates a just in time system whereby a centralised system produces daily manufacturing schedules, which are transmitted to computers on the production lines – which in turn transmit orders direct to component manufacturers as components are required.

E-contracting

3.12 Electronic contracts can be created and transmitted to suppliers (and other relevant stakeholders). This has particular value-adding benefits, in:

- Enabling the 'cutting and pasting' of standard contract terms, and the variation of draft terms, in an efficient and flexible way
- Enabling strong controls over confidentiality (eg by password-protected access to contract drafts and details)
- Enabling strong contract variation, change and version control (eg with clearly flagged variations and versions; 'read only' versions, which cannot be amended by non-authorised users; and the ability to make amendments confined to authorised individuals)
- Integration with a contract management database, enabling contract managers to access contract details, manage versions, capture supplier performance data and so on.

4 E-catalogues

4.1 Catalogue sourcing has been around for a long time in paper-based form. Many suppliers offer a catalogue of their products, prices and terms of trade, with facility for the customer to order by phone, fax or email. Stationery companies such as Viking are good examples of this. Provided the buyer is happy that the catalogue represents good value, this method of ordering is very cheap and convenient. In many cases the supplier will invoice periodically (say monthly) instead of invoicing with every supply.

4.2 An online catalogue is the electronic equivalent of a supplier's printed catalogue, providing product specifications and price information. However, an interactive e-catalogue also includes:

- Integrated stock database interrogation (to check availability and location)
- Integrated ordering and payment (e-commerce) facilities.

This allows for efficient and cost-effective procurement of proprietary goods and services – especially since, with the aid of internet search engine tools, price comparisons of specified products can be obtained within seconds.

Internet, extranet and intranet catalogues

4.3 E-catalogues may be posted on the supplier's website: either on the *internet* or on a dedicated *extranet*, with user-ID and password-controlled access only for registered external customers and buyers.

4.4 Alternatively or additionally, an approved supplier's catalogue may be downloaded and posted on the buyer's *intranet* or internal network, for use by authorised individuals involved in sourcing and procurement (eg to issue call-off or pre-approved orders).

4.5 To be effective online catalogues should provide the following facilities.

- User-friendly navigation, allowing buyers to find the product or service required without going through endless levels of indexes or menus
- Comprehensive, focused information content, to support buyer data-gathering and decision-making. This may include technical specification, price and availability details, pictures, the opportunity to order samples – so on.
- E-commerce facilities, such as a 'trolley' (goods earmarked for order, with running cost subtotal); 'checkout' (opportunity to review, edit and confirm the order, with all relevant information, including delivery costs and instructions); and payment (via a pre-arranged credit account, for later invoice, or the use of a pre-approved purchasing card).

4.6 One potential downside to the use of e-catalogues is the lack of human contact, which might be necessary for clarification or negotiation of terms or special delivery instructions. Most online catalogues have integrated help-line facilities to assist the buying process when needed.

5 E-auctions

5.1 There are two main approaches to e-auctions.

- In a standard auction, suppliers offer goods online, and potential buyers bid competitively. All bids are 'open' (visible to all participants, minus the names of the suppliers), so buyers may raise their offers competitively during the auction. At the end of the specified bidding period, the highest bid (as evaluated by the auction software) wins. You may be familiar with this system from e-Bay, for example.
- In a *reverse auction,* the *buyer* specifies its requirements, and *suppliers* submit competitive quotes. Again, all bids are open, so suppliers may lower their prices competitively during the auction. At the end of the bidding period, the lowest bid compliant with the specification (as evaluated by the software and/or according to agreed 'auction rules' eg whether the lowest bid must be accepted) wins.

5.2 The increasingly common practice of using online reverse auctions has attracted much comment in the procurement literature. Many benefits are claimed for online auctions (particularly by software firms marketing online auction systems!), including the following.

- Efficient administration and reduction in acquisition lead time, through eliminating time-consuming manual processes of supplier engagement, quotation requests and comparisons, negotiations and so on
- Savings for buyers, over and above those obtained from negotiation, as a result of competition
- Improved value for buyers, by giving a 'wake up' call to existing suppliers on the need to reconsider their cost base and pricing in order to remain competitive
- Access for buyers to a wider range of potential suppliers and sources of market information, including a global supply base
- Less time 'wasted' on interpersonal interaction eg meeting supplier representatives (although, of course, this may be a *drawback* where a buyer wishes to develop closer, more collaborative relationships with its supply chain)
- Opportunities for suppliers to enter previously closed markets or accounts (especially valuable for smaller suppliers)
- Opportunities for suppliers to gather competitor and market pricing data (and a clear indication of what is required in order to win business) in order to develop and maintain their own competitiveness.

5.3   Online auctions have also come in for criticism, on the following grounds.

- Online auctions are based on a zero-sum, adversarial or 'win-lose' approach: profit for either party is at the other's expense. This may get in the way of collaborative supply chain relationships, and the value gains available from collaboration.
- Suppliers are vulnerable to coercion (being forced to participate on threat of lost business) and manipulation (eg 'fake' bids by a buyer to force down prices; or forcing prices lower by 'apparent' competition, while always intending to use a pre-selected supplier). Suppliers may feel exploited, leading to loss of trust and goodwill in the buyer-supplier relationship.
- There may be long-term adverse effects on the economic performance of the supplier: forced to competitive price reductions which are unsustainable.
- There may be long-term adverse effects on the economic performance of the buyer: eg if supplier failure (and/or loss of goodwill) reduces the future supply base and incurs further costs (eg quality problems).
- Promised savings may not materialise, due to factors such as: the costs of switching suppliers, or retaliatory pricing by alienated suppliers (especially when buyers have urgent requirements).
- Suppliers get the message that price is the most important factor in winning business, and may therefore downgrade the quality, innovation or sustainability of their offerings, in order to compete on cost.
- The process leaves little scope to take adequate account of non-price criteria (eg quality, customer service or sustainability) and stakeholder input.

5.4   Lysons & Farrington argue that: 'Lowest-price reverse auction processes should be used only where there is little concern about production specifications or the suppliers selected. They are not appropriate for complex products or projects requiring collaboration or considerable negotiation.'

6   E-tendering

6.1   The use of e-tendering replaces traditional manual paper-based processes for competitive tendering (discussed in Chapter 8) with electronically facilitated processes based on best tendering practices. For example:

- The invitation to tender (ITT) is published on the buyer's e-tender web portal, for potential suppliers to view. Bid-related documents are posted for interested suppliers to download.
- Suppliers respond to the ITT by sending their bids using secure email to the e-tendering system's 'electronic vault', and are registered as bidders.
- Buyers can observe and manage the tendering process through a 'front end' web function, enabling them to answer queries for clarification and so on.
- In-built security features prohibit access to any of the tender responses until a specified time. Once the tender deadline has been reached, the tender evaluation team can 'open' (view) the tenders and collaborate online to evaluate the submitted bids.
- The system may include automatic scoring and evaluation capability. Alternatively, data can be cut and pasted from e-tender documents to a spreadsheet for ease of comparison.
- Successful and unsuccessful bidders can be automatically notified of the award.

6.2   In addition to these core functions, most e-tendering systems provide additional support such as archiving, document management, early warning of opportunities to suppliers, and maintenance of approved and/or potential supplier lists. If such a system is integrated with the organisation's contract management system, the complete lifecycle of the contract can be managed, and re-tendering (when the contact comes up for renewal) co-ordinated.

Benefits of e-tendering

6.3 A number of benefits are typically claimed for e-tendering, both tangible (eg in terms of cost savings, efficiency gains and added value) and intangible (eg in terms of relationship development and sustainability).

6.4 E-tendering systems can help to ensure consistency of tendering procedures and embed tender best practice in an organisation. They can promote procurement centres of excellence, responsible for defining and applying the tender process and specifying standard tender documents, such as terms and conditions of contract.

6.5 The embedding of best practice procedures may help to support the devolution of tendering tasks to non-procurement specialists, by empowering buying organisations with the tools to maintain control over tender procedures. Through reporting tools, managers are able to assess the status of all tenders, with end-to-end visibility.

6.6 A major benefit of e-tendering is the potential for process efficiencies, as a result of reducing tender cycle times, and reducing labour-intensive tasks and paperwork. E-tendering systems automate or eliminate many repetitive, routine administrative tasks, including: general administration; alerts for imminent tenders; contract notice creation; opening procedures; document preparation (eg expressions of interest, invitations to tender); document distribution; tender evaluation; supplier enquiries; and contract award notifications.

6.7 The combination of automation of routine tasks and controlled devolution of tasks to non-procurement specialists may help to free up the time of procurement specialists to focus on more value-adding activities, such as strategic sourcing; negotiating better contracts; aggregating demand; supplier management and development; handing high-risk and high-value contracts; sharing and embedding best practice.

6.8 Paperless tendering functions (to the extent that they are taken advantage of) can help to reduce the overhead costs of tendering, such as printing, copying, paper, postage and stationery. They may also free up valuable storage or office space eg for the storage of paper-based contract information and tender histories. (This can be significant, as in some circumstances, tender histories must be kept for as long as the contract period, which can be anything from one year to 20 years and beyond.)

6.9 E-tendering provides a platform for cross-functional collaboration, facilitating internal communication and data sharing about procurement projects. In its simplest form, it provides a single point of information for contractual aspects such as standard terms and conditions. For more complex projects and contracts, it provides tools to support collaboration through workflow and edit notification alerts, and by having a single repository for all required documentation. Increased collaboration and centralisation of the sourcing process may also help to encourage value-adding sourcing strategies such as the aggregation of demand.

6.10 E-tendering facilitates the fast and accurate screening of bids against pre-qualification data, enabling the efficient rejection of suppliers that fail to meet the tender specification. Automation reduces the time spent in analysis of numerical information, having parts of the responses already in spreadsheet format, ready to manipulate and compare. Sophisticated systems have functionality that can perform the evaluation task automatically (particularly effective for fixed commodity contracts) and can automatically send out an email notification to suppliers that fail to meet defined pre-qualification criteria.

6.11 Integrated communication tools (such as tender-dedicated email facilities) enable faster response to questions and points of clarification during the tender period. Bidders may also be supported in other ways, such as:

9

- By notifications of impending deadlines (sent automatically if they have not downloaded or submitted required documentation)
- By elimination of the risk of responses arriving late as a result of courier delays, incorrect addressing or routing, or responses being rejected as a result of envelopes inadvertently being stamped with supplier identification details.

6.12   Integrated document management functionality enables secure and efficient storage and retrieval of tender-related documents. All documents for a particular tender, or of a particular type, can be held in a logical structure for ease of retrieval and interrogation. Folder repositories may include policies and procedures for tendering, standard terms and conditions, standard Pre-Qualification Questionnaires (PQQ) and previous Invitations to Tender (ITT) and responses. These can be cross-referenced to encourage consistency with subsequent tenders, to assist with future negotiations, or to monitor price and performance variations over time.

6.13   Automation generally improves the transparency and fairness of the tendering process: ensuring that all suppliers get the same information, operate to the same (automatically enforced) time-scales, are evaluated on the same criteria, are able to track the progress of the tender – and so on. This is particularly important for public sector procurements, due to factors such as: public accountability and audit scrutiny to ensure value for taxpayers' money; the obligation to provide leadership in ethical sourcing and trading; and strict rules (arising from the EU Public Procurement Directives) for tender processes and time scales.

6.14   The quality of integrated information capture and storage also provides an improved 'audit trail': the recorded history of events and decisions leading up to contract award. An audit trail and contract histories:

- Enable managers to evaluate procurement decisions and learn lessons for future sourcing projects
- Provide data for the 'de-briefing' of unsuccessful bidders, where feedback is given to enable them to compete more effectively for future contracts
- Provide evidence of best practice in the event of a legal challenge to the contract award decision by an unsuccessful supplier
- Enable internal auditors to investigate the causes of subsequent budget or schedule variances (eg if contingencies have not been factored into a tender, or if poor specification or contracting practices have led to costly post-contract change requests)
- May be used by procurement staff to support supplier development and contract renewal decisions. They can see which suppliers expressed interest during the original process; where suppliers require capability development to compete more effectively for future contracts; and where tender documentation and selection criteria may need to be updated for the following contract period.

6.15   E-tendering systems typically include reporting capabilities, providing suitably formatted information to support future sourcing decisions and tendering processes. Examples of useful reports might be:

- Information on an individual tendering process, such as the number and profile of suppliers that have expressed interest.
- Information on cross-functional take-up and leverage of the e-tendering system, in order to identify additional resource requirements, or groups in need of further training or support.

6.16   Among more intangible benefits of e-tendering, there are key benefits for suppliers and potential suppliers.

- E-tendering provides a single point of contact to access and view all tender opportunities and information. Suppliers are able to see contract renewal dates, tender deadlines and status, and the rationale for award of the contract. The site can be accessed 24 hours a day and is 'self-service': eliminating response delays. Early tendering notification can also provide advance warning to suppliers, enabling them to prepare tender responses or to apply for approved list status.
- E-tendering offers non-discriminatory access to the tender process – via the internet – for SME suppliers and international suppliers: making tendering opportunities more widely known; reducing

the burden of tender documentation handling; and improving the quality of tender and pre-qualification information (to avoid time wasted on unwinnable tenders). Opening up contracts to SMEs and international suppliers may also, of course, offer cost or innovation benefits to the buyer – and may support the organisation's strategies for SME supplier development or international sourcing.

Integrating e-tendering within the supply chain

6.17 There may be resistance within the buying organisation to adopting the e-tendering process. The procurement department should work with other internal departments to minimise this issue as much as possible, eg through a structured communication programme to internal customers, demonstrations of the new approach, and support and facilitation (eg through user training and documentation).

6.18 The success of an e-tendering project is also strongly linked to supplier buy-in to the system. The key reasons for supplier resistance are often: lack of technical know-how and equipment; perceptions of lack of security with an electronic system; and the possibility of the buyer charging for use of the e-tender exercise. All these issues can be addressed through communication, training, technical support – and eliminating cost to suppliers who use the e-tender process.

Drawbacks of e-tendering

6.19 Drawbacks to e-tendering include:

- Limited access for suppliers lacking the technical know-how or equipment to bid electronically. Suppliers with little experience of e-tendering may lose out (or be deterred from bidding) because of the technical nature of the process – perhaps to suppliers who offer less value or less innovative solutions, but are simply better able to manage the tender process.
- Issues around the security of commercial information and intellectual property shared in the course of the tender exercise
- Significant initial investment costs associated with specialist equipment, software, staff training and so on.

Chapter summary

- Developments in information technology have radically changed the way people do business. In particular, use of the internet has transformed the way buyers work.
- E-purchasing is defined as 'the combined use of information and communication technology through electronic means to enhance external and internal purchasing and supply management processes'.
- The internet is now one of the most-used sources of information on supply markets. Buyers also make extensive use of intranets and extranets.
- Electronic requisitioning is designed to simplify the process whereby the procurement function captures requisitions from users.
- EPOS systems involved the use of barcoding and RFID tagging to simplify inventory management and provide sales reports.
- An online catalogue is the electronic equivalent of a supplier's printed catalogue, but also includes interactive features.
- Online reverse auctions have become a common part of a buyer's work, but despite their advantages they have also attracted criticism.
- Many benefits are claimed for e-tendering, both tangible (eg in terms of cost savings, efficiency gains and added value) and intangible (eg in terms of relationship development and sustainability).

Self-test questions

Numbers in brackets refer to the paragraphs where you can check your answers.

1   In what ways have developments in ICT changed the way people do business? (1.1)

2   What are the benefits of the internet for buyers? (1.5)

3   List major types of e-sourcing tools. (1.9, Table 9.1)

4   What is (a) an intranet and (b) an extranet? (2.3, 2.6)

5   List potential benefits of using extranet systems. (2.11)

6   Give examples of requirement planning and specification tools. (3.3)

7   What are the main benefits of EPOS systems? (3.8)

8   Describe interactive elements of an online supplier catalogue. (4.2)

9   What facilities should an online catalogue provide to ensure effectiveness? (4.5)

10   List benefits of online reverse auctions. (5.2)

11   List common criticisms of online reverse auctions. (5.3)

12   List benefits of e-tendering. (6.3ff)

13   List drawbacks of e-tendering. (6.19)

CHAPTER 10

Sourcing in the Private and Third Sectors

Assessment criteria and indicative content

 5.1   Analyse the main legislative, regulatory and organisational requirements when sourcing in the not for profit, private and public sectors

- Regulatory bodies that impact on the private sector
- Organisations that impact on product and safety standards

Section headings

1. Private sector organisations
2. Objectives of private sector organisations
3. The regulation of private sector procurement
4. Key features of private sector procurement
5. Third sector organisations
6. Key features of third sector procurement
7. Organisations that impact on product and safety standards

Introduction

In this chapter we focus on the particular requirements of procurement in the private and third sectors. We leave consideration of the public sector to the following chapter.

Much of the good practice and generic processes discussed throughout this Course Book – as in the procurement literature in general – are drawn from the private sector. In this chapter, therefore, we merely draw out the additional points specified in the syllabus content. We also add some discussion of the regulation of private sector procurement, in line with the overall emphasis on 'compliance' in this section of the syllabus.

We give a brief overview of third sector procurement.

Finally, we describe organisations that impact on product and safety standards.

1   Private sector organisations

1.1   To get a handle on the numerous types of organisation in the private sector, there are various classifications we can use.

- We can distinguish on the basis of ownership and control – for example, sole traders, partnerships and limited companies.
- We can distinguish on the basis of size – for example, SMEs (small and medium-sized enterprises), to large, multinational corporations such as Unilever or Microsoft.
- We can distinguish on the basis of business activity – for example, **primary industries** engaged in the

extraction of raw materials, **secondary industries** engaged in manufacturing, and **tertiary industries** engaged in services.

We will look at each of these classifications, and their impact on procurement.

The constitution of private sector organisations

1.2 Private sector organisations may be formed or 'constituted' in various different ways.

- An individual may carry on a business as a **sole trader**.
- A group of individuals may carry on a business together by legal agreement, as a **partnership**.
- A potentially very large number of people may carry on a business according to specific legal requirements for 'incorporation' as a **company**.

We will look at each of these types of organisation in turn.

Sole tradership

1.3 A sole tradership may be an appropriate business type for a tradesperson, say, or a shopkeeper or freelance designer. There is no legal distinction between the individual person and the business entity: the individual supplies all the capital for the business, and is personally liable for its debts. (This is *not* the case for a company, as we will see later...)

1.4 The advantages and disadvantages of sole tradership are summarised in Table 10.1.

Table 10.1 *Evaluating sole tradership*

ADVANTAGES	DISADVANTAGES
Few costs or legal requirements to establish the business	The proprietor is personally liable for the business's debts
No public accountability (though financial records are required for tax purposes)	It may be difficult to get finance for the business (eg a loan by personal guarantee)
The proprietor controls all decisions for the business – and enjoys all the profits	Resources are limited to what the proprietor can personally generate

Partnership

1.5 Many sole traders find that a logical way of expanding without the formalities of incorporation is to take on one or more partners, who contribute capital and expertise to the business, and who share the managerial and financial responsibilities. A partnership is defined in UK law (Partnership Act 1890) as 'the relation which subsists between persons carrying on a business in common with a view of profit'. There must be at least two to a standard maximum of 20 partners, for a commercial partnership. (A professional practice, such as a firm of accountants or solicitors, can have any number of partners.)

1.6 Like a sole tradership (and *unlike* a company), a partnership does not have a separate legal identity from its members. This means, for example, that:

- Partners jointly own the assets of the partnership and are personally liable for its debts
- Partners are entitled to participate in management and act as agents of the firm (unlike in a company, where shareholders do not necessarily have this status)
- A change of partners terminates the old firm and begins a new one (unlike in a company, where shares can be transferred from one person to another).

1.7 The advantages and disadvantages of partnerships are summarised in Table 10.2.

Table 10.2 *Evaluating partnership*

ADVANTAGES	DISADVANTAGES
Partners contribute capital and expertise	Decision-making has to be shared/negotiated
Partners share managerial and financial responsibilities and liability	Profits have to be shared among the partners
With greater asset backing, it is often easier to raise loans than for a sole trader	Partners are generally personally liable 'without limit' for the partnership's debts
Suits professions, as members are prohibited from practising as limited companies	

Limited company

1.8   By far the most common trading vehicle in the private sector is the *limited company*. A limited company is an 'incorporated' body: that is, it is considered a separate legal entity (or 'person') from its individual owners (shareholders).

- The company can own assets, enter into contracts and incur liabilities in its own name.
- If the company incurs a debt, payment will come from the assets owned by the company. The individual owners cannot be asked to contribute to the payment from their personal funds: their liability is *limited* to the amount they have invested in the company – usually by buying shares. (Hence, a 'limited company'.)

1.9   The people who pay for shares in a company are the shareholders, also known as the members of the company. These are the company owners. As time goes by, others may be invited to subscribe for shares in the company. Any money subscribed for shares belongs to the company. The company will not normally return the money to the shareholders, other than in exceptional circumstances (eg when the company ceases to trade and is wound up).

1.10   A company may be registered as a *public limited company* ('plc') or as a *private limited company* ('Ltd'). The key differences are as follows.

- A *public* limited company may offer its shares to the general public. (A relatively small number of public companies – known as listed companies – trade their shares on The Stock Exchange.) This is not the case for a *private* limited company, whose shareholders are generally directors of the company, or connected to it in some way. This means that PLCs are able to raise significantly larger sums of capital than private limited companies.
- A *public* limited company must have a minimum authorised share capital (the value of shares the company is allowed to issue) of £50,000, with allotted shares of at least that value, and a minimum of two members and two directors. There are no minimum capital requirements for a private limited company, and the minimum number of directors is just one.
- A *public* limited company is subject to detailed company law requirements in regard to shares, directors, annual general meetings, accounting and so on. For *private* limited companies, there is much less red tape – because the owners and managers are generally the same people.

1.11   The advantages and disadvantages of incorporation are summarised in Table 10.3.

10

Table 10.3 *Evaluating incorporation*

ADVANTAGES	DISADVANTAGES
Limited liability protects owners from personal liability for contracts and debts	Expense and red tape of incorporation, and the constraint of a written constitution
Shares are a stable source of finance: the amount of capital is unaffected by trading, and is not subject (like loans) to finance costs	Subject to regulation eg re public disclosure (in financial reports and accounts etc)
Directors provide the expertise the business needs, without 'diluting' ownership	Share trading can result in unwanted change of ownership

1.12 In the UK, limited companies are set up by filing a Memorandum of Association and Articles of Association with the Registrar of Companies, who (for a small fee) issues the Certificate of Incorporation. All these documents are placed on file, maintained by the Registrar, and open to inspection by the public.

- The **Memorandum of Association** defines the constitution and set up of the company. It must include the name of the company, the location of its registered office, its objects/business, a statement of limited liability, and the amount of authorised share capital.
- The **Articles of Association** define the company's internal administration, rules and procedures: how shares will be issued and managed, the rights of shareholders, requirements for shareholder meetings, the powers and remuneration of directors, payment of dividends, and division of assets if the business is wound up.

Small and medium enterprises (SMEs)

1.13 From your own experience, you will have gathered that private sector organisations vary widely by size: from one-person operations to small businesses to vast global conglomerates. According to a 2005 European Union definition (used for grant-aid purposes):

- A 'micro' enterprise is one which has fewer than 10 employees and an annual turnover of less than 2 million euros.
- A 'small' enterprise is one which has 10–49 employees and an annual turnover of less than 10 million euros.
- A 'medium-sized' enterprise is one which has 50–249 employees and an annual turnover of less than 50 million euros.
- A 'large-scale' enterprise employs more than 250 employees, with an annual turnover of more than 50 million euros.

1.14 Particular attention has been given to small and medium enterprises (SMEs) in recent years, because (a) they are a significant contributor to economic activity (by the above definition, some 99% of enterprises in the EU in 2005, providing around 65 million jobs), and (b) because they require financial guidance and support in order to overcome lack of economic strength in competition with larger players.

1.15 Worthington and Britton *(The Business Environment)* ascribe the resurgence in the importance of the small-firm sector in the UK to a range of factors.

- The shift from manufacturing to service industry: many services are dominated by small firms
- Increasing consumer demand for more specialised and customised (as opposed to mass produced) products, to which small firms are better able to respond
- The growth of outsourcing, where non-core activities are contracted to small specialist firms
- Reorganisation and job cutting to reduce costs, creating 'downsized' organisations
- Government policy, with initiatives designed to support SMEs in creating economic activity and jobs
- More accessible technology, allowing small firms to reach global markets (via ICT) and eroding larger firms' technological edge and economies of scale

1.16   SMEs may have an advantage over large firms in clearly defined, small markets: it would not be worth large firms entering markets where there is no scope for cost-effective mass production. Such an advantage may apply in a geographically localised market, say, or in a 'niche' market for specialist, customised or premium-quality products. In addition, the entrepreneurial nature and speed of communication in small enterprises makes them particularly well suited to innovation and invention, and they may have an advantage over larger, less flexible firms in fast-changing, high-technology markets.

1.17   On the other hand, SMEs are at a disadvantage in areas such as: raising loan and share capital (because they are a greater risk); managing cashflow (being harder hard hit by late payment or non-payments); ability to take financial risks (including investment in research and development); and dealing with bureaucratic requirements.

1.18   Large organisations are able to take advantage of economies of scale.

- Technical economies, which arise in the production process. Large undertakings can afford larger and more specialised machinery, for example, and can take advantage of the cost efficiency of mass production.
- Commercial economies, such as purchasing economies (eg through bulk purchase discounts)
- Financial economies, such as obtaining loan finance at attractive rates of interest – or being able to raise large amounts of capital via the sale of shares to the public (as a public limited company).

A firm in an industry with a large consumer market may have to grow to a certain size in order to benefit from such economies of scale, and thus to be cost-competitive with larger players.

1.19   UK government support has focused on the problems and disadvantages of SMEs, in these areas, with initiatives designed to:

- Encourage on-time payment of bills by PLCs and public sector bodies
- Relax rules and regulations applicable to SMEs
- Reduce the tax burden (eg levels of corporation tax) on small business
- Provide grants to assist SMEs in rural areas or areas of industrial decline (eg the EU SME Initiative and the Enterprise Fund)
- Provide information, advice and support (eg through the Small Business Service and Business Link network).

1.20   From the above discussion, you may be able to identify particular challenges for the procurement or supply chain function in SMEs.

- A procurement officer in an SME will work within a limited expenditure budget and tight cost controls; will need to manage cashflow closely (eg securing long credit terms from suppliers); and may have to develop a supply chain which can respond to innovation, short product lifecycles and small-quantity, fast-turnaround requirements.
- A procurement officer buying *from* an SME will need to take into account the firm's limited capacity to handle volume; its potential financial instability (if it hits problems in the midst of a supply contract); and its cashflow issues (the ethical response to which would be to pay invoices on time in full).

Sources of finance in the private sector

1.21   There are a number of key sources of finance for private sector organisations.

- Initial capital investment by the owners of the business (eg in the case of a sole trader or partnership) or by venture capitalists
- Share capital: that is, the sale of shares in the company. A public limited company (plc) will, as we have seen, be able to sell shares to the general public on the Stock Exchange. A private limited company (Ltd) can raise finance by selling shares to investment syndicates and associates (eg friends and family members).

10

- Retained profits resulting from the profit-generating activities of the business, such as sales: that is, profits that are 'ploughed back' into the business (rather than being withdrawn by the owners or paid out to shareholders as dividends)
- Loan finance, such as bank overdraft facilities, or bank loans and debentures (usually secured against the assets of the business)
- The sale of unneeded assets
- Government grants (eg for small business development or other projects and capital purchases).

2 Objectives of private sector organisations

Profitability

2.1 As we have already seen, the primary objective for a private sector organisation is normally to maximise profits. Profit is the difference between the selling price of a product (or the total revenue earned from selling a product) and the cost of producing the product. In other words, it is the gain or surplus left over after the manufacturer or service provider has paid all its costs.

2.2 Both buyers and suppliers seek to make a profit for a number of reasons.

- Profit means that the business has covered its costs and is not 'bleeding' money in losses. This is important for the business to survive in the long term.
- Profit belongs to the owners or shareholders of the business, as a return on their investment: a share of profits is paid to them in the form of a 'dividend' on their shares. Strong and consistent profits are therefore important to encourage shareholders to continue to invest in the company, and to maintain the share capital of the company through a high share price (reflecting market demand for the shares).
- Profits which are not paid to shareholders ('retained profits') are available for reinvestment in the development of the business, enabling it to acquire assets, meet long-term borrowings, update plant and equipment, and build up reserves for future contingencies – without the cost and risk of borrowing funds for these purposes.

2.3 Procurement staff in a profit-seeking firm may well feel pressure to achieve the lowest possible cost when purchasing supplies – but this does not mean that they will sacrifice all other considerations in order to choose the lowest-cost option. Even in the short term this might not be the best way to achieve profits. For example, a more expensive material of higher quality might lead to lower levels of waste, rework and scrap: in the long run, it may work out cheaper than an inferior material.

2.4 More importantly, buyers must look to the longer-term benefit of their organisation, and more complex definitions of 'value'. This could mean an in-depth assessment of potential suppliers along a number of dimensions, not just price. For example, the long-term profitability of the organisation might be best served by a partnership relationship with a supplier offering technology sharing, just in time delivery, ongoing collaboration on cost reduction and process improvements – and/or other non-price advantages.

2.5 Procurement teams can, however, contribute measurably to profitability through savings on materials, inventory, and contracting and transaction costs (eg through effective negotiation and contract development, efficient management of the procurement process, and effective use of inventory management and e-procurement tools). These savings in turn contribute to bottom line profit.

2.6 If cost reductions are retained within the business, there is an immediate improvement in the bottom line. If the surplus resource is used up by budget holders, there is no direct impact on the bottom line – but there is added benefit.

Market share

2.7   One of the key features of the private sector is the very strong influence of competition. In nearly all cases, a private sector firm will be one of several, or many, firms offering goods or services of a particular type. Securing competitive advantage, in order to win *more* customers and *better quality* customers (higher lifetime value) is therefore a key focus of private sector strategy, including supply chain management.

2.8   Competitive advantage may be defined as the ability (gained through the development, protection and leverage of distinctive competencies and resources) to deliver value to customers more efficiently or effectively than one's competitors.

2.9   Strategy guru Kenichi Ohmae *(The Mind of the Strategist)* argued that: 'What business strategy is all about is, in a word, competitive advantage. The sole purpose of strategic planning is to enable a company to gain, as efficiently as possible, a sustainable edge over its competitors.' Ohmae argued that competitive advantage is achieved by matching the strengths and resources of the corporation with the needs of the market, in such a way as to achieve superior performance, relative to competitors in the market, in areas which are perceived as critical for success in the market.

2.10 Firms may measure the success of their competitive efforts in various ways: for example, sales volume growth, sales revenue growth, or growth in the number of customers. However, the most common measure of competitive success is market penetration or market share: the percentage of the total value of sales in a market (or market segment) which is accounted for by a given product or organisation. Market share may be defined in terms of either volume (units) or value (revenue).

2.11 Market share is a key indicator of performance for many private sector organisations in competitive markets. It enables firms to identify whether increases in their sales result from the market expanding – or from their capturing customers and sales from competitors.

Shareholder value

2.12 As we noted earlier, the purpose of securing or maximising corporate profitability is not just 'profitability' for its own sake. The aim of profitability is to generate a return on the value of shareholders' investment of capital in the business, in the form of:

- Dividends, through which a share of profits is distributed directly to shareholders
- Growth in the capital or equity value of shareholders' investment, through:
  - Retained profits being reinvested in the business
  - Maintaining or enhancing the value of the company's shares in the financial markets (eg due to positive market perceptions of the company's value, management and future prospects)
  - Maintaining or enhancing the value of the company's assets, such as land and buildings, plant, reputational capital, intellectual property (designs and patents), brand equity (the power of strong brands to command sales and profits) and so on – increasing the overall value or worth of the corporation.

Corporate social responsibility (CSR)

2.13 Corporate social responsibility is increasingly prioritised as a corporate objective in the private sector, owing to public, media and consumer pressure, and the risk of reputational damage as a result of the exposure of irresponsible corporate (and supply chain) behaviour.

2.14 It is worth noting that the value of CSR may be contested in the context of private sector organisations.

2.15 Milton Friedman and Elaine Sternberg have argued the view that 'the social responsibility of business is profit maximisation': to give a return on shareholders' investment. Spending funds on objectives

10

not related to shareholder expectations is irresponsible: regard for shareholder wealth is a healthy discipline for management, providing accountability for decisions. The public interest is served by profit maximisation, because the State levies taxes. 'Consequently,' argued Friedman, 'the only justification for social responsibility is enlightened self interest' on the part of a business organisation.

2.16   So how does CSR serve the interest of the firm?

- Law, regulation and Codes of Practice impose certain social responsibilities on organisations (eg in relation to health and safety, employment protection, consumer rights and environmental care). There are financial and operational penalties for failure to comply (eg 'polluter pays' taxes).
- Voluntary measures (which may in any case only pre-empt legal and regulatory requirements) may enhance corporate image and build a positive brand. A commonly quoted example is the environmental and sustainability strategy adopted by The Body Shop. (You might like to check out the website of the Medinge Group, which publishes profiles of each year's top *Brands with a Conscience*: http://www.medinge.org.)
- Above-statutory provisions for employees and suppliers may be necessary to attract, retain and motivate them to provide quality service and commitment – particularly in competition with other employers/purchasers.
- Increasing consumer awareness of social responsibility issues creates a market demand for CSR (and the threat of boycott for irresponsible firms)
- Social responsibility helps to create a climate in which business can prosper in the long term. In the same way, ethical sourcing helps to create a climate in which mutually-beneficial long-term relationships with suppliers can be preserved.

3   The regulation of private sector procurement

The influence of government

3.1   There are four main areas in which a nation's government influences private sector organisations (quite apart from its direct influence on public sector organisations).

- Governments influence the operation of organisations: what they can and cannot produce, and how they produce it (eg in laying down restrictions on production processes in order to protect the environment).
- Governments influence the costs and revenues incurred by organisations: by the application of taxes and duties on the production and sale of certain goods, and by the effect of taxes on the general level of consumer spending.
- Governments influence organisations by the actions they take in pursuing macroeconomic objectives (eg in establishing exchange rates and interest rates, by the extent to which they stimulate aggregate demand in the economy).
- Governments influence the values and norms that are regarded as acceptable within the national culture, and hence indirectly affect the outputs produced by organisations and the ways in which organisations behave.

3.2   Governments of all persuasions accept that some regulation of the private sector generally is desirable, for the following reasons.

- Governments wish to preserve a balance between consumers and firms. Consumers must be protected in terms of service, quality and price, while firms must be prevented from charging excessive prices for essential services.
- Governments wish to promote competition, eg by preventing mergers or acquisitions which result in monopolies or the abuse of a dominant market position.
- Governments wish to assist firms to prosper, because their prosperity makes for the prosperity of the nation generally.

- Governments wish to protect national interests, eg by protecting domestic companies from unfair competition from overseas companies.

Law and regulation

3.3 There is a wide variety of law and regulation affecting the conduct of business, deriving (in the UK) from three main sources: regulations and directives issued by the European Union; statute law (Acts of Parliament); and case law (law deriving from the decisions of judges in the courts, which set principles and precedents for future decisions). In addition, there are voluntary codes of practice developed by professions and industries, and scrutiny by various regulatory bodies.

3.4 This is a particularly important area for monitoring and management by procurement organisations, because:

- The organisation's response is not 'optional' or left to managerial discretion: compliance is required and enforced by various sanctions and penalties.
- The requirements are constantly changing, as courts and tribunals define them through their decisions, and as legislators and regulatory bodies issue new provisions and amendments.

3.5 Despite attempts to increase competition and innovation in markets through a process of de-regulation (eg in financial services), there are increasing legal and political constraints on managerial decision making, in areas such as the following.

- Restricting practices that tend to stifle competition, such as the formation of agreements between corporations (eg cartels) that would prevent, restrict or distort competition; and the control of monopolies, mergers which would result in monopolies, and the abuse of a dominant market position. UK legislation in this area includes the Competition Act 1998 and the Enterprise Act 2002 – and similar provisions apply in European law (Articles 81 and 82 of the Treaty of Rome)
- Protecting the rights of minority groups in regard to equal opportunity and diversity in employment. This is covered by a range of equal opportunity law, which in the UK currently outlaws discrimination and harassment on grounds of sex, marital status, sexual orientation, race, colour, ethnicity, religious belief, disability and age. A range of UK law and regulation in these areas is currently being integrated, starting with the Equality Act 2010.
- Protecting the rights of employees in the workplace and employment relationship. There is a wide range of employment law, embracing issues such as workplace health and safety; working hours and leave entitlements; family-friendly flexible working arrangements; rights of consultation for worker representative or trade unions; equal treatment of part-time workers; and employee rights in the event of unfair dismissal, redundancies or transfer of undertakings.
- Protecting the rights and safety of consumers, through consumer protection law; the outlawing of unfair contract terms (eg limiting manufacturers' liability for faulty or unsafe goods); regulations on product health and safety; and so on.
- Enforcing environmental protection standards and commitments, which cover an increasing body of issues including: air and water quality, climate change and greenhouse gas emissions, agriculture, biodiversity and species protection, pesticides and hazardous chemicals, waste management, remediation of environmental impacts, impact review, and the conservation of public lands and natural resources. UK legislation includes the Environmental Protection Act 1990, the Environment Act 1995, the Climate Change Act 2008, the Energy Act 2008, and the Environmental Damage (Prevention and Remediation) Regulations 2009.
- Restricting the types of products that firms can supply (eg forbidding the supply of dangerous goods) or materials and ingredients that can be used (eg forbidding the use of poisonous lead in paints used in toy manufacture)
- Restricting the uses to which firms can put personal data (eg forbidding firms from passing on customer details without their consent, under the Data Protection Act 1998).

10

- Enforcing good corporate governance: eg via corporate, finance and tax law (and voluntary regulation such as the Stock Exchange Combined Code)
- Preventing corruption. In the private sector, this mainly concerns the prevention of money laundering: obtaining, concealing or investing funds or property known or suspected to be the proceeds of criminal conduct or terrorist funding (eg the Money Laundering Regulations 2007)

Regulation of privatised firms

3.6   Privatised firms are those such as British Telecom that used to be in public ownership but were sold by the government into private hands. In order to ensure that public services continue to be delivered (and priced) fairly, the government has imposed a regulatory regime on these firms.

3.7   The main power wielded by Ofcom (the telecommunications regulator) and similar bodies is concerned with limiting price rises. The regulator simply instructs the firm concerned that its price rises for a particular period must not exceed a certain percentage, which invariably is less than the general rate of inflation for that period.

3.8   Another important power arises from publicity. Naturally, the activities of an organisation such as British Telecom affect very large numbers of people. There is widespread interest if Ofcom finds fault with any of those activities, which means that the regulator has no difficulty in gaining publicity in the media. This clearly puts pressure on the monopolist firm to fall into line and pursue 'fair' policies.

3.9   Other powers include the following.

- Issuing and renewing licences for firms wishing to operate in the market. In exceptional circumstances the regulator may withdraw a licence to operate, but this would only be in extreme cases involving (for example) a threat to public safety or persistent and large-scale failure to comply with regulatory standards.
- Setting standards of good practice
- Monitoring the activities of firms operating in the market, responding to customer complaints, and seeking to ensure that firms operate to high standards.
- Communication and promotion of market activities to maintain consumer confidence.
- Making periodic reports to the government.

4   Key features of private sector procurement

Brand values

4.1   A 'brand' is defined by marketing guru Philip Kotler as 'a name, term, sign, symbol or design, or combination of them, intended to *identify* the goods or services of one seller or group of sellers, and to *differentiate* them from those of competitors [in the perceptions of customers]'.

4.2   By developing an identifiable and distinctive brand identity, branding allows customers to develop perceptions of the brand's values (eg prestige, quality, good value, style) which support purchase decisions and – ideally – foster customer loyalty. The task of the organisation marketing a brand is to ensure that the values associated with the brand, product – or organisation as a whole – are positive, attractive, and in line with how it wants to be seen, especially in relation to its competitors.

4.3   The term 'brand values' refers to what a product or corporate brand 'stands for' in the minds of customers and other stakeholders: the core values and characteristics associated with the brand. Brand values might include value for money (as with Aldi Supermarkets), quality (as with Rolls Royce cars), design (as with Apple consumer electronics), technological innovation (as with Dyson engineering products), corporate ethics (as with The Body Shop), heritage and tradition (as with Cadbury's chocolate), entrepreneurship (as with the Virgin group) – and so on.

4.4 The term 'brand positioning' is given to the way consumers define or 'place' a brand on important attributes (like price, value, quality or trendiness), or how the brand is perceived or 'placed' relative to competing products and organisations. An organisation will often seek to determine – and influence – how its corporate image and products are perceived by customers in relation to its competitors.

4.5 The key point made by the mention of this topic in the syllabus is that procurement strategies, policies, practices and decisions will be concerned to *support* (or not undermine) the brand values and positioning created or desired by the organisation, as part of its marketing and competitive strategy.

4.6 So, for example:

- Procurement decisions should support any quality values attached to the brand, by securing high quality inputs and contributing to quality assurance processes.
- If the brand is competitively positioned on the basis of low price or value for money, procurement will have to support this by reducing or managing the costs of inputs and supply processes, so that the organisation can keep consumer prices down and maintain some kind of profit margin.
- If the brand's core values are corporate social responsibility, ethics or environmental responsibility, procurement will have to ensure that all inputs are ethical, fairly traded and environmentally friendly, and that the supply chain is managed in an ethical and responsible way.

And so on: you should be able to develop your own examples, from everything you have learned in this Course Book so far.

Alignment with suppliers

4.7 A key feature of private sector innovative procurement is the extent to which the interests of buyers and suppliers have become integrated or 'aligned'.

4.8 Dyadic supply relationships (with direct suppliers) have been replaced by supply chain relationships and supply chain management: an orientation which emphasises the continuous flow of value towards the customer from first producers to end users. Rather than firms competing, the modern view is that whole supply chains compete to offer customer value (and meet customer demand) more efficiently and effectively than their competitors. Suppliers are therefore seen as essential collaborators in value delivery, competitive advantage and business success.

4.9 For this reason, traditional adversarial, transactional (one-off, commercially driven) relationships have increasingly been replaced, for important and strategic procurements, by longer-term, collaborative relationships, or supply chain partnerships.

4.10 The interests of buyers and suppliers are no longer seen as mutually exclusive, or competitive – usually based around a win-lose battle to gain the advantage over the other party on price. Instead, the interests of buyers and suppliers are viewed as potentially 'aligned': that is, broadly compatible, or aiming towards the same goals. Everyone benefits from improved supply chain performance and competitive advantage. Supply chain management is often used to pursue mutual benefits, through mechanisms such as:

- Supplier development: enhancing the capacity and capability of suppliers to meet the buyer's needs – while at the same time enhancing their business development and earning potential with other (ideally non-competing) customers
- Collaborative waste and cost reductions through the supply chain: enhancing the efficiency of all parties' operations
- Collaborative process and quality improvements through the supply chain, or continuous improvement programmes: developing all parties' performance
- Collaborative efforts to improve labour and environmental management standards through the supply chain (eg through policy development, monitoring, or seeking certification under

international standards schemes): improving all parties' sustainability, reputation and reputational risk management.

4.11 In addition to 'alignment', supply chains may also seek positive 'synergy', a state in which benefits are secured by collaboration, over and above what each party could secure on its own: a possibility sometimes summed up as '2 + 2 = 5'. While each party will want to maximise its own share of value gains (its 'slice of the pie'), this end can equally well be served by working together to 'enlarge the pie'. So, for example, buyers and suppliers may bring unique resources, competencies or technology to the relationship, to enhance the success of the supply chain as a whole. Meanwhile, the *pursuit* of supply chain alignment or integration may itself be synergistic, as it increases trust, information sharing and communication, joint problem-solving and other value-adding processes.

Innovative supply chain approaches

4.12 A number of supply chain approaches developed in the private sector have come to be regarded as innovative best practice which could benefit public sector procurement.

- **Early involvement of procurement**. Treasury (2007) argues that government departments and agencies should: 'ensure that procurement professionals are brought in at the earliest stages of projects, where their skills and knowledge are likely to have most impact.'
- **Early involvement of suppliers**. Treasury also makes it a general principle that the objectives of a procurement should be 'communicated to potential suppliers at an early stage, to gauge the market's ability to deliver and explore a range of possible solutions.'
- **The use of electronic procurement.** The Office of Government Commerce identified e-procurement as a significant opportunity to grasp quick savings, and Treasury emphasised the successful adoption of a number of specific mechanisms in the private sector, such as e-auctions, e-marketplaces and procurement cards.
- **Pro-active contract management**. The National Audit Office (1999) argued the need for 'active contract management' for high value and strategically important procurement. 'This involves ensuring that reliable and comprehensive information is available to monitor the performance of the contractor, and taking action quickly when delivery, price and quality is at risk. It also requires a clear understanding of shared responsibilities so that when the client department has agreed to provide facilities, support or other inputs essential for the supplier to meet the terms of the contract these are provided at the right time...'
- **Flexibility in the use of competition.** Formal competitive procedures are being adapted in a number of ways including: early procurement involvement; working more closely with suppliers; giving suppliers better access to information about contracts; greater use of e-procurement; explicit statement of non-price selection criteria and weightings; and improved supplier debriefing.

5 Third sector organisations

The not for profit (NFP) sector

5.1 The 'third sector' of an economy comprises non-governmental organisations (NGOs) which are operated on a not-for-profit (NFP) basis, generally reinvesting any 'surplus' from their activities to further social, environmental, cultural or other value-driven objectives. Such organisations include: charities, churches, political parties, museums, clubs and associations, co-operatives, interest, pressure and advocacy groups, trade unions and professional bodies such as CIPS.

5.2 Organisations in the NFP sector have typically been set up to achieve a defined objective (eg for a charitable or awareness-raising purpose, or to represent the interests of members) rather than to maximise profit.

5.3 NFP organisations usually derive their funding from voluntary donations, legacies (money left to the organisation in someone's will), sponsorships and government grants and subsidies. They may also have a profit-seeking trading arm to generate revenue (as in the case of 'charity shops', say).

5.4 They may be owned by their members (as in a club or association) or by a trust (as in a charity). They are typically managed by a board of trustees or directors.

The voluntary and subscription sectors

5.5 NFP organisations are sometimes subdivided into further sectors, according to their membership and funding.

- In the **voluntary sector** (eg churches, charities and interest groups), the organisations are generally controlled by a few individuals (eg trustees), but operate by voluntary contributions of funding (eg donations and grants, plus sales of product where relevant) and participation (volunteer labour). The funds are used to maintain the work.
- In the **subscription paid sector** (eg clubs, trade unions and professional bodies), the organisations are owned by the people who pay subscriptions to be members.

Objectives of third sector organisations

5.6 Obviously, the range of third sector organisations is very wide, and they may have a range of different specific purposes.

- Raising public awareness of a cause or issue (eg environmental or social pressure and interest groups)
- Political lobbying and advocacy on behalf of a cause, issue or group
- Raising funds to carry out activities (perhaps using commercial operations to generate profits, in addition to requesting grants, donations or subscriptions)
- Providing material aid and services to the public or specific beneficiaries (eg homeless or aged care charities, wildlife protection and conservation groups)
- Providing services to members (eg trade unions advocating employment rights, and professional bodies securing ethical and technical standards)
- Mobilising and involving members of the public in community projects, for mutual benefit (eg Volunteer Service Overseas).

5.7 As with public sector organisations, the range of an NFP organisation's stakeholders can therefore be wide, including: contributors (staff, volunteers, members, donors); funding bodies (sponsors, funding authorities); beneficiaries of the services or activities; the media (since activities are often 'in the public interest'); and regulatory bodies (such as the Charities Commission). This means that there will be multiple influences on organisational policy and decision-making.

5.8 In order to avoid loss of direction, or pressure to change direction from influential stakeholders (especially sponsors and donors), third sector organisations generally set out their objectives, policies, rules and regulations in some form of governing documents – similar to the Articles of Association of a corporation. These may take the form of a written constitution, charter, trust deed or memorandum and articles of association, setting out:

- The purpose and objectives of the organisation
- Governing principles, policies, rules and regulations for operation
- Responsibilities for management of the organisation (eg the board of trustees)
- Protocols for changing administrative provisions or ceasing operations.

5.9 Johnson, Scholes & Whittington (*Exploring Corporate Strategy)* summarise some of the key characteristics of the third sector as follows: Table 10.4.

10

Table 10.4 *Key characteristics of the third sector*

Objectives and expectations	• May be multiple service objectives and expectations • Expectations of funding bodies are usually very influential • May be subject to political lobbying • Multiple influences on policy: complicates strategic planning • Consultation and consensus-seeking becomes a major activity • Decision-making can be slow
Market and users	• Beneficiaries of services are not necessarily contributors of revenue or resources • Multiple stakeholders and customers • Service satisfaction is not measured readily in financial terms
Resources	• Multiple sources of funding • High proportion from sponsors and donors • Resources received in advance of service delivery, often with attached expectations • Tends towards strategic emphasis on financial or resources efficiency rather than service effectiveness • Strategies and communications may be addressed as much towards sponsors and donors as clients

5.10 You may like to browse the websites of some NGOs in areas that interest you, and see how clearly articulated their values and objectives are, and how these flow down to procurement, sourcing and corporate social responsibility policies.

6 Key features of third sector procurement

The stewardship role

6.1 A significant factor affecting procurement in NFP organisations is that they are seen as performing a 'stewardship' function. That is, they are spending money that has been derived not from the organisation's own trading efforts, but from someone else's donations or taxes. In fact, funding will often come from persons or organisations not themselves benefiting from the services provided.

6.2 Procurement functions are therefore more closely scrutinised and regulated than in the private commercial sector, with a strong emphasis on accountability and stewardship.

6.3 Johnson & Scholes *(Exploring Corporate Strategy)* argue that this may cause a focus on resource efficiency at the expense of service effectiveness. In other words, there is a danger that such organisations will be less concerned to identify and satisfy the needs of their 'customers' – and more concerned with demonstrating absence of waste in their use of sponsors' funds.

6.4 Third sector organisations generally establish clear governance structures for their management – and procurement – in order to provide clarity, accountability, checks and controls on the use of funds.

Regulations impacting on charities

6.5 Third sector organisations are subject to the same general laws and regulations as private and public sector enterprises, as discussed earlier. The syllabus therefore focuses here specifically on regulations impacting on charities.

6.6 The Charities Commission is the statutory regulatory body for charities in England and Wales. Its objectives (as stated on its website: www.charity-commission.gov.uk) are as follows.

- To register charities (like the registry of companies at Companies House)
- To ensure that charities meet the legal requirements for being a charity (in order to register with the Commission), and are equipped to operate properly and within the law

- To check that charities are run for public benefit, and not for private advantage
- To ensure that charities are independent and that their trustees take their decisions free of control or undue influence from outside agencies
- To detect and remedy serious mismanagement or deliberate abuse by or within charities
- To work with charities and other regulators, to enhance public confidence in charities and the work they do (in order to ensure continuing volunteer labour and funding).

6.7 The Commission has a range of responsibilities, including:

- Gathering and maintaining information about charities on the charities register, and making information available to the general public on request
- Offering advice and guidance to charities (via a help line and site visits) on governance and compliance
- Auditing charity activities to check governance and compliance arrangements
- Investigating complaints about charities, and – in the case of mismanagement or abuse – intervening to protect the charity's assets.

What do third sector organisations buy?

6.8 With such a wide range of activities, the range of items procured may be correspondingly wide.

- An NFP organisation may provide services – in which case, its requirements will be the same as those for other service organisations.
- An NFP organisation may have a retail arm, in order to help it raise funds – in which case, its requirements will be the same as those for other retail organisations.
- More generally, NFP organisations will have general operating requirements: office supplies and equipment, IT support, premises management services and so on.
- More specifically, NFP organisations may have requirements for specialist supplies related to their activities. A church will need premises, furniture and supplies for its religious services, say. A charity may need collecting tins, volunteer badges, merchandise for sale and so on.

Key drivers for third sector procurement policy

6.9 Key drivers for procurement policy in third sector organisations therefore include the following.

- The values of internal and external stakeholders (including founders, staff, voluntary workers, donors and supporters), which are often directly related to the mission and purpose of the organisation. The range of a third sector organisation's stakeholders can be wide, including: contributors (staff, volunteers, members, donors); funding bodies (sponsors, funding authorities); beneficiaries of the services or activities; the media (since activities are often 'in the public interest'); and regulatory bodies (such as the Charities Commission). This means that there will be multiple influences on procurement policy and objectives.
- The need to align procurement policies and procedures with the core values, cause, issue or theme promoted by the organisation (eg to support 'green' procurement, if the organisation is an environmental charity or lobbying group).
- The management of reputation and reputational risk. Public relations crisis, caused by some internal failure of policy or implementation, is both more likely for third sector organisations (because of the extent of scrutiny and high standards) and more significant in its impact (because of the dependence on volunteer labour, political support and discretionary funding – most of which will, in turn, be intentionally directed to the values for which the organisation purports to stand). One high-profile example of reputational damage, for example, concerned the exposure of labour exploitation practices in the supply chain for Oxfam's 'Make Poverty History' wristbands.
- The need to source inputs for a very wide range of activities, some of which pose significant logistical challenges (eg foreign aid and development work, disaster relief and so on).
- The need to act as retail or merchandise buyers, if goods are resold to raise funds. Procurement officers will therefore have to source goods of a quality, variety and distinctiveness which will appeal

10

to consumers, at a price which allows them to make a significant 'surplus' on the sale. At the same time, there will often be ethical issues involved in dealing fairly with suppliers, and providing suppliers with a fair price for their goods (especially if, like Oxfam, for example, the organisation specifically obtains goods from developing countries and small rural suppliers, as part of their charitable activity).

- The need for differentiation (eg via best practice sustainable procurement policies, or distinctive merchandise for re-sale to raise funds) in order to compete for attention, volunteers and funding
- Limited resources. Some third-sector organisations (such as the International Red Cross) have very large procurement budgets. However, many have limited funds, and are anxious to devote as much as possible of their funding to the work for which they were formed: there is therefore a strong emphasis on cost control.
- The need for economic sustainability. The term 'non-profit' or 'not-for-profit' should not be interpreted as implying a disregard for commercial disciplines. On the contrary, such disciplines may be more important than in the private commercial sector, because of the scarcity of funds; pressure to devote as much as possible of their income to beneficiaries; or expenditure limits set by funding authorities (eg grant providers) or trustees. It is worth noting, too, that NFP organisations can enjoy a 'surplus' of income over expenditure, even if it is not described as a 'profit'. Procurement professionals therefore have a key role to play.
- The need for transparency, accountability and stewardship in the management of funds – and resulting oversight and regulation: as discussed earlier.

7 Organisations that impact on product and safety standards

7.1   A standards organisation is one whose primary activities are developing, coordinating, revising, or amending technical or safety standards that are intended to meet the needs of a wide number of users. Most standards are voluntary in that they are offered for adoption by organisations operating in the industry, but failure to adopt them is not necessarily illegal. (In some cases, there is a legal obligation to observe published standards.)

7.2   Standards organisations can be classified by their role, their position and the extent of their influence on the local, national, regional and global standardisation arena. By geographic designation, there are international, regional, and national standard bodies. By technology or industry designation, there are standards developing organisations (SDOs) and also standards setting organisations (SSOs) also known as consortia. Standards organisations may be governmental, quasi-governmental or non-governmental entities.

7.3   The three largest and most established international organisations are the International Organisation for Standardisation (ISO), the International Electrotechnical Commission (IEC), and the International Telecommunication Union (ITU), which have each existed for more than 60 years (founded in 1947, 1906, and 1865, respectively). Each of these is based in Geneva, Switzerland.

7.4   Together they have established tens of thousands of standards covering almost every conceivable topic. Many of these are then adopted worldwide, replacing various incompatible 'homegrown' standards. Many of these standards are naturally evolved from those designed in-house within an industry, or by a particular country, while others have been built from scratch by groups of experts who sit on various technical committees. These three organisations together comprise the World Standards Cooperation (WSC) alliance.

7.5   ISO standards in particular are common in purchasing. The ISO is composed of the national standards bodies (NSBs), one per member economy. The IEC is similarly composed of national committees, one per member economy. In some cases, the national committee to the IEC of an economy may also be the ISO member from that country or economy. ISO and IEC are private international organisations that are not established by any international treaty. Their members may be non-governmental organisations or governmental agencies, as selected by ISO and IEC (which are privately-established organisations).

7.6 In addition to these, there are many independent international standards organisations which develop and publish standards for a variety of international uses. In many such cases, these are not based on the principle of one member per country. Rather, membership in such organisations is open to those interested in joining and willing to agree to the organisation's by-laws, having either corporate or individual technical experts as members.

7.7 Regional standards bodies also exist, such as the European Committee for Standardisation (CEN), the European Telecommunications Standards Institute (ETSI), the Pacific Area Standards Congress, the Pan American Standards Commission and many others.

7.8 Within the European Union, only standards created by CEN, CENELEC, and ETSI are recognised as 'European standards' (CE). EU member states are required to notify the European Commission and each other about all the draft technical regulations concerning ICT products and services before they are adopted in national law. These rules were laid down with the goal of providing transparency and control in regard to technical regulations.

7.9 In general, each country or economy has a single recognised national standards body. A national standards body is usually the sole member from that economy in ISO, which currently has 161 members. National standards bodies usually do not prepare the technical content of standards, which instead is developed by national technical societies. The UK standards body is the British Standards Institution.

The British Standards Institution (BSI)

7.10 The British Standards Institution is the world's first national standards body and is now a global independent business organisation that provides standard-based services in more than 140 countries.

7.11 BSI publish British Standards and standards-related information products and services aimed at enabling companies to implement and manage the wide range of product and service standards suitable for differing sectors of business.

7.12 Standards can be used across a wide range of business, industry and technology. There are two main types of standard.

- Technical standards consist of technical specifications or other precise criteria that ensure products, manufacturing processes and services meet fixed benchmarks for quality and health and safety.
- Management system standards provide a framework for a business to manage its business processes and activities.

7.13 **Technical standards** can be used to:

- ensure quality and safety requirements for products and services
- improve compatibility between products and services
- provide information about products and services
- make the most out of innovations.

7.14 **Management system standards** can help businesses improve their efficiency by providing a best practice model for them to follow. Showing that your company, product or service meets a specific standard can also help you compete for business from larger businesses or government departments, many of whom have strict standards or criteria that suppliers must comply with. In some instances customers may insist that a business uses standards before they feel comfortable purchasing their products or services.

10

7.15 Adopting particular standards can bring a range of benefits.

- **Differentiating** your products, services and business
- Accessing **new markets**
- Increasing **efficiency** and improving the quality of your products and services
- Ensuring you **comply** with regulations
- Managing your business more effectively

Chapter summary

- Private sector organisations include sole traders, partnerships and limited companies (both public and private). Many enterprises are now classed as small medium enterprises (SMEs), which face particular challenges and receive public sector support.
- Objectives of private sector organisations typically include maximisation of profits and shareholder wealth, and increase in market share. Increasingly, such organisations recognise objectives of corporate social responsibility.
- There are increasing legal and political constraints on the activities of private sector organisations.
- Private sector organisations frequently adopt a supply chain approach in which the interests of buyers and suppliers are aligned for mutual advantage.
- The third (not-for-profit) sector includes charities, churches, political parties, interest and pressure groups, clubs and associations. They may have a range of purposes and activities. The main challenges for purchasing will be limited funds and accountability in the use of those funds.
- There is a wide range of national and international bodies committed to the development of standards affecting both products and health and safety.

Self-test questions

Numbers in brackets refer to the paragraphs where you can check your answers.

1   In what ways may private sector firms be constituted? (1.2)

2   List advantages and disadvantages of incorporating a private sector firm. (1.11, Table 10.3)

3   What factors account for the resurgence in importance of the small-firm sector? (1.15)

4   Why is the lowest-cost option not always optimal even for a buyer pursuing profit maximisation? (2.3)

5   How does CSR serve the interests of private sector firms? (2.16)

6   How do governments influence private sector organisations? (3.1)

7   How are privatised firms regulated? (3.6–3.9)

8   Account for the growth in collaborative buyer-supplier relationships in recent years. (4.7–4.10)

9   Distinguish between the voluntary sector and the subscription paid sector. (5.5)

10   List key characteristics of the third sector in terms of objectives and expectations. (Table 10.4)

11   What are the objectives of the Charities Commission? (6.6)

12   Distinguish between technical standards and management system standards. (7.13, 7.14)

CHAPTER 11

Public Sector Sourcing

Assessment criteria and indicative content

 Analyse the main legislative, regulatory and organisational requirements when sourcing in the not for profit, private and public sectors

- The use of competitive tendering processes
- The impact of timescales on tendering processes
- Procedures for contract award

Section headings

1   The public sector
2   Public sector sourcing
3   Legislative and regulatory requirements
4   The EU Public Procurement Directives
5   The National Sustainable Procurement Agenda

Introduction

So far in this Course Book we have focused broadly on best practice sourcing, as it relates to the most generally applicable context for procurement: the private sector. At this point, however, the syllabus turns its attention to the legislative, regulatory and organisational requirements of more specialised sourcing contexts: public sector sourcing (addressed in this chapter) and international sourcing (addressed in chapters 12 and 13).

There is considerable variety in public procurement contexts, including different requirements for central government departments and agencies, and local government authorities. We endeavour to give a general overview of the procurement climate and structure in each context.

Since the learning outcome for this section of the syllabus focuses on compliance with legislative and regulatory requirements, we focus specifically on a key framework for public sector sourcing: the EU Public Procurement Directives, and their enactment in UK law as the Public Contracts Regulations.

We also emphasise some of the key values and objectives of public sector sourcing, such as competition, accountability and value for money – which may have rather different connotations in the public sector than they do in the private sector.

1 The public sector

The private and public sectors

1.1 As most readers will be aware, a private sector organisation is one that is owned by private individuals, either few in number (such as a small family business) or very numerous (as with a large company owned by millions of private shareholders). Public sector organisations on the other hand are 'owned' by the public in general: the UK National Health Service, for example, is headed by a Government minister whose responsibility is to run the service efficiently and effectively on behalf of the State.

1.2 Some key differences between the private and public sectors, as a context for sourcing, can be summarised as follows.

1.3 In the *private sector*:

- Organisations are owned by their investors (proprietors or shareholders), and controlled by directors or managers on their behalf
- Activity is funded by a combination of investment, revenue (from the sale of goods or services) and debt
- The primary purpose is the achievement of commercial objectives: generally, maximising profits for their owners, or for reinvestment in the business. Managerial decisions are assessed on the extent to which they contribute to organisational profit or shareholder wealth.
- Competition is a key factor. Several, or many, firms may offer goods or services of a particular type, with consumers free to choose between their offerings: consumer choice ensures that quality and efficiency are maintained at an acceptable level.
- The core 'constituency' served by firms is shareholders, customers and employees, all of whom are involved with the firm by choice. Firms can and must, therefore, focus their activity on meeting the needs of these few key stakeholders.

1.4 In the *public sector:*

- Organisations are owned by the government on behalf of the State, which represents the public
- Activity is financed by the state, mainly via taxation – as well as any revenue the organisation's activities may generate
- The primary purpose is achieving defined service levels: providing efficient and effective services to the public, often within defined budgetary constraints and sustainability strategies
- There has traditionally been little or no competition, although, since the 1980s, successive UK governments have sought to introduce some market disciplines (eg competitive tendering). In the absence of consumer choice, quality and efficiency are imposed by mechanisms such as regulation, customer charters, performance targets and competition for funding allocations.
- The 'constituency' of concerned stakeholders is wider and more diverse, including government, taxpayers, funding bodies, those who consume services – and society as a whole. There is a far greater need for accountability and stakeholder consultation in managing the organisation.

1.5 Although the private sector is the focus of most procurement and supply chain literature – and arguably represents best practice in some areas of sourcing – the public sector is an important context for procurement operations. The spending power of public sector enterprises is enormous, and the sheer range of public sector service provision is vast.

Private and public sector procurement environments

1.6 Public and private sector organisations and environments are different in some key respects, as we noted above. The key implications for procurement have been summarised by Gary J Zenz (*Purchasing and the Management of Materials),* whose analysis forms the basis of Table 11.1, with our own points added.

Table 11.1 *Differences between public and private sector purchasing*

AREA OF DIFFERENCE	PRIVATE SECTOR	PUBLIC SECTOR
Objectives	Usually, to increase profit	Usually, to achieve defined service levels
Responsibility	Buyers are responsible to directors, who in turn are responsible to shareholders	Buyers are responsible ultimately to the general public
Stakeholders	Purchasing has a defined group of stakeholders to take into account.	Purchasing has to provide value to a wider range of primary and secondary stakeholders.
Activity/process	Organisational capabilities and resources used to produce goods and services	Add value through supply of outsourced or purchased products and services. (Tend not to purchase for manufacture.)
Legal restrictions	Activities are regulated by company law, employment law, product liability law etc	Most of this applies equally to public sector, but additional regulations are present too (eg EU procurement directives)
Competition	There is usually strong competition between many different firms	There is usually no competition
Value for money	Maintain lowest cost for competitive strategy, customer value and profit maximisation.	Maintain or improve service levels within value and cost parameters.
Diversity of items	Specialised stock list for defined product and service portfolio.	Wide diversity of items or resources required to provide diverse services (eg local government authority).
Publicity	Confidentiality applies in dealings between suppliers and buyers	Confidentiality is limited because of public interest in disclosure
Budgetary limits	Investment is constrained only by availability of attractive opportunities; funding can be found if prospects are good	Investment is constrained by externally imposed spending limits
Information exchange	Private sector buyers do not exchange information with other firms, because of confidentiality and competition	Public sector buyers are willing to exchange notes and use shared e-purchasing platforms, consolidate purchases etc.
Sourcing policies/ procedures	Tend to be organisation-specific. Private sector buyers can cut red tape when speed of action is necessary	Tend to follow legislative directives. Public sector buyers are often constrained to follow established procedures
Supplier relationships	Emphasis on long-term partnership development where possible, to support value chain.	Compulsory competitive tendering: priority to cost minimisation and efficiency, at the expense of partnership development.

1.7 The differences between public and private sector sourcing should not be overemphasised, however. Differences in objectives, organisational constraints and so on may not necessarily lead to differences in operational *procedure*.

- Public sector buyers may not be seeking to maximise profit, for example, but they will still be concerned to achieve value for money.
- Public sector buyers may not seek competitive advantage, but they will still aim to ensure the quality of inputs in order to support the quality of outputs (to fulfil the terms of a customer charter, say).
- Meanwhile, private sector buyers may not have non-economic goals as their primary objective, but they are increasingly being challenged to consider the interests of wider stakeholders in society (through pressure for corporate social responsibility).

1.8 An article in *Procurement Professional* journal (CIPS Australia) recently noted that: 'Key issues for the procurement profession... are as relevant for the public sector as they are for the private sector... Work is currently underway in public sectors around the world to address these issues, centred on:

- Developing standards for the assessment and ongoing development of public procurement professionals
- The greater application of strategic sourcing principles to public procurement
- The introduction of e-procurement systems.'

11

1.9 It should be noted that there is increasing best practice sharing between sectors, with best practice models and recommendations published by public sector bodies such as the Organisation for Government Commerce (OGC) and Sustainable Procurement Task Force, and with commitment from the public sector to learn from private sector best practice (in areas such as closer supplier relationships, supply chain innovation and procurement professionalism).

1.10 Key priorities, such as corporate social responsibility, sustainability, customer service improvement and the reduction of cost inefficiencies, operate across sectoral boundaries.

2 Public sector sourcing

Central government procurement

2.1 The 1999 Gershon Efficiency Review recommended centralised co-ordination of central government procurement, through the Office of Government Commerce (OGC), which was established in 2000. OGC's three main priorities were defined as: improving public services by working with departments to help them meet their efficiency targets; delivering savings in central government civil procurement; and improving the success rate of mission-critical programmes and projects. OGC therefore operates a wide-ranging programme supporting three significant activities: improving efficiency; programme and project management (PPM); and procurement.

2.2 OGC Buying Solutions is an executive agency of the OGC, providing procurement services to help public sector organisations and their private sector agents and contractors achieve value for money from procurement.

2.3 For those working in the public sector, the implications of the OGC include: greater pressure to achieve efficiency savings from procurement; greater emphasis on aggregating requirements and collaborative contracting; stronger focus on the status and role of procurement; stronger focus on professional and career development in procurement; increased involvement in contracting across the organisation; and increased involvement in cross-functional contracting teams.

Local government procurement

2.4 Unlike in central government, there is no central co-ordination of local authority procurement. Functional departments and committees are influential, and procurement's role is often limited to advising on procedures and managing clerical processes. A 2002 Audit Commission report noted that: 'It is encouraging that some authorities are using procurement as a tool for improvement, and that there is evidence of good practice. However, many authorities still need to ensure that their approach to procurement makes full use of competition and challenges current services.'

2.5 Local Government Improvement & Development (formerly known as the Improvement and Development Agency or IDeA) provides advice and guidance. It provides a range of tools and services to local authorities, including: a procurement competency framework; procurement training and development for members and officers; an e-procurement service and portal/marketplace; best practice guidance; and a procurement toolkit.

National Health Service procurement

2.6 Until recently, the Purchasing and Supply Agency (NHS PASA) acted as a centre of expertise, knowledge and excellence in purchasing and supply matters for the UK health service. It advised on policy and the strategic direction of procurement, and its impact on developing healthcare, across the NHS. It also contracted on a national basis for products and services which were strategically critical to the NHS, and where sectoral aggregation of demand was thought to yield greater savings than local or regional collaboration.

2.7 The agency was closed down in April 2010, to be replaced by a more commercially-focused regime. All of its non-clinical core categories (including energy, fleet, estates and outsourcing, ICT, professional services, temporary staffing and audit) are now being handled by Buying Solutions: the national procurement partner for UK public services, and an executive agency of OGC. A series of Regional Support Units, owned by the NHS, has been set up to provide a single point of contact to suppliers in each region.

Public sector supply chain drivers

2.8 In contrast to the profit focus of private sector concerns, public sector organisations have a primary orientation to achieving defined service levels: providing efficient and effective services (education, transport, healthcare) and utilities (water, power) to the public, often within defined budgetary constraints and environmental or sustainability strategies. This less intensely competitive environment allows greater information exchange, best-practice sharing and collaborative or consolidated sourcing and supply arrangements, such as shared e-procurement platforms and buying groups.

2.9 The range of stakeholders in public sector organisations is more diverse, including funding and user groups. This creates a more complex network of stakeholder expectations, relationships and accountabilities to be managed. A much wider diversity of items and services may also be sourced: consider a local government authority in the UK, which may be a purchaser of construction materials for use in housing or road maintenance, of dustbin lorries for refuse collection, of sporting equipment for a community leisure centre, and much more.

2.10 Public sector buyers are subject to a high level of accountability. They must ensure that appropriate processes have been followed to acquire best value for taxpayers' money; that a full 'audit trail' exists so that their actions and decisions can be vetted; and that appropriate service levels are achieved in the provision of services to members of the public. These objectives are thought to be best achieved by an insistence on competitive tendering, for contracts over a certain size (measured by contract value).

2.11 Public sector sourcing policies are governed by EU Directives in areas such as the compulsory use of competitive tendering, the use of e-auctions, ethical requirements (eg in regard to gifts and hospitality as possible inducements to sourcing decisions) and public interest disclosure of information (limiting the confidentiality of the dealings between buyers and suppliers).

2.12 As we suggested earlier, the distinction between private and public sector procurement should not be over-emphasised, since both sectors deal with inputs and broadly aspire to good practice in terms of the 'five rights'. However, you should be aware that there are some distinctive challenges in public sector sourcing.

- Public sector buyers generally have the overall objective of achieving defined service levels (rather than increasing profits, as in the private sector). 'Value' is thus defined by maintaining or improving service levels within value and cost parameters – rather than by minimising cost as part of a strategy of profit maximisation and competition.
- They have to satisfy a wider range of stakeholders: managers, customers, beneficiaries of services, taxpayers, communities and so on. There will usually be a stronger emphasis on pre-qualification criteria such as ethics, social sustainability (eg using diverse, small and local suppliers), environmental protection and so on.
- They may have a wider range of activities, and therefore a wider range of sourcing requirements. (Think of the range of items required by a school, or a local government organisation, say.)
- They are subject to established sourcing procedures, and legislative directives (including the EU Public Procurement Directives, enacted in UK law as the Public Contracts Regulations). This means, for example, that open competitive tendering is compulsory for placing supply contracts over certain value thresholds.
- They will often be subject to budgetary constraints, cash limits and/or efficiency targets, to maximise the value obtained from public funding.

11

Competition

2.13   A key issue in the public sector is to ensure that suppliers are selected not on the grounds of political expediency, socio-economic goals, favouritism or fraud, but by transparent procedures which are open to audit and give all eligible suppliers an equal opportunity. There has been a particular emphasis on ensuring that competitive procedures are followed, as part of a process of developing the professionalism of the purchasing function.

2.14   It has also been recognised that public procurement has an important role to play in ensuring the efficient use of public funds. Policy dictates that this is to be achieved wherever possible via competition, as the best guarantee of quality and value for money.

2.15   Some form of competitive tendering is therefore used within the public sector for almost all goods purchased. For small items this usually takes the form of written quotations from selected suppliers. However, the greater the value of goods purchased, the more formal the tendering procedure. EU public procurement procedures (discussed in Section 3 of this Chapter) are based on formal competitive tendering to ensure openness and equality of opportunity within a competitive framework.

2.16   It is important to note that the aim of competitive sourcing is not just 'competition' for its own sake, but its judicious use to achieve *competitive supply*: the extent to which a supply arrangement provides supply which matches or exceeds requirements at a cost which represents best value in relation to a given supply market. *Competitiveness* is the strength and intensity of competition within a market, which results in genuine customer choice and potential for gains in price, quality and innovation.

2.17   One key issue is whether levels of competitiveness in a supply market result in bids which represent competitive supply, or whether there is a need to *generate* greater competition eg through: encouraging new entrants or substitute products and processes; expanding the market (eg from regional to EU or global); collaborative sourcing to increase buyer power; or making contracts more accessible and attractive to potential suppliers (such as small and medium sized enterprises, third sector suppliers, or minority-owned suppliers).

2.18   Compulsory competitive tendering is designed to ensure fair, non-discriminatory and competitive supplier selection, based on equality of access to tender information, selection of suppliers based on clear price (and non-price) criteria, and accountability for decisions (including feedback to unsuccessful bidders). It also supports value-for-money procurement – and procurement cost savings (as part of government efficiency targets) – by improving and maintaining the competitiveness of supply.

2.19   It has been recognised, however, that restrictive or inflexible use of competitive procedures may: discourage more innovative approaches; reinforce a risk-avoidance culture; provide an excuse for lack of expertise and professionalism; limit opportunities to achieve wider socio-economic goals through procurement; and place obstacles in the way of developing close relationships with suppliers.

2.20   The main focus has been on compliance with the EU Public Procurement Directives, emphasising the transparent use of competitive procedures, rather than necessarily the achievement of competitive supply or added value outcomes. An initial restrictive interpretation of the Directives by the OGC resulted in a negative view of the use of procurement for socio-economic purposes. EU rules do not therefore always encourage best practice procurement, in areas such as sustainability, SME and minority business participation, longer-term supply partnership relations – or indeed competitive supply.

2.21   One key challenge for public procurement is that inflexible use of competitive tendering may inhibit the development of the kinds of long-term collaborative relationships which underlie strategic procurement models. Consideration must be given to the benefits and feasibility of developing close supplier relationships within the regime.

2.22 It has long been recognised that there needs to be more constructive co-operation between customers and suppliers and that – particularly in highly specialised markets, and for complex and continuously developing requirements – longer-term partnering arrangements may be appropriate. Such partnerships will still be established by competitive tender and re-opened periodically to competition *(Treasury, 1995)*: a policy sometimes called 'partnership within competition.'

2.23 Whilst in principle 'partnership within competition' provides a viable alternative for the public sector, it risks undermining the principles of transparency, competitiveness and fraud prevention. Such risks need to be recognised and managed, eg through greater professionalisation of the procurement function, and through the development of procedures combining dialogue with potential suppliers and formal procedures for the submission of bids. Once competitive tendering processes have been completed, close relationships may be developed between clients and suppliers on the basis of continuing competitiveness, innovation, cost and quality improvement over the duration of the contract.

2.24 Another challenge is the inflexible use of price and 'value for money' criteria in awarding competitive contracts – potentially at the expense of important criteria such as whole life costs, sustainability, or relational compatibility (eg potential for EDI links). Particular efforts may have to be made to include such criteria in specifications – which is the latest stage at which non-price criteria can be introduced.

Public accountability

2.25 This level of accountability in the public sector impacts strongly on public procurement. One key effect is an insistence on detailed procedures and record keeping: it may be difficult later to justify a course of action which breaches defined procedures or which is poorly documented.

2.26 Reports of the Public Accounts Committee illustrate the kinds of behaviour which are required by public accountability, in areas such as: the need to record the reasons for all sourcing decisions; the need for procurement officers to declare any personal interests in sourcing decisions; the need to avoid conflicts of interest; the need to secure proper authorisations; and the need generally to monitor and manage fraud risk.

2.27 However, it is often argued that the scrutiny and accountability regime also creates a 'risk avoidance' culture among public sector officials. The National Audit Office has stated that a lack of flexibility and innovation, in seeking to minimise risks, may itself cause failure to achieve value for money. Examples include:

- Rigid application of procedures, and use of the same terms and conditions for all contracts regardless of the nature of the requirement, market conditions and relationship with potential suppliers
- Reluctance to involve procurement specialists at an early stage of the sourcing process, working with clients, technical experts and users in cross-functional teams
- Reluctance to use innovative approaches such as early dialogue with suppliers over market availability and specification, visits to or presentations by potential suppliers.

Value for money

2.28 Traditionally, supplier selection and contract award measures have been based on prices paid and cost savings. However, a more holistic concept of 'value for money' (VFM) was advocated in the 1995 White Paper *Setting New Standards,* and OGC guidance. 'All public procurement of goods and services, including works, must be based on value for money... Value for money is not about achieving the lowest initial price: it is defined as *the optimum combination of whole life costs and quality.*'

2.29 This reflects an increased emphasis on:

- The importance of taking into account all aspects of cost over time, rather than lowest purchase price (discussed in Chapter 3) and

- The importance of defining 'value' from the perspective of the customer, and meeting service level and quality requirements
- The importance of achieving efficiency (making best use of available resources) and effectiveness (accomplishing objectives) – in addition to economy (using the least possible resources).

3   Legislative and regulatory requirements

3.1   The impact of law and regulation on public sector sourcing is broadly as follows.

- To ensure that bought-in materials, goods and services comply with defined public standards and specifications
- To ensure that all sourcing exercises are compliant with public policies, standing orders and statutory procedures – with the general aim of securing competitive supply, value for money and ethical procurement
- To ensure that all resulting supply chain operations are compliant with law, regulation and standards in areas such as health and safety (eg in regard to manual handling or transport of dangerous goods); environmental sustainability (eg in regard to carbon emissions); employment rights (eg in regard to equal opportunity or employment protection); data protection and freedom of information.

3.2   Such regulations are common to both the public and private sectors. Public sector procurement is, however, subject to additional regulation and scrutiny, including:

- **EU Public Procurement Directives**, now enacted in UK law as the Public Contracts Regulations 2006 and the Utilities Contracts Regulations 2006
- **Anti-corruption law**, which broadly outlaws the offering and receiving of bribes and inducements which might influence, or be seen to influence, decision making by public officials (eg the Public Bodies Corrupt Practices Act 1989 and the Prevention of Corruption Act 1916)
- **Freedom of information** law (eg the Freedom of Information Act 2000), which gives the public the right to access information held by public authorities (including emails, the minutes of meetings, research and reports) – *unless* it is determined that the public interest in withholding the information is greater than the public interest in disclosing it: the 'public interest test'. Public authorities must respond promptly (within 20 days) to FOI requests, although they have 'reasonable time' to consider whether the disclosure would be in the public interest. Complaints and disputes are arbitrated by the Information Commissioner's Office
- Government **policy agendas, action plans and targets**: eg on procurement efficiency, value for money (or Best Value), and sustainable procurement (eg the National Sustainable Procurement Action Plan).

4   The EU Public Procurement Directives

4.1   The EU Public Procurement Directives were implemented into UK law by the Public Contracts Regulations 2006, the Utilities Contracts Regulations 2006, the Defence and Security Public Contracts Regulations 2011 and their Scottish equivalents.

4.2   The rules apply to procurements by public bodies, above certain financial thresholds, which are updated every two years. From 1 January 2012 to 31 December 2013, the principal thresholds are as follows (net of VAT).

- Supply (goods) and service contracts awarded by central government: £113,057
- Supply and service contracts awarded by other contracting authorities: £173,934
- Works contracts: £4,348,350.

4.3   The purposes of the EU procurement directives are broadly as follows.

- To open up the choice of potential suppliers for public sector organisations and utilities, in order to stimulate competition and reduce costs
- To open up new, non-discriminatory and competitive markets for suppliers

- To ensure the free movement of goods and services within the European Union
- To ensure that public sector purchasing decisions are based on value for money (via competition) and that public sector bodies award contracts efficiently and without discrimination.

Tender advertisement

4.4 All contracts covered by the 2006 Regulations must be awarded in a fair and open manner. Nearly all large contracts must be advertised in the Official Journal of the European Union (OJEU). There are certain defined exemptions to this advertisement rule, eg for geographically-fixed services (such as hotel and restaurant services) and for reasons of national security.

Contract award criteria

4.5 In all cases, contracts must be awarded on the basis of objective award criteria which are clearly set out, ensuring transparency, non-discrimination, equal treatment, and competition. Buyers are generally obliged to award contracts on the basis of:

- Lowest price *or* (more commonly)
- Most economically advantageous tender (MEAT).

The initial contract advertisements must state which criterion is to be used.

4.6 If MEAT is used, buyers must make this known to tender candidates and must explain the criteria that will be used to assess 'economic advantage'. Such criteria might include: quality, deliverability within target time scales, technical merit, innovation, risk sharing, health and safety or environmental performance, or the promotion of equality or diversity. Such criteria must be listed in all contract notices or invitations to tender, and must be meaningfully ranked and weighted. This is usually done by directing bidders to a website where the award criteria are listed in order of importance, with weightings to show how important each criterion is (eg price 50%; quality of personnel 30%; implementation 20%).

4.7 The award criteria that are used in deciding which is the most economically advantageous tender must be relevant to the purpose of the contract, and the technical specifications provided. For example, the level of performance is directly relevant: the nationality of the bidder's staff is not.

4.8 The buyer may exclude bidders if they fail to meet certain defined criteria in regard to suitability, financial standing and technical competence.

- **Personal situation of the supplier**: eg bankruptcy, liquidation or similar situations under international laws; conviction of an offence relating to professional ethics or competence, or failure to pay taxes; or false declaration of professional qualifications during the tender process
- **Financial capacity.** The purchasing authority may fix the level of financial or economic capacity required to fulfil the contract, and may determine the nature of evidence to justify this capacity (eg bank declarations, submission of balance sheets)
- **Technical capacity.** A buyer is permitted to seek information about matters such as: professional qualifications held by the supplier or senior employees; principal services, products or works carried out in the last three years; material and technical equipment used to carry out tasks; methods of assessing the quality of the project; whether and how the work will be subcontracted
- **Professional qualifications.** A buyer can ask bidders to evidence that their professional qualifications are registered with the appropriate professional body.

4.9 In relation to non-price (eg sustainability) criteria:

- Public bodies can specify sustainable options, provided that doing so does not unreasonably distort competition or discriminate against products or suppliers from any EU member state. It is possible, for example, to specify recycled paper or energy-efficient IT equipment. Fair Trade options can be 'welcomed' – and an authority might require caterers to supply fair trade coffee or tea products, for

11

example, as this would not affect competition between caterers.

- In relation to contract award, only two criteria are allowable: lowest price or 'most economically advantageous tender'. This allows issues such as resource consumption and disposal costs, for example, to be taken into account. Any social or environmental sustainability criteria used must be directly related to the performance of the contract, and appropriately weighted.
- EU rules do not permit preference being given to any sector of suppliers such as local suppliers, social enterprises or SMEs (except for 'supported businesses' where particular rules apply). It is permissible, however, to remove any *obstacles* that might be preventing such groups from competing for public business. This might be done by, for example, ensuring they are aware of where opportunities will be advertised and making tendering documentation and procedure as simple as possible for all suppliers.
- The best opportunity to incorporate sustainability criteria may be at the need definition, specification and pre-qualification stages of the procurement cycle – and through post-contract negotiated improvement agreements.

Procedures and time limits

4.10   There are four basic procedures permissible under the public procurement rules.

- Open procedure
- Restricted procedure
- Negotiated procedure
- Competitive dialogue.

Buyers can choose between open and restricted procedures, but negotiated and competitive dialogue procedures are only allowed under certain circumstances.

4.11   Subject to certain exceptions, public bodies must use the **open procedure**.

- The invitation to tender must be advertised according to rules designed to secure the maximum publicity across the EU, including advertisement in the Official Journal of the European Union (OJEU). This should set out the requirement and invite bids.
- Suppliers respond to the tender notice by the date specified, and invitation to tender (ITT) documents must be issued or made accessible to *all* potential suppliers within six days.
- The closing date for bids (tender documents) to be received by the purchasing authority must be at least 52 calendar days after the tender advertisement appears.
- If the buyer issues a 'prior information notice' or PIN (advertising in advance that a contract or group of contracts is to be advertised shortly, to give prospective bidders a chance to pre-prepare), the time limit can be reduced to 26 days – enabling the buyer to speed up the procedure in the event of urgent requirements.
- Closing dates can also be brought forward by the use of electronic systems: by seven days if contracts are drawn up and transmitted in electronic form; and by an additional five days if all contract and supporting documentation is accessible by electronic means.
- Tenderers are appraised (according to defined selection criteria) and tenders evaluated (according to defined award criteria), and the contract is awarded.
- A maximum of 48 days after contract award, the contract award notice must be despatched for publication in the OJEU.

4.12   The advantage of the open procedure is that it opens the contract to the widest possible supplier base, and maintains maximum transparency and open competition – with the potential to secure competitive value solutions. The main disadvantage of the open procedure is the lack of supplier pre-qualification, and the sheer volume of suitable and unsuitable bids that must be opened and evaluated.

4.13   Under the **restricted procedure:**

- The initial advertisement in the OJEU is followed by a pre-qualification or supplier appraisal stage, in which bidders are generally required to respond to a pre-qualification questionnaire (PQQ).

- The closing date for prospective bidders to register their interest and submit the completed PQQ must be at least 37 days after the advertisement (or 15 days under the 'accelerated restricted procedure', if justified by operational urgency which makes normal time scales impracticable. The use of the accelerated procedure must be stated and justified in the OEJU notice).
- There must be a pre-stated range of suppliers (5–20) to whom invitations to tender will be sent, following pre-qualification.
- Selected qualified bidders must be allowed at least 40 days to respond to the invitation to tender. This can be reduced to 36 days, if a prior information notice is issued. It can also be reduced by the use of electronic tendering (as with the open procedure) or by use of the 'accelerated restricted procedure' (minimum of 10 days).
- The contract is awarded, as for the open procedure, and the contract award notice sent for publication in the OJEU within 48 days.

4.14 The key advantage of the restricted procedure is the potential to pre-qualify suppliers prior to the bidding process. This minimises the administrative burden on buyers (opening and evaluating a restricted number of bids) and on suppliers (who are not put to the time and expense of bid preparation if they lack suitability on pre-qualification grounds).

4.15 Under a **negotiated procedure:**

- The tender may be conducted without OJEU advertisement in strictly defined circumstances: eg in the case of urgency, existing exclusivity agreements, no tenders being received under open or restricted procedures, or sole supply (eg if for technical, artistic or intellectual property rights reasons, the contract can only be carried out by a particular bidder).
- Where advertisement is used, prospective bidders must be given a minimum of 37 days to register their interest in entering into negotiation.
- A minimum of three parties must generally be selected, where possible, to participate in negotiation.
- Suppliers' best and final offers are evaluated (competitively, where applicable) on the basis of stated award criteria.

4.16 The OGC urges 'extreme caution' before the use of negotiated procedures, in order to ensure that competition and best value are maintained. Use of the procedure must be justified if challenged.

4.17 The **competitive dialogue procedure** was introduced in the Public Contracts Regulations 2006, reinforcing best practice principles for large, complex projects (such as Private Finance Initiative or Public Private Partnership projects). For such projects, the requirement cannot be specified in detail or priced in advance; price may not be the most important variable in a complex requirement; specifications may change over time; and solutions may have to be developed in collaboration with the supplier. In such circumstances, the open and restrictive procedures cannot be used effectively.

4.18 Prior to 2006, such projects were mainly sourced under the negotiation procedure – but, as we have seen, this was only available in exceptional circumstances. Competitive dialogue was developed as a more flexible procedure, and has (in effect) replaced the negotiated procedure. Its use must still be justified, if challenged. Utility companies are not permitted to use competitive dialogue, but have a free choice between open, restricted and negotiated procedures.

4.19 Under competitive dialogue:

- The requirement is advertised in the OJEU, and suppliers must be given at least 37 days to register an expression of interest.
- The buyer opens a 'dialogue' with selected pre-qualified suppliers. The purpose of dialogue is to identify and define the means best suited to satisfying the requirement: all aspects of the contract may be discussed at this stage. The authority may not reveal the solutions proposed by one participant to the others, nor disclose any confidential information communicated by a participant without its agreement.

11

- Dialogues may be conducted in successive stages, in order progressively to reduce and refine the number of solutions: phased de-selection is permitted, providing pre-determined criteria (set out in the contract notice or descriptive document) are used.
- Once dialogue has identified the solution or solutions, the authority informs the participants that the dialogue is concluded. Participants are then asked to submit final tenders on the basis of the solutions presented and specified during the dialogue, and these are competitively evaluated.
- No post-closure negotiation is permitted. Tenders may only be clarified, specified or fine-tuned at the request of the contracting authority, without changing the basic features of the tender or call for tender.

4.20 Here are some advantages of the competitive dialogue procedure.

- It is easier to justify its use than the negotiated procedure, particularly given OGC and CIPS guidance favouring its use.
- Complex solutions (and associated contracts and models) can be developed in collaboration with potential suppliers, allowing access to supplier expertise and innovation.
- Phased de-selection minimises the risks and costs of lengthy ineffective discussions.
- There is freedom to structure the dialogue to meet the circumstances of the procurement.

4.21 The main disadvantage of the competitive dialogue is that it is still comparatively new and unfamiliar, which may deter participation – or create uncertainty about legal interpretation and compliance issues. For participant suppliers, there is a higher initial cost of engagement, and they may be reluctant to disclose information and solutions during the dialogue, despite confidentiality rules.

Post-contract award procedures

4.22 The results of the tender (a contract award notice) must be notified to the Official Journal of the EU within 48 days.

4.23 The purchasing organisation must include a 10-day **standstill period** between the decision on contract award and the point when the contract is signed. This is often called the 'Alcatel' period, because of the name of the court case that originally gave rise to it. The standstill period allows bidders to seek debriefing from public authorities, and gives time for unsuccessful bidders to challenge the award decision if they feel it is unfair or that the tender has been non-compliant or unfairly conducted.

4.24 Unsuccessful bidders have the right to a de-brief within 48 days of request. The focus should be on the weaknesses that led to rejection of the bid (to support the development of capability and competitiveness for future contracts), as well as strengths. The debrief should *not* be used to justify the award of the contract to the successful tenderer – and, in particular, confidential commercial information about the successful bid should *not* be disclosed.

4.25 Government guidelines have suggested that de-briefing might include topics such as: cost (eg number of bidders who offered lower prices); schedules and lead times; design quality; organisational or administrative weaknesses; experience; personnel and management; facilities and equipment; reliance on subcontractors and the adequacy of control arrangements; cost and schedule control; industrial relations record; quality management systems; contract terms; and after-sales service and support offering.

4.26 The results of debriefing interviews must always be recorded in case there is a subsequent challenge by the unsuccessful bidder.

E-tendering

4.27 Contracting authorities may use tendering and auction systems. Devices for the electronic receipt of tenders, requests for participation and plans and projects must (through technical controls and appropriate procedures) guarantee:

- Precise determination of the exact time and date of receipt of tenders, requests to participate and the submission of plans and projects (to ensure compliance with timescales and deadlines, and equal treatment of submissions)
- No access to data before the time limits and schedules laid down for the process – and clear detectability of any infringement of access prohibitions
- Access to data submitted (after the prescribed deadline for submission) only by simultaneous action by authorised persons (ie simultaneous 'opening' of tenders)
- Control over the confidentiality of all data received and opened, with access only for authorised persons.

4.28 If e-tendering is used, as noted earlier, there are implications for the time scales set for tender stages.

- Where contract notices are drawn up and transmitted by electronic means, the Regulations allow for the time limits for the receipt of tenders in open procedures (and the time limit for the receipt of requests to participate in restricted, negotiated or competitive dialogue procedures) to be shortened by seven days.
- The time limit for receipt of tenders may be reduced by a further five days, where the contracting authority offers unrestricted and full direct access by electronic means to the contract documents and any supplementary documents from the date of publication of the notice, by specifying in the text of the notice the internet address at which this documentation is accessible.
- If contracting authorities seek to take advantage of the above opportunity to shorten the time limits for the receipt of tenders on the basis of electronic availability of their contract documents, they must publish the specifications and the additional documents in their entirety on the internet.

E-auctions

4.29 Contracting authorities which decide to hold an electronic auction must state that fact in the contract notice. The specifications must include the following details.

- The features, the values of which will be the subject of electronic auction, provided that such features are quantifiable and can be expressed in figures or percentages
- Any limits on the values which may be submitted, as they result from the specifications relating to the subject of the contract
- The information which will be made available to tenderers in the course of the electronic auction and, where appropriate, when it will be made available to them
- The relevant information concerning the electronic auction process
- The conditions under which the tenderers will be able to bid and, in particular, the minimum differences which will, where appropriate, be required when bidding
- The relevant information concerning the electronic equipment used and the arrangements and technical specifications for connection.

Remedies for breach of the directives

4.30 The main means by which a breach of the EU Directives may be remedied are:

- Legal action by an aggrieved supplier or contractor against the purchasing authority, pursued in the High Court
- Legal action pursued by the European Commission against the member state in the European Court of Justice (ECJ).

4.31 Possible 'remedies' resulting from such an action, if procedures are found not to have been followed properly, include:

- Suspension of a contract award procedure that has not yet been completed
- Setting aside of the contract award decision (only by the ECJ)
- An award of damages.

11

5 The National Sustainable Procurement Agenda

5.1 Sustainable procurement has been defined as:

- 'A process whereby organisations meet their needs for goods, services, works and utilities in a way that achieves value for money on a whole life basis in terms of generating benefits not only to the organisation, but also to society and the economy, whilst minimising damage to the environment.' (The Sustainable Procurement Task Force)
- 'Policy on procurement issues where public procurement is seen as a lever to achieve wider socio-economic policy objectives, including: environmental or green issues; SME and MOB [minority-owned business] support; fair trade issues; adult basic skills; disability, race and gender equality; innovation; and promotion of on-going and contestable markets.' (Office of Government Commerce)

5.2 The public sector has particular reasons for demanding greater levels of sustainability from its supply chain: it is directly and explicitly responsible for ensuring that public money spent on goods and services (€150 billion per annum in the UK) is applied in such a way as to maximise benefits to society.

Benefits and opportunities arising from sustainable procurement

5.3 The UK government has outlined eight good reasons for sustainable sourcing, and the procurement of sustainable products, for the public sector.

- To achieve best value for money over the whole lifecycle of assets (eg by using whole life costing)
- To fulfil the government's commitment to sustainable development
- To be able to withstand increased public scrutiny
- To meet international obligations (such as the Kyoto Protocol and EU Sustainable Development Strategy)
- To stimulate the market for sustainable technologies
- To maintain and improve our standard of living
- To improve health and the environment
- To save money (through long-term eco-efficiencies).

5.4 Other benefits and opportunities arising from adoption of a sustainable procurement policy are listed in Table 11.2.

The UK Sustainable Procurement agenda

5.5 The UK's Sustainable Procurement Task Force was established in 2005 and charged with drawing up an action plan to bring about a step-change in public procurement to put the UK among the sustainability leaders in the EU by 2009.

5.6 The task force drew on a range of governmental and non-governmental organisations to analyse the key barriers to sustainable procurement and presented a National Action Plan for overcoming them. The report *Procuring the Future* (also known as the Simms report, after Taskforce chairman Sir Neville Simms) delivered its findings and recommendations in June 2006.

- *Lead by example.* The lack of consistent leadership on sustainable procurement emerged as a key barrier. Many public sector procurers lack clear direction from the top of their organisation on the priority to be given to delivering sustainable development objectives. To address this a clear commitment from government should be cascaded down through both government targets and performance management systems that are independently monitored.
- *Too much guidance.* Procurers complained of guidance and information presented in an incoherent manner – a 'one size fits all' approach. The proposal was to rationalise policies into a single integrated framework which meets the needs of procurement.
- *Raise the bar.* The existing minimum standards for central government should be properly enforced

Table 11.2 *Potential benefits/opportunities of sustainable procurement*

Compliance	Law and regulation impose certain social and environmental responsibilities on organisations (eg in relation to workplace health and safety, employment protection, consumer rights and environmental care). There are reputational, financial and operational penalties for failure to comply.
Reputational benefits and reputational risk management	Voluntary measures on sustainability may enhance corporate image and reputation, enabling the organisation to attract and retain quality employees, funders, delivery partners and suppliers. The risk of reputational damage extends to 'responsibility by association' in supply chains: buying organisations are increasingly held responsible for unsustainable behaviour by their suppliers.
Supply continuity and risk management	Support for the financial viability and sustainable practices of suppliers protects the ongoing security of supply, which might otherwise be put at risk.
Cost management and efficiency	A emphasis on whole life value can contribute to cost management and efficiency. The environment-friendly focus on resource-efficiency and the reduction or elimination of waste products and processes can also lead to measurable efficiencies and cost savings.
Improvement and innovation	Sustainable procurement initiatives often require increased supply chain communication, and investment in problem-solving and innovation: this may open up new avenues for performance improvement, cost reduction, enhanced collaboration, supplier development and product/service innovation, with flow-on benefits.
Competition and competitive supply	Emphasis on innovation and accessibility of public contracts to small and diverse suppliers also supports competition and contestable supply markets. There may be particular opportunities arising from increased use of SME suppliers (as argued in the report Smaller supplier... better value? (OGC, 2006). 'Opening the market to a wider supplier base means that: • you will not miss out on potential suppliers who may be more competitive • you might find innovative solutions you might otherwise have missed • you will avoid the danger of the market stagnating through an ever decreasing number of large suppliers • simplifying the procurement process and removing unnecessary obstacles can help to make your life easier.'
Social policy objectives	Sustainable procurement supports key public sector goals such as equal opportunity and diversity and job creation.

and extended to the rest of the public sector. The task force recommends working with suppliers to identify future needs and to phase out products and services that fall below minimum standards.

- *Build capacity.* The public sector must develop its capabilities to deliver sustainable procurement. Sustainable procurement cannot be undertaken effectively unless procurement activities are carried out professionally and effectively; all procurement should be carried out by people whose skills have been developed appropriately.
- *Remove barriers to sustainable procurement* – whether actual or perceived. Whole life costing was not being implemented in practice, the focus being on lower upfront costs. Rules, budgetary constraints, and entrenched viewpoints were all barriers. All public organisations were called upon to examine their budgeting arrangements to make sure they encourage and support sustainable procurement.
- *Innovation.* The public sector must capture opportunities for innovation and social benefits and must manage risk better through smarter engagement with the market. Many suppliers questioned felt that it was difficult to penetrate the public sector with innovative solutions and that there were missed opportunities.

5.7 The Task Force put forward three key building blocks for moving the sustainable procurement agenda forward.

- A *flexible framework* that guides public sector leaders in actions to develop capability and maturity in implementing sustainable procurement.
- *Prioritisation of spend.* Ten priority areas were identified for action nationally.
- *Toolkits* providing expert advice and support to public sector procurers, including the 'Quick Wins' minimum and best practice specifications for commonly purchased goods and services.

11

Chapter summary

- A private sector organisation is owned by private individuals; a public sector organisation is owned by the public in general.
- Differences in objectives and organisational constraints do not necessarily lead to differences in purchasing procedures in the two sectors. In many respects, best practice is the same in all sectors.
- While private sector firms usually have the overriding aim of maximising profit and shareholder wealth, public sector organisations have a primary aim of achieving defined service levels.
- In the public sector, there has been a regulatory emphasis on ensuring that competitive procedures are followed.
- The level of accountability in the public sector requires an insistence on detailed procedures and record keeping.
- Public sector buyers are subject to a range of regulation in addition to that of private sector buyers.
- The EU procurement directives require the use of competitive tendering for public sector contracts in excess of a defined (low) threshold.
- The public sector has particular reasons for demanding greater levels of sustainability from its supply chains.

Self-test questions

Numbers in brackets refer to the paragraphs where you can check your answers.

1   In the context of sourcing, list key differences between the public and private sectors. (1.3, 1.4)

2   Give reasons why such differences do not necessarily lead to differences in operational procedure. (1.7)

3   List priorities of the OGC. (2.1)

4   List some of the distinctive challenges of public sector procurement. (2.12)

5   What is the aim of compulsory competitive tendering in the public sector? (2.18)

6   Why is a culture of risk avoidance in the public sector sometimes counter-productive? (2.27)

7   Explain the main impacts of legislation on public sector sourcing. (3.1)

8   What are the purposes of the EU procurement directives? (4.3)

9   What are the four tendering procedures permissible under the EU directives? (4.10)

10 What is meant by a 'standstill period' in public sector procurement? (4.23)

11 List reasons given by the UK government for sustainable sourcing. (5.3)

12 Describe the findings of the Simms report. (5.6)

CHAPTER 12

International Sourcing

Assessment criteria and indicative content

 5.2 Analyse the main legislative, regulatory and organisational requirements when sourcing from international suppliers

- Documentation relating to imports
- Import duties and tariffs
- Payment mechanisms
- The use of incoterms
- Customs control and clearance

Section headings

1 International and global sourcing
2 Import processes within the EU
3 Imports from outside the EU
4 Import duties and tariffs
5 The use of incoterms
6 Payment mechanisms
7 Dispute resolution

Introduction

In this chapter we begin to look in detail at a topic raised earlier in the syllabus, in connection with sourcing strategies: the implications of international sourcing.

We start by looking briefly at the nature of international sourcing, and some of the drivers for an increasing trend towards international sourcing – although this topic will be addressed in more detail in Chapter 13, where we consider the opportunities and risks of sourcing internationally.

In this chapter we look at the more practical implications of sourcing from international suppliers, or 'importing' goods. The European Union was formed to operate as a single market, with the aim of eliminating restrictions to the free flow of goods, finance and labour between member countries. In an EU context, therefore, different regimes apply to importing goods from within the EU and from outside the EU – to which more complex tariff and non-tariff restrictions apply. We will look at each regime in turn.

We then go on to look at some key tools and techniques for developing international contracts, resolving currency and risk issues in international payments, and resolving international contract disputes.

1 International and global sourcing

1.1 International sourcing is about sourcing goods and services from 'overseas' or other-country suppliers: essentially, 'importing'.

The term 'global sourcing' does not just mean sourcing from a more widespread network of international suppliers. It has a more strategic flavour, involving the development of an international supply network, from which the company's sourcing requirements can be met flexibly, competitively and in a co-ordinated way.

1.2 Either way, there has been a notable increase in international sourcing in recent decades, driven by factors such as the following.

- Improvements in transport technology, creating the 'shrinking' of distance (and related risks) for logistics
- Improvements in ICT, abolishing distance for the purposes of communication, relationship development, delivery tracking and performance monitoring
- Progressive reductions in trade barriers (eg through trading blocs and agreements), facilitating direct investment and the movement of goods and labour
- Sourcing efficiencies: with the ability to select the lowest-cost supplier from anywhere in the world
- Country or region-specific supply factors: some goods (especially raw materials and commodities) may only be available from particular countries, or may be supplied more efficiently by particular countries, due to specialisation (eg of call centres and IT services in India)
- Harmonisation of technical standards, which has enabled the sourcing of standardised components, compatible systems and so on.

1.3 We will discuss the specific advantages and disadvantages of international sourcing for buying organisations in Chapter 13. However, a number of general arguments may be put forward in favour of international sourcing, as part of the wider process of international trade.

- International trade stimulates local economic activity (due to the theory of comparative advantage). This leads to improved productivity and output, and helps to create employment, leading to greater prosperity, educational development and other standard-of-living benefits (particularly if foreign investors also operate community development policies). Smaller developing nations particularly benefit from the wider scope of markets, since their domestic economy may have represented too small a market to allow development and resulting economies of scale.
- There may be improvements in human rights and labour conditions in developing economies, where foreign buyers enforce ethical and CSR policies and monitoring in their supply chains (even if this is primarily done to protect their own reputations).
- Global consumers benefit from more product and service choice and competitive pricing.
- It has been argued that international trade is a primary mechanism for positive international relations and a deterrent to conflict.

1.4 It should be obvious from TV footage of violent protests outside World Trade Organisation meetings, however, that there is a contrary viewpoint. Those opposed to globalisation argue that global sourcing may:

- Encourage the exploitation of labour in developing nations (poor wages, poor conditions, child labour and so on) for lower-cost production. This is partly supported by more relaxed intellectual property, employment protection and health and safety laws.
- Export pollution, deforestation, urbanisation and other environmental damage to developing nations
- Cause unemployment in developed nations, where justified expectations of pay and conditions make labour 'uncompetitive' with cheap-labour competitors
- Squeeze small domestic suppliers out of the supply market, with negative effects on competition, communities and cultures.

The role of trading blocs and trade restrictions

1.5 A 'trading bloc' is an economic arrangement created among a group of countries. There are more than 30 trading organisations and blocs around the world, including: ASEAN (The Association of Southeast Asian Nations); EFTA (The European Free Trade Agreement); and NAFTA (the North American Free Trade Agreement). Trade *within* each of these three major trading blocs is expanding on a vast scale – while trading *between* blocs, or indeed with non-members, tends to decline.

1.6 Unlike the European Union, which has moved towards political integration, most trading blocs are solely about economic integration. This type of integration can take various forms.

- A **free-trade area** (such as EFTA and NAFTA) represents the least restrictive economic integration between nations. Essentially, in a free-trade area all barriers to trade among members are removed, and no discriminatory taxes, tariffs or quotas are imposed.
- A **common market** (such as the Andean Common Market – Ancom – comprising Venezuela, Columbia, Ecuador, Peru and Bolivia) is the closest form of integration: a trading group with tariff-free trade among members *and* a common external tariff on imports from non-members, *and* collective regulation on quotas and other non-tariff barriers. Commercial law is also drafted centrally, and overrides the domestic laws of member states.

1.7 Outside trading blocs, international trade may be subject to barriers in the form of taxes and duties (tariffs) and non-tariff measures, such as the following.

- Quotas: limits on the quantities of specified products that are allowed to be imported
- Complex customs procedures and paperwork, for goods to cross borders
- The need to comply with different quality, health and safety, environmental protection and other regulations in different countries
- Government subsidies to domestic producers (which make it more difficult for overseas firms to compete on price)
- Exchange controls: limits on the ability of a domestic importer to obtain the foreign currency needed to pay his overseas suppliers.

1.8 Although the trend is now to reduce trade restrictions (supported by bodies such as the World Trade Organisation), they can perform a useful function: protecting strategic industries (in order to preserve the economies which depend on them); protecting emerging industries (in order to encourage development); and improving a country's 'balance of payments' (the ratio of its exports to imports).

1.9 The main effect of trade restrictions is to create customs procedures, and import duties and tariffs. We will now look at some of the practical implications of this, as they apply to imports both within the EU and from outside the EU.

2 Import processes within the EU

The role of HM Customs & Excise

2.1 International trade involves the complex flow of goods and services between countries. Each country will have its own customs and excise service to monitor and control the flow of goods both for import and export.

2.2 The function of the UK body (HM Customs & Excise or HMCE – nowadays a part of HMRC) is to control the import and export of goods, in order to:

- Ensure that no unauthorised goods are allowed to enter or leave the country
- Ensure that all relevant import and export duties are paid
- Compile trade statistics.

These controls are achieved by licensing the import or export of certain goods or by requiring importers and exporters to submit 'entries' (required details) to HMCE.

2.3   Declarations are required by HMCE:

- To ensure that import and export licensing requirements are met
- To provide accurate details for trade statistics
- To prevent the unauthorised return of duty-free or VAT zero-rated goods (VAT means value added tax, a tax on sales of goods or services)
- To provide information to assist VAT verifications
- To enable checks to be carried out on goods that are subject to controls
- To check that only valid CT (Community Transit) documents are authenticated.

Imports within the European Economic Area

2.4   The Single Market Act led to the introduction of a single European market in January 1993, facilitating the free movement of people, capital, services and goods within the European Union. To support the free movement of goods, the customs tariff was harmonised across EU member countries so that the same import duties and quotas apply over every member country.

2.5   There are basically two types of goods, for the purposes of Customs procedures.

- Goods with Community status. (The term 'Community' refers to the European Community: the former name of the European Union.) These may be goods manufactured within the EU ('of European Union origin') *or* goods for which import formalities have been completed and import duty paid upon their first import into an EU country, and which are thereafter deemed to be in 'free circulation': not subject to further duties as they move across borders to other EU countries.
- Goods without Community status: goods which are from outside the EU, and for which no import formalities have yet been completed and no duty paid.

2.6   Goods that meet the criteria of 'free circulation' can now be moved freely within Europe without attracting duties or quota restrictions (restrictions by weight or number), although customs and excise authorities throughout Europe require evidence as to the status of goods while they are in transit and upon arrival. The effects of these changes are as follows.

- Goods moving from the UK to European member countries are no longer classified as exports but are now officially referred to as 'despatches'.
- Imports from European member countries into the UK are now referred to as 'acquisitions'.
- Goods that are in 'free circulation' and are transported between European member countries are no longer subject to Customs procedure but are still required to evidence their status with either an invoice, a 'movement document' or a completed 'Copy 4' of a SAD (Single Administrative Document) form. Customs authorities always have the right to investigate the status further if they feel there is a need.

2.7   Goods *not* in free circulation may simply be transiting through the EU to a destination outside the EU, or they may have excise duty yet to be paid (eg cigarettes and alcohol). The 'Community Transit' (CT) system is a Customs procedure that allows goods not in free circulation to move within the EU and EFTA areas, with the payment of customs duties suspended until a later point.

Movement documents

2.8   All goods transiting EU countries require a 'movement document' or 'T' (for Transit) form: Table 12.1.

Table 12.1 *Movement or 'T' documents*

TYPE OF T-DOCUMENT	USE	COPY OF SAD REQUIRED
T1	Where the goods are not in 'free circulation' within the EU	1, 4, 5 and 7
T2	Where the goods are in 'free circulation' within the EU	1, 4, 5 and 7
T2L	For 'free circulation' goods but where the 'community transit' (CT) system is not required	1 and 4

2.9   It is not always necessary for a T-form to accompany goods; only that the appropriate status is declared on the SAD (Single Administrative Document) form. However, if goods are moved under the full CT procedure, the T-form must accompany them: an import entry cannot be made to Customs prior to arrival of the goods. This will cause delays as Customs process the entry, since the T-form will need to be presented at the appropriate import office.

The Single Administrative Document (SAD)

2.10   The SAD form was introduced to simplify documentation, facilitate trade and allow for computerised communications throughout the European Union. In its full eight-copy format, the SAD form is intended to be used as a combined export, community transit and import document, used for declarations for exports and imports from non-EU countries.

2.11   However, traders are not required to present all eight copies in every circumstance. SAD sets (known as 'spilt sets') are available containing only those copies that are appropriate for particular circumstances. Within the EU, only the following copies are required: Table 12.2.

Table 12.2 *SAD split set for movement of goods within the EU*

COPY NO	DESCRIPTION OF COPY	LOCATION OF COPY
1	Copy from customs office of departure	Despatch (export) country
3	Consignor/exporter's copy	Despatch (export) country
4	Copy for the customs office of destination or EU status (T2L declaration)	Travels with goods
5	Return copy from customs destination office to evidence arrival	Travels with goods; returned to despatch country as evidence of arrival
7	Statistical copy in country of destination	Travels with goods

2.12   The SAD form sounds a complex document, but becomes familiar with use. Its purpose is:

- To allow customs to monitor the movement of goods;
- To ensure all relevant duties have been paid;
- To ensure regulations, such as statistical declaration, have been complied with (statistical information is required to show balance of trade and industry trend information among other purposes).

New Computerised Transit System (NCTS)

2.13   The New Computerised Transit System (NCTS) is a Europe-wide automated system for traders to enter transit declarations (and other details, such as the arrival of goods) electronically, as part of the Community Transit system. Connected traders receive electronic responses advising of decisions during the procedure, such as acceptance of the declaration, release of goods etc, at both departure and destination.

2.14   Through NCTS, a customs declaration is delivered electronically to customs authorities, and receives a unique registration number. The goods can then be released and moved, accompanied by the customs document, to the place of destination. Meanwhile, the Customs office of departure sends details of the consignment to the Customs office of arrival. After checking and acceptance on arrival, the goods will be released and confirmation passed back to the office of departure.

2.15   NCTS was designed to provide better control of goods in transit through EU and EFTA states, following European Parliament findings that paper-based systems were vulnerable to transit fraud, and incapable of providing a reliable level of control and management.

2.16   For organisations the NCTS brings the following advantages.

- An improved quality of service with less waiting time at Customs points, and greater flexibility in presenting declarations
- Speedier control and release of goods at the office of destination
- Reduction in costs, time and effort when compared to the paper based system
- The opportunity to integrate electronic transit declaration procedures with the organisation's existing computerised system
- Greater clarity and consistency in requirements.

Customs Handling of Import and Export Freight (CHIEF) system

2.17   Import procedures are supported by a range of international computer systems. 'CHIEF' is one of the largest and most advanced declaration processing systems in the world, controlling and recording the UK's international trade movements across transport modes, and linking with several thousand businesses. The CHIEF system allows required customs data to be input electronically by exporters and importers or their agents.

2.18   CHIEF embraces a range of customs entry methods (which we will look at briefly in the following paragraphs).

- Full pre-entry or pre-shipment declarations
- Low-value procedures
- Simplified clearance procedure (SCP) for post-shipment declaration (prior approval required)
- Local export and import control.

Pre-entry or pre-shipment declaration

2.19   Pre-entry or pre-shipment declaration involves making a physical declaration to HMCE at the point of export or despatch of the goods. This can be time-consuming and delaying, and is often replaced by computer-based entry methods. It is the usual method for making full export declarations for customs clearance using the SAD form. To aid declarations, shipment information such as shipment date, vessel name/flight number and port of export can be omitted.

Low-value procedure

2.20   HMCE has no interest in goods with a value of less than £600 and a net weight of less than 1,000 kg – although it retains the right to inspect and investigate. Goods that fulfil these criteria may be presented for export with reduced documentation: either a copy of an approved commercial document (usually an invoice) or a transit document with, for example, 'LV 350' stated: this declares the goods suitable for the low value procedure, and with a value of £350. Alternatively, a partially completed 'Copy 2' of the SAD can be used.

2.21   The low-value procedure cannot be used when goods are restricted or subject to duty.

Simplified clearance procedure (SCP)

2.22 The Simplified Clearance Procedure (SCP) is intended to be used when an exporter does not have enough information to make a full export declaration on a SAD at the time of export.

2.23 In order to use the SCP, traders must register in advance with the Tariff and Statistical Office, and the exported goods must not be dutiable or restricted. Approved exporters will be issued with a five-digit Customs registered number (CRN), and are then permitted:

- To declare goods for export by means of pre-shipment advice (an approved standard commercial document or partly completed SAD Copy 2) containing a minimum of information – instead of a full pre-shipment declaration
- To submit a full statistical export declaration *after* shipment (within 14 days of export).

Local import control (LIC)

2.24 LIC is available to those importers and agents who regularly import goods as consolidated 'unit loads' (such as containers) and who wish to have customs clearance facilities at their premises. This can often be integrated with other special facilities such as 'authorised consignor' status, under which a trader can authenticate its own Community Transit documentation. An equivalent procedure exists for goods being exported (local export control or LEC).

2.25 LIC goods should normally be in secure containers, including road vehicles and trailers. When Customs-approved seals are required, these must have unique identifying numbers and containers must be capable of being sealed effectively.

2.26 Full post-shipment statistical declaration of the exports must be sent to Customs Statistical Office no later than 14 days after the export clearance takes place and may be made by a SAD export declaration, printed schedule or computerised entry (eg via CHIEF).

3 Imports from outside the EU

3.1 Imports from outside the EU will need to fulfil more rigorous criteria than with 'acquisitions' from EU countries. The importer of any goods is required to deliver to the proper customs officer an entry on the appropriate form containing prescribed details of the goods, carrying ship or aircraft, port of importation, and so on. Goods may be entered for:

- Consumption (ie the products will be sold or otherwise used in the importing country or trade bloc) – in which case, duty becomes payable
- Temporary import for warehousing, transit or transhipment, testing, trade fairs and so on.

3.2 For imports from outside the EU, a buyer would usually use the services of an import agent or freight forwarder, who presents Customs entries, usually by computer. Entries need to be lodged four clear days before the anticipated date of arrival or within seven working days after arrival (for air imports), or four clear days before the anticipated date of arrival or within 14 days after arrival (for sea or land imports). When goods reach a port of entry, they are held until the entry process is complete, after which they are released into the country.

3.3 A typical import transaction, for goods arriving from outside the EU, might therefore be as follows.

- Apply for an import licence (if required).
- Open a 'letter of credit' or arrange for any other special finance requirements (as explained in Section 6 of this Chapter).
- Place the order: agree an International Commercial Term (or Incoterm: see Section 5), payment details and the law that applies to the contract.

- Send full details of the documents to the supplier, including documents required to enable the movement of the goods (eg certificates of origin, if required). Provide specific detail if any special packing, marking, invoicing, delivery or other instructions are required.
- Receive shipping documents and details from the supplier: advise the clearing agent.
- Release the bill of lading, for sea freight (see below).
- Pass customs entry, paying duty where necessary.
- Arrange collection, storage and delivery.

Documentation requirements for non-EU imports

3.4   Table 12.3 gives the names and brief descriptions of some of the main 'shipping documents' you may see references to.

Table 12.3 *Documentation for overseas imports*

DOCUMENT	DESCRIPTION
Invoice	Evidence of a contract between the buyer and the seller. (Standard pro-forma invoices are available for this purpose.)
Bill of lading	A multi-purpose document: evidence of a contract for carriage; a receipt for the goods; a statement of the condition of the goods; and, in some cases, a document of title (ownership) as well.
Seaway/airway bill	Evidence of contract for carriage by sea or air, and receipt for the goods.
Insurance policy/ certificate	Evidence that insurance has been effected
Certificate of origin	Evidence of the country of origin of the goods

Bill of lading

3.5   A bill of lading (for sea freight) is 'a document signed by a ship owner (or by the master or other agent on behalf of the ship owner) which states that certain goods have been shipped on a particular ship, or have been received for shipment' (*Charlesworth's Business Law*). As noted above, a bill of lading acts as:

- A document of title (ownership). The owner or exporter of the cargo assigns the bill to the buyer or importer, resulting in the passing of ownership to the buyer. The importer must present the original bill of lading to the carrier at the destination port, in order to claim the goods (as their new owner).
- A receipt for the goods (in a stated quantity and condition), issued by or on behalf of the carrier. (If defects not noted on the bill are found at the destination, there is a clear inference that they arose in transit, and are therefore the responsibility of the carrier.)
- Evidence of the terms of the 'contract of carriage' between the exporter and the carrier, by which the shipper agrees to pay freight costs (among other standard terms) and the carrier must provide a seaworthy vessel and proceed without delay to the destination port by the agreed route.

4   Import duties and tariffs

Import duties and tariffs

4.1   Customs duties are indirect taxes levied on imports at the point of entry. They are assessed on the 'landed value,' ie the value of goods *plus* freight and insurance, as they arrive in the United Kingdom. Duties can be calculated in two ways.

- *Ad valorem* (by value)
- **Specific** (by unit measurement or weight).

4.2   Import duties are levied according to the details defined in the *Integrated Tariff of the United Kingdom*, which specifies duties chargeable, preferential rates and quotas together with procedural methods.

4.3 The Tariff is a three-volume annual publication that is updated monthly containing essential information about customs import and export requirements.

- Volume 1 contains general information regarding import and export matters.
- Volume 2 contains the Schedule of Duty and trade statistical descriptions, codes and rates.
- Volume 3 contains information about customs freight procedures including directions for completing the SAD.

4.4 The right 'class' or commodity code for goods in accordance with the UK Tariff must be identified, a process known as 'classifying'. The importer or exporter is legally responsible for the correct tariff classification of the goods. This applies even if an agent is employed to handle customs entries on behalf of the actual importer or exporter.

Relief from import duty and VAT

4.5 Various goods brought into the EU and then re-exported have total or partial relief from import duty and VAT provided certain conditions are met.

4.6 **Inward Processing Relief (IPR)** applies to goods imported from outside the EU, which are processed and then re-exported to countries outside the EU: it is used most frequently when components are imported to manufacture an end product for export, or when goods are returned for maintenance or repair and re-export.

4.7 IPR is therefore designed to assist EU exporters to compete in the world market: if they source materials and components internationally and export their finished products, they can save the customs duty and VAT normally payable at import.

4.8 Other exemptions can be granted for reimported goods, temporary imports, goods imported under direction and goods entitled to end-use relief.

4.9 VAT becomes chargeable on the importation of goods into the UK at the rate of tax prescribed by the VAT Act 1994. There are rules to establish the value of goods and there can be a requirement to provide evidence to support the valuations.

4.10 There are reliefs from VAT on imports in certain circumstances.

- Where the importation is of a temporary nature
- Where the importation is transacted within an approved relief zone or approved Customs warehouse (see below)
- On permanent importations of specified goods such as goods for handicapped persons, coffins and urns containing human remains, or low-value, non-commercial imports (among others)

4.11 Where goods are returned from abroad unaltered, they can also be reimported free of VAT and customs duty provided specific HMCE requirements can be met.

Customs warehousing

4.12 Customs warehousing is a procedure that enables the suspension of import duty and/or VAT for imported non-EU goods by storing them in premises or under an inventory system authorised by HMCE.

4.13 Companies can choose to store the goods at their own 'defined location' (eg a private warehouse) using their inventory system to control the goods, or they can pay a third party to store them in a 'defined location' (eg a public warehouse). A 'defined location' can be a whole building, a small compartment in a building, an open site, a silo or a storage tank.

12

4.14 Being able to suspend the payment of import duty and/or VAT, with no time restrictions, can be very beneficial to companies, not least for cashflow reasons. The duty to comply with prescribed procedures, however, may be a drawback.

Carnets

4.15 Carnets are important in the movement of goods both within and outside the European Union. A carnet is a permit or a form of licence designated for a particular purpose, usually temporary importation for a specific purpose such as film equipment, equipment for trade fairs and exhibitions, and equipment for sporting events. The import can then be made into a country, or it can be permitted to transit through a country, without payment of any duties that would otherwise be due. This is subject to full documentary requirements being met and evidence of the goods subsequently leaving the country concerned.

4.16 The two most commonly used carnets are as follows.

- **Carnet de passage en douane**. Within Europe, most countries allow the importation of vehicles and containers free of duty or duty deposit. However, certain countries require a 'carnet de passage' to enable their temporary importation, including:
  — Vehicles and trailers entering the majority of middle-eastern countries
  — Vehicles and trailers remaining in Pakistan for a period exceeding three months
  — Vehicles and trailers remaining in Italy for more than three months
  — Vehicles remaining in Greece for more than ten days.
- **ATA carnets**. These are used extensively on a worldwide basis. An ATA carnet is issued by a Chamber of Commerce and is valid for 12 months from the date of issue. It requires pre-planning as individual pages are raised for each movement – eg 'exit UK, enter Singapore, exit Singapore, enter Japan, exit Japan, enter UK' – and they should be used in sequence. Breaches can lead to fines or applicable duty being levied. The ATA carnet does not relieve the user of observing customs requirements in each country. At the end of use, the goods and the ATA carnet are returned to the country of origin and the correctly stamped carnet is returned to the appropriate Chamber of Commerce.

5   The use of incoterms

The purpose of incoterms

5.1 When sourcing from abroad, a buyer may find istelf involved in up to four separate contracts: the actual purchase contract, a contract of carriage, a contract of insurance, and a contract of finance.

5.2 The communication difficulties involved in international trade have long been recognised as a problem. The translation and interpretation of contractual terms is of key importance to both buyers and suppliers, since both parties' understanding of contract requirements must be absolutely free from ambiguity in order for a contract to be fulfilled successfully – and without dispute.

5.3 With this in mind, the concept of incoterms (International Commercial Terms) was introduced by the International Chamber of Commerce (ICC) in 1936. It was felt that if the parties concerned in an international transaction adopted standard terms, many problem areas could be averted, as all parties would be clear on their areas of risk and responsibility at all stages of transaction – and there would be no ambiguity of law or jurisdiction in the event of a dispute.

5.4 Incoterms is a set of contractual conditions or terms that can be adopted into international contracts, which are designed to be understood and interpreted on a worldwide basis. A booklet published by the ICC sets out agreed explanations of many of the terms used in international trade to define the obligations of seller and buyer. The booklet is regularly updated in line with developments in commercial practice: the most recent edition being *Incoterms 2010* (effective from 1 January 2011).

5.5 There is no legal requirement to use incoterms when drawing up an international commerical contract: buyers and suppliers may contract with each other on whatever terms they think most suitable. However, if they specifically refer to an incoterm (or 'adopt' an incoterm into the contract), both parties agree to be bound by the detailed specifications laid out in *Incoterms 2010*: in the event of a dispute, the courts will 'imply' the standards of incoterms in law.

5.6 The use of incoterms in a contract can save pages of detailed negotiation as, when adopting incoterms into the contract, the detailed specifications relating to the relevant incoterm will apply, defining areas of risk and responsibility. Areas detailed within incoterms specify the obligations of buyer and seller in regard to, among other things:

- where delivery should be made
- who insures
- what level of insurance is required
- who raises particular documents.

5.7 Parties may negotiate to determine which type of incoterm agreement is most suitable.

The basic structure of incoterms

5.8 Incoterms are perhaps best viewed from the exporter's or supplier's perspective, as they are arranged in order of increasing responsibility for the exporter. This is seen in the four main groups of incoterms below: Table 12.4.

Table 12.4 *The four groups of incoterms*

GROUP	DUTIES OF BUYER/SELLER
'E' terms	The seller's only duty is to make the goods available at its own premises: it may assist with transit, but this is not a requirement.
'F' terms	The seller will undertake all pre-carriage duties, but main carriage arrangements are the responsibility of the buyer.
'C' terms	The seller arranges for carriage of the goods, but once they are despatched it has fulfilled its obligations.
'D' terms	The seller's obligations extend to delivery of goods at the specified destination; it is therefore liable for damage or loss in transit, insurances in transit and so on.

5.9 For convenience, incoterms are referred to using three letter designators that should be linked with the relevant point where risk and responsibility pass. Incoterms 2010 includes elevent pre-defined terms: Table 12.5.

Table 12.5 *Incoterms summary*

INCOTERM	NAME	RISK AND RESPONSIBILITY PASS AT:
EXW	Ex works ...	named place
FCA	Free carrier ...	named place
FAS	Free alongside ship ...	named port of shipment
FOB	Free on board ...	named port of shipment
CFR	Cost and freight ...	named port of destination
CIF	Cost, insurance and freight ...	named port of destination
CPT	Carriage paid to ...	named place of destination
CIP	Carriage and insurance paid to ...	named place of destination
DAT	Delivered at terminal ...	named terminal at place of destination
DAP	Delivered at place ...	named place of destination
DDP	Delivered duty paid ...	named place of destination

Table 12.6 *Incoterms*

EXW
(ex works) ...
named place
	This is the easiest form of export that can be used by the seller: the buyer collects the goods, and the EXW price is for the goods alone, free of any delivery charges, insurances etc.
	    The obligations of the seller are to place the goods under the contract at the factory gate or other named area in the factory vicinity that will enable the buyer to uplift the goods. The buyer must then make all arrangements to uplift the goods from the premises and ship them to the destination at its own risk and expense.
	    If the buyer cannot carry out export formalities, FCA may be required.

FCA *(free carrier)* *... named place*	Unlike FOB, this term is applicable to all modes of transport to a specific carrier or specific destination: it is particularly relevant for multi-modal, containerised transport. The seller retains responsibility and risk until it has handed the goods over, cleared for export, into the charge of the carrier named by the buyer at the named place. The place stipulated by the buyer could be an inland clearance depot (ICD), rail or airport terminal, shipping berth, or freight agent's warehouse.
FAS *(free alongside ship) ...* *named port of shipment*	Similar to FCA, but used only for sea or inland waterway traffic. The goods must be delivered to the berth or quay alongside a shipping vessel nominated by the buyer or his agent: the buyer takes on responsibility for getting the goods from the quayside to the vessel, plus all costs and risks after that point. Again, if the buyer cannot carry out export formalities, FCA may be used.
FOB *(free on board)...* *named port of shipment*	Suitable for conventional cargo (eg break-bulk) shipments sent by sea or inland waterway: for other transport modes, the term FCA is more appropriate. The seller has responsibility for delivering to the port and vessel nominated by the buyer, and responsibility and risk remain with the seller until the goods have actually passed the ship's rail at the port of shipment.
CFR *(cost and freight) ...* *named port of* *destination*	The seller bears the responsibility and cost of delivery from its premises to the port of *destination*, using sea and inland waterway freight. The seller is therefore required to provide all export documents (certificate of origin, export licence, pre-shipment inspection certificates and so on) if required. However, *risk* is transferred to the buyer when the goods pass over the ship's rail at the port of *shipment*, so the cost of marine insurance is borne by the buyer.
CIF *(cost, insurance and* *freight) ... named port of* *destination*	Similar to CFR, but the seller is also responsible for marine insurance (for the benefit of the buyer) to protect the goods against loss or damage during carriage to the named place of destination. If the buyer requires a higher level of insurance than the supplier would arrange as standard (often a minimum level), this should be clarified when drawing up the sales contract.
CPT *(carriage paid to)* *... named place of* *destination*	Designed for use with containerised and multi-modal transport. Responsibility and costs of transit are borne by the seller, up to the point at which the goods are delivered to the place of destination designated in the sales contract. However, responsibility for insurance is borne by the buyer.
CIP *(carriage and insurance* *paid to) ...* *named place of* *destination*	Similar to CPT, except that the seller also arranges all insurances for transit.
DAT *(delivered at terminal) ...* *named terminal at* *destination port/place*	The seller pays all costs of carriage to the named destination terminal, including taxes and delivery charges, but *not* including costs related to import clearance. The seller also assumes all risks up to the point at which the goods are unloaded at the terminal. The buyer needs to arrange customs clearance and onward transport.
DAP *(delivered at place) ...* *named place of* *destination*	The seller pays all costs of carriage to the named place (eg the buyer's premises), *excluding* costs related to import cleareance, customs duty, VAT and so on. The seller also assumes all risks up to the point at which the goods are ready for unloading by the buyer. The buyer carries out all customs formalities, unless the contract states otherwise. (This is similar to a previous term called 'DDU': delivered duty unpaid.)
DDP *(delivered duty paid) ...* *named place of* *destination*	The seller is responsible for delivering the goods to the named place in the buyer's country (eg the buyer's premises), and pays all costs in bringing the goods to that destination, *including* all import duties and taxes. If the seller cannot obtain an import licence, this term should not be used. DDP represents the ultimate extension of responsibility to the supplier – with the advantage that capital costs are tied up until payment is received. The corresponding advantage for buyers is that they know exactly what they are paying, particularly if quoted in local currency.

5.10 The choice of relevant incoterm will depend to an extent on the mode of transportation used.

- Seven of the terms (EXW, FCA, CPT, CIP, DAT, DAP and DDP) are designed to reflect the increasing use of inter-modal transport, by applying flexibly to any mode of transportation: hence the reference to a named 'place' of destination, which enables delivery to depots or freight forwarders, for example.
- Four terms (FAS, FOB, CFR and CIF) apply only where transportation is conducted entirely by sea or inland waterway, referring to a 'named port'.
- Some terms (FCA, CPT and CIP) reflect the increasing use of containerised shipments, eg when goods are delivered to an inaland clearance or container depot for transfer to onward sea or road freight, or when they are delivered to an airfreight forwarder who consolidates and containerises the consigment.
- Some terms (FOB, CFR and CIF) reflect more traditional methods of freight, as being sent 'break-bulk' (eg packed in wooden crates for transport in the hold of a non-container vessel), with terms suitable for port-to-port transit.

5.11 Table 12.6 contains a brief overview of all eleven incoterms. (The International Chamber of Commerce publishes full details, if you are interested.)

6 Payment mechanisms

6.1 An overseas supplier may not be entirely confident that it will be paid for goods, once the buyer has got hold of them. The seller may be vulnerable because of the distances involved; the risks of international transportation; limited direct contact with the buyer; and the difficulty of conducting payment disputes through different legal jurisdictions. International trade therefore recognises the need to protect the seller's position, to give exporters some guarantee of payment by their customers.

6.2 There are various ways of arranging international payments.

- **Open account trading**: ordinary credit terms, where the seller bears the risk of non-payment. This is only used where there is a good level of trust between buyer and supplier.
- **Payment in advance**: simple and low risk for the seller – but high risk for the buyer (given the risk of non-delivery, or loss of value in transit)
- **Bills of exchange:** similar to a post-dated cheque, guaranteeing payment at a defined future date (eg 90 days from the date of creation)
- **Letters of credit:** the buyer's bank guarantees payment to the supplier, once the terms and conditions of the sales contract have been shown to be satisfied (eg by presentation of a bill of lading or other documentation).

Letters of credit

6.3 Using letters of credit is essential in international trade, and importers need a reasonable understanding of how they work. However, the procedure is somewhat complex and to help your understanding it is worthwhile to bear in mind what the system attempts to achieve.

- The seller's aim is to ensure that it will get paid, without the need for costly and time-consuming litigation or arbitration (particularly in a foreign jurisdiction).
- The buyer's aim is to ensure that payment is *not* made until it is sure that the goods have been safely transferred to its possession.

6.4 In order to achieve this, two local banks are used as intermediaries.

- The buyer instructs the *issuing bank* (in the buyer's country) to open credit with the *advising bank* (in the seller's country) in favour of the seller.
- The seller can draw on that credit (ie obtain funds) at the advising bank, once it has delivered to the advising bank any documents specified by the buyer (eg a clean bill of lading).
- The advising bank then forwards the documents to the issuing bank, and is re-imbursed for the credit sum it advanced.

12

- Finally, the issuing bank presents the documents to the buyer, in return for settlement.
- The end result is that the buyer has paid, and the seller has received, the contract price – while the intermediary banks have received fees for handling the transactions.

6.5 The Letters of Credit process is depicted in Figure 12.1 (drawn from the explanatory booklet *Letters of Credit* by HBOS).

6.6 From the supplier/exporter's point of view, a 'confirmed irrevocable' letter of credit is the most secure method of payment in international trade, as it offers a legal guarantee of payment.

- 'Confirmed' means that the advising bank has confirmed the arrangement with the seller in its own country, and the seller therefore has confidence in receiving funds from a local source, once it has delivered the required documents.
- 'Irrevocable' means that the issuing bank receives an authority which cannot be revoked or withdrawn by the buyer (even in the event of a contractual dispute) – and undertakes irrevocably to honour the credit.

7 Dispute resolution

Applicable law and jurisdiction

7.1 It is essential to know the applicable law governing an international contract of sale, and which country's courts have jurisdiction (or power) in any subsequent dispute. The EC's Rome Convention On The Law Applicable to Contractual Obligations 1980 (The Rome Convention) was designed to replace common law rules to determine the law that applies to a contract, in any situation involving a choice between the laws of different countries. It was enacted into UK law by the Contracts (Applicable Law) Act 1990.

7.2 The Rome convention allows the parties to the contract to agree on which law will be applicable. They may do this by an express clause in the contract – and this is certainly the safest option – even if it is difficult to negotiate! Any stipulation as to applicable law must always be undertaken via negotiation, and with the express agreement of both parties.

7.3 If the applicable law is not expressed in the contract, and questions or disputes arise, it may be inferred from the nature of the contract and the prevailing circumstances. The general rule is that the choice of law should be the law with which the contract is most closely associated: generally, the law of the country in which the contractual work is to be performed.

7.4 The Convention applies to any kind of contract, including contracts for the sale of goods, and employment contracts. However, it does *not* apply to arbitration agreements and agreements on the choice of court (among other exemptions).

The use of arbitration

7.5 Litigation (taking legal action through the courts) can be complex and involved – particularly when international considerations are involved. To reduce the risks involved, parties involved in dispute may seek to avoid legislation and seek to use an alternative means of dispute settlement, such as arbitration.

7.6 Arbitration is the most commonly used form of dispute resolution for international disputes. There are well established frameworks for international dispute arbitration, using the court of arbitration of the International Chamber of Commerce (ICC) or the United Nations Commission on International Trade Law (UNCITRAL). Arbitration brings a measure of neutrality, so that no party is unfairly disadvantaged by the location of the proceedings, the language used, the procedures applied and so on.

7.7 The parties to the contract have to agree to arbitration before it can be applied. The parties can agree

Figure 12.1 *Letters of credit flowchart*

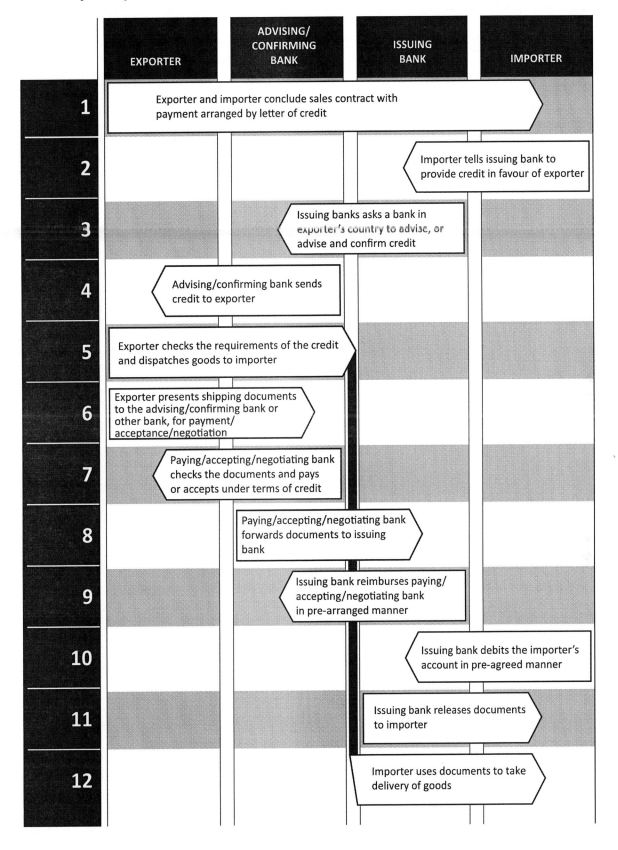

	EXPORTER	ADVISING/ CONFIRMING BANK	ISSUING BANK	IMPORTER
1	Exporter and importer conclude sales contract with payment arranged by letter of credit			
2				Importer tells issuing bank to provide credit in favour of exporter
3			Issuing banks asks a bank in exporter's country to advise, or advise and confirm credit	
4		Advising/confirming bank sends credit to exporter		
5	Exporter checks the requirements of the credit and dispatches goods to importer			
6	Exporter presents shipping documents to the advising/confirming bank or other bank, for payment/ acceptance/negotiation			
7		Paying/accepting/negotiating bank checks the documents and pays or accepts under terms of credit		
8		Paying/accepting/negotiating bank forwards documents to issuing bank		
9			Issuing bank reimburses paying/ accepting/negotiating bank in pre-arranged manner	
10				Issuing bank debits the importer's account in pre-agreed manner
11			Issuing bank releases documents to importer	
12				Importer uses documents to take delivery of goods

12

to this either before or after the dispute has arisen, but good risk management would ensure this is considered prior to entering into an international purchase contract.

7.8 Arbitration is a formal procedure and the award given by the arbitrator is in most cases enforceable. However, it does not always provide a quick solution to a dispute: in fact it is not uncommon for arbitration proceedings to last as long as court hearings.

7.9 Arbitration does have some positive advantages over litigation.

- The contracting parties have the freedom to choose who they desire to arbitrate. These can be people who, for example, possess expertise in a particular trade and might be best suited to resolving the dispute. This often makes for smoother resolution of the dispute.
- The parties can choose rules of procedure, such as rules published by the International Chamber of Commerce (ICC).
- The parties can often choose the time and place to hold arbitration proceedings.
- The parties can keep the dispute between themselves as arbitration proceedings are undertaken behind closed doors, as opposed to litigation which is in the public domain.
- Arbitration awards are generally final, meaning there is little likelihood of protracted dealings through appeals.

7.10 Although the adoption of incoterms into a contract will mean that courts will imply the standards of incoterms in law, the ICC will arbitrate on disputes. If this course of action is considered worthwhile the ICC recommends inclusion of the following term in the contract:

'All disputes arising in connection with the present contract shall be finally settled under the Rules of Conciliation and Arbitration of the International Chamber of Commerce by one or more arbitrators appointed in accordance with the said Rules'.

Chapter summary

- Various drivers have given rise to an increase in international sourcing in recent years.
- Outside trading blocs, international trade may be subject to barriers such as quotas and exchange controls.
- In the UK, the control of imported and exported goods is the responsibility of HM Customs & Excise, a division of HMRC.
- Within the EU, goods may in principle circulate with minimal controls and paperwork.
- Imports from outside the EU are subject to more rigorous controls.
- Customs duties are indirect taxes levied on imports at the point of entry.
- Firms trading across international boundaries may benefit from using incoterms to clarify the terms on which they are contracting.
- Letters of credit are a common payment mechanism in international trade, giving security to both buyer and seller.
- In international trade, it is important to clarify which country's law will apply in the event of dispute.
- Arbitration is the most common form of dispute resolution in international trade.

 ## Self-test questions

Numbers in brackets refer to the paragraphs where you can check your answers.

1   What factors have driven the modern increase in international trading? (1.2)

2   What are the arguments in favour of international trade? (1.3)

3   List possible barriers to international trade. (1.7)

4   What is meant by goods 'in free circulation' within the EU? (2.6)

5   Explain the more rigorous criteria applying to goods imported from outside the EU. (3.1ff)

6   What is a bill of lading? (3.5)

7   Describe 'inward processing relief'. (4.6)

8   Describe the four groups of incoterms. (5.8)

9   What is meant by (a) FOB and (b) CIF terms? (Table 12.6)

10 Describe the use of intermediary banks in the letter of credit mechanism. (6.4)

11 Why might parties to an international trading contract wish to use arbitration? (7.5, 7.6)

CHAPTER 13

Risks and Opportunities in International Sourcing

Assessment criteria and indicative content

5.2 Analyse the main legislative, regulatory and organisational requirements when sourcing from international suppliers

- Ethical sourcing and fair trade standards
- Currency regulations
- Applicable law

Section headings

1 Opportunities in international sourcing
2 Risks in international sourcing
3 Ethical sourcing in international markets
4 Managing currency and exchange rate risk
5 Managing cross-cultural supply chains

Introduction

In this chapter we follow up our coverage of the practical and administrative issues of international sourcing with an exploration of the broader, more strategic issues. What are the benefits, costs and risks of international sourcing? What considerations will an organisation have to bear in mind when considering sourcing from international suppliers? How can the risks and costs of international supply chains be managed?

We start by weighing the opportunities inherent in international sourcing (and the main reasons for the development of international sourcing) against the key categories of risk, across a range of areas.

We then proceed to examine how a buying organisation can manage some of the key categories of risk, looking at: the challenges of ethical trading and enforcing supplier compliance with corporate social responsibility policies; risks arising from currency fluctuations; communications challenges; and issues in the management of cross-cultural supply chains.

1 Opportunities in international sourcing

The motivation for sourcing overseas

1.1 In this section we look at an important factor involved in the choice of suppliers: the question of whether to choose suppliers locally or internationally.

- Local sourcing implies using suppliers who are 'based within easy reach of the buyer' (*CIPS Knowledge Summary: Using Local Suppliers*), whether geographically or by other measures of accessibility. In the present context, however, it may be taken to mean sourcing within the local region or country – as opposed to international sourcing.

- International sourcing implies using suppliers across national borders – although it can also be distinguished from 'global' sourcing (which, as we noted in Chapter 12, implies the co-ordination of requirements among the worldwide business units of a firm).

1.2 Certain obvious advantages of sourcing *locally* may present themselves immediately. With shorter distances or 'lines of supply', communications are likely to be easier; delivery costs should be lower, and delivery lead times should be faster and more reliable. Unforeseen 'rush' orders are easier to cope with, and just in time (on-demand) supply may be possible, to minimise stockholding. There are likely to be few problems of language, or cultural or legal differences.

1.3 Given all this, why should firms even consider sourcing from international suppliers? Some of the opportunities available from international sourcing can be identified as follows.

- Access to required materials, facilities and/or skills, which may not be available (or available at the right price) in local supply markets. There may simply be no local or national supplier which can meet the requirements, in the case of agricultural products (which favour certain climatic conditions) or raw materials (such as minerals) which are not evenly distributed geographically.
- Availability of diverse and culturally-distinctive goods (eg for retailers purchasing for re-sale), which may only be available – or attract premium prices – if obtained at source
- Access to a wider supplier base, with opportunities to select the most competitive offering – and the flexibility to switch sources of supply, if requirements are not reliably available in any single market (due to supply fluctuations, disruptions or the imposition of import quotas, say)
- Opportunities for cost savings. Historically, this has been the prime motivator of international sourcing. Certain overseas countries have been strongly price competitive with domestic supply markets, because of cheap wage rates, sourcing economies (eg easy access to abundant supplies of local raw materials), scale economies, government export subsidies or beneficial exchange rates.
- Exchange rate advantages. Cost savings may be further enhanced by exchange rate differences: if the buyer's currency is strong, imports from countries with weaker currencies will be cheaper.
- Competitive quality, arising from suppliers' ability to take advantage of raw material quality, skill and technology specialisation, or quality values and management techniques in other cultures. In previous decades, for example, the quality revolution was largely pioneered in the Far East, and especially in Japan: Western purchasers found that reliability and quality considerations favoured suppliers from such countries, for manufactured products such as consumer electronics and cars.
- Specialisation. Some countries attract concentrated investment in infrastructure or capability development for the supply of particular goods and services, creating focused, innovative, high-quality and efficient supply markets. One well-known current example is the focus of certain regions of India on the provision of IT and call-centre services.
- Reduced regulatory and compliance burden. Some overseas countries may have more lax regulatory regimes in relation to quality standards, health and safety, minimum wages, environmental protection, or the protection of intellectual property. Although this may (as we will see later in the chapter) be a source of reputational and compliance risk for the importer, it may also enable it to 'cut corners' on costs.
- Leveraging available ICT developments for virtual organisation, e-sourcing and e-procurement, contract management and supplier relationship management and communication
- Reciprocal trading: companies purchasing materials from suppliers in a foreign country may be entitled under a counter-trade agreement to export their products to that foreign country (or to those suppliers)
- Ability to compete with competitors who are benefiting from any or all of the above advantages.

1.4 As we saw in Chapter 11, international sourcing may be a compliance issue for public sector procurements over the threshold for application of the EU Public Procurement Directives. Such contracts must be advertised throughout the EU: it is not an option for a buyer to source locally, without inquiring widely for potential suppliers.

1.5 International sourcing may also be more or less imposed under counter-trade agreements, where a company exporting to a foreign country may be 'requested' to purchase materials from organisations in that country. Typically, these agreements have taken place with countries suffering from lack of hard currency, including the developing economies of Eastern Europe.

Arguments for and against

1.6 The arguments for and against international sourcing are summarised in Table 13.1. We will be looking at some of the drawbacks of international sourcing listed, in the next section of this chapter.

Table 13.1 *Arguments for/against local and international sourcing*

BENEFITS OF INTERNATIONAL SOURCING	DRAWBACKS OF INTERNATIONAL SOURCING
Availability of required materials and/or skills: increased supply capacity or competitiveness	Exchange rate risk, currency management issues etc
Competitive price and cost savings (scale economies, low labour costs)	High sourcing and transaction costs (risk management, tariff and non-tariff barriers)
Less onerous constraints and costs re environmental and labour compliance	Cost savings and lower standards may create sustainability, compliance or reputational risk
Leverages technology (eg for virtual organisation, e-sourcing)	Different legal frameworks, time zones, standards, language and culture
International trade (arguably) promotes development, prosperity, international relations etc	Additional risks: political, transport (lead times, exposure), payment, supplier standards monitoring
Public sector: compulsory to advertise contacts within the EU	Environmental impacts of transport and haulage (especially by air freight)
BENEFITS OF LOCAL SOURCING	DRAWBACKS OF LOCAL SOURCING
Investment in local community, employment, skills etc (plus reputational or brand benefits)	Materials, skills or capabilities may not be available locally (or may be more costly)
Accessibility for supplier development and contract management (eg site visits)	Ethical and reputational risks of close social ties with suppliers, common spheres etc
Supplier knowledge of local market, sustainability issues, regulatory standards etc.	Smaller suppliers: no economies of scale (higher costs), greater dependency issues
Reduced transport, payment, cultural risks and costs	Local sourcing policy may make local suppliers complacent or un-competitive
Short supply chain eg supporting JIT, fewer environmental impacts of transport	*Public* sector: not allowed to discriminate on basis of geography
Avoids 'evils' of globalisation	*Public* sector: may not offer 'value for money'

2   Risks in international sourcing

2.1 Now for the downside: the reasons why not every company sources internationally – and why the decision to source internationally must be taken, with care, at a strategic level. We will briefly survey some of the risks and costs of international sourcing, using some of the headings mentioned in the syllabus – although it is worth noting that the risks can be categorised in various ways, and frequently overlap. (For example, most risks will have a potential impact on costs, through losses and remedial action if the risk event happens – or the costs of preventing it from happening.)

Price and cost risks

2.2 International sourcing creates a number of risks in relation to price and cost – despite the strong price and cost advantages available.

- Additional costs of identifying, evaluating and developing new sources of supply, in situations where information may be difficult to obtain (eg inaccessibility for site visits and performance monitoring)

13

and where quality standards and regulatory regimes may differ (and may offer inadequate compliance assurances)

- High transaction costs, given the complexity of international transaction documentation, time zone differences, the need for detailed contracting, specification and contract management and so on. (These will be mitigated to some extent by e-procurement and e-commerce technologies – but this, in itself, represents an extra investment.)
- Costs caused by transport risks and delays, because of distance, lead times in transit, and the potential for deterioration, damage and loss of goods in handling, storage and transit. There will be additional costs of risk management measures to mitigate these risks, such as special packing, refrigeration, insurance, expediting systems and so on.
- Exchange rate risk, as a result of fluctuations in the value of buyer- or supplier-side currencies (discussed further in Section 4 of this chapter) and currency management costs (obtaining foreign currencies, arranging letters of credit and so on).
- Payment risk, with reduced confidence for suppliers of being paid due to distance (especially bearing the risk of non-delivery, loss of goods or rejection of goods paid for in advance) and the complexity of risk management measures (eg letters of credit, bills of exchange)
- Costs associated with tariff and non-tariff barriers to trade (discussed in Chapter 11), such as onerous customs procedures and documentation; import duties and taxes; import quotas and so on.

2.3 Overseas economies may have lower costs of production (labour costs, environmental compliance costs), which can be passed on to purchasers as lower prices. This is the overwhelming reason why companies now source internationally, or outsource production to low-labour-cost countries. However, there is increasing pressure for buyers not to *exploit* overseas workers, with an emphasis on Fair Trading (fair prices paid to suppliers) and ethical monitoring of suppliers (to ensure that their workers have fair terms and conditions).

2.4 International sourcing will incur additional costs of: procurement staff training and systems preparation; larger order and stock quantities (because of longer lead times for delivery); transport and logistics; compliance (with different laws and regulatory regimes); transport and exchange rate risk (and risk management: insurances, forward contracts and so on); contracting and payment (given the complexity and distance); supplier selection and monitoring; quality assurance; and so on. As we saw in Chapter 3, low prices are only one part of the total purchasing cost.

Quality risks

2.5 Quality risks arise from a number of factors.

- The difficulty of obtaining verified supplier pre-qualification information (eg via site visits or financial statements) at a distance or with different reporting regimes
- The difficulty of monitoring suppliers' quality management systems, or sampling verified outputs, at a distance
- The difficulty of 'drilling down' through suppliers' own supply chains, in situations where there may be poor supply chain documentation and lack of communication infrastructure
- Perceived emphasis on price competition encouraging a 'cutting of corners' on quality
- Differences in regulatory regimes in regard to consumer protection, labelling and other quality issues (eg the inclusion of poor-quality materials or ingredients)
- Differences in quality standards, and related factors such as vocational education and management development, technology infrastructure, access to quality inputs, awareness of quality management standards and techniques, working conditions, investment in quality, and culturally-conditioned values and perceptions of quality.

2.6 The emphasis in managing such risks may be on: rigorous supplier pre-qualification and monitoring; rigorous specification of quality requirements, tolerances, service levels and KPIs; contract incentives and penalties to support quality performance; and the use of third-party local agents or consultancies to perform supplier appraisal and performance management tasks.

Time, quantity and place risks

2.7 As you may remember from your studies of the 'Five Rights' of procurement for other modules, issues of time, quantity and place are often interdependent. The 'right quantity' will depend on how often an item is used, how soon it is needed, and its lead time to obtain from a supplier ('right time') – which in turn depends on where the supplier is, where the item has to be delivered to, and by what means ('right place').

2.8 Time, quantity and place risks are therefore, essentially 'supply risks'. They may include:

- Potential disruptions to supply, and risk of supplier failure, caused by factors such as political instability, civil unrest, war or terrorism, trade policy changes (such as the imposition of export or import quotas), industrial unrest or natural factors (eg drought, flood, earthquake or disease) in overseas areas
- Transport risks: the risk of loss, deterioration, damage or theft of goods in transit, given the longer distances and lead times involved – as well as the inherent risks of increased handling, storage and transport conditions (dust, pressure, water and so on). Piracy or war damage may be a risk to sea freight or road haulage in some areas of the world. Natural factors may also cause delays: recent examples include snow disrupting road haulage, and the eruption of a volcano disrupting air freight.
- Increased lead times for supply, due to transport distance (particularly if slower modes of transport such as sea freight or road haulage are used); delays due to weather or transport congestion; delays due to customs clearances and inspections; delays due to inefficient transport planning; and so on.
- Risks of misunderstanding of requirements (in relation to quantity, time, place or other matters), due to differences of language or interpretation (different meanings attached to terms and concepts in different cultures) in negotiation, specifications or supply contracts.
- Problems caused by communication delays (eg due to slow communication infrastructure or time zone differences).

2.9 The management of such risks will generally focus on measures such as the following.

- Proactive demand forecasting and procurement planning, taking into account realistic lead times for international supply
- Proactive transport planning, in order to maximise the security and efficiency of deliveries, customs clearances and so on
- Rigorous risk identification, monitoring and assessment, including the regular updating of supply risk registers, and planning for risk management and mitigation
- Contingency planning: developing action plans and mitigating measures for unlikely but foreseeable risk events (including, where appropriate, developing alternative local 'back-up' sources of supply)
- The purchase of appropriate insurances to cover likely and/or high-impact contingencies, and the use of Incoterms to establish buyer and supplier responsibilities for insurances, and liability for risk events during storage, transport and handling
- Collaborating with suppliers to minimise identified risks – and/or to help with disaster recovery and supply continuity (eg Toyota supporting its supply network in rebuilding after an earthquake or tsunami)
- Using third party service providers (eg agents, freight-forwarders or logistics providers), in order to access international expertise and local offices – and share or transfer responsibility for risks
- The use of incoterms to minimise contract ambiguities
- The use of local agents or consultants, or translation and interpretation services, in negotiating and developing contracts and agreements.

13

Negotiation and relationship risks

2.10   A number of risks are incurred in cross-cultural negotiation and relationships, especially due to the following factors.

- Differences in language and interpretation. Linguistic barriers may impact on the negotiation of contract terms, general business relations, the interpretation of specifications and so on.
- Differences in culture, tastes and values eg in regard to business customs, ethics, management style, communication and conflict styles, negotiation styles, the role of gifts and hospitality, gender roles in business – and so on. These will impact on negotiations, impressions management and supplier relations. (Crucially for downstream operations, they will also affect market perceptions of the product.)

2.11   We will discuss these issues in more detail in the final section of this chapter.

Compliance, legal and reputational risk

2.12   A further category of risks in international sourcing may arise from:

- Differences in legal frameworks (eg on contract law, health and safety, employment, environmental protection and intellectual property protection).

    Such differences may cause direct commercial and project risks: for example loss of intellectual assets (eg if the buyer submits specifications or designs to suppliers); or breach of the supply contract and costs of litigation or arbitration; the use of unsafe materials or components (with the buyer ultimately liable for loss or damage to consumers, as in Mattel's massive product recall of toys made in China with illegal lead paint).

    There may also be reputational damage to the buyer as a result of exposure of poor labour standards or adverse environmental impacts by its supply chain: a high profile recent example was the damage caused to Oxfam by the revelation that its overseas suppliers of 'Make Poverty History' wristbands were imposing poor conditions on their workers.
- Issues around 'applicable law': the determination of which country's legal system will have jurisdiction over disputes between parties to international contracts. Efforts are being made, especially within trading blocs, to harmonise legal frameworks and establish international arbitration systems.
- Differences in ethical standards and the cost and complexity of managing them, eg by ethical monitoring of suppliers. As well as impacting directly on business practices (eg costs and ethical conflicts relating to bribes or 'grease money'), ethical issues pose the risk of reputational damage, given increasing public concern about human rights, ethical trading and so on.

2.13   As we have seen, some risks can be managed operationally: through supplier monitoring, insurances, incoterms and so on. At a more strategic level, sourcing professionals will need to establish policy guidelines (eg on ethics and risk management) and implement on-going environmental monitoring and research. They will also need to make key strategic decisions about the configuration of the supply network: eg using agents, freight forwarders, logistics lead providers, strategic alliances or local strategic business units (or divisions) to help manage international supply chain relationships.

Summary of issues in international sourcing

2.14   An article in *Supply Management* ('10 tricky decisions', 16 February 2006) helpfully highlighted some key practical considerations in international sourcing, which offers a good summary of the foregoing discussion.

Do you really want to go overseas?

('Global sourcing for cost reasons alone may not be sustainable in the long term, and closing down more local options may lead to sourcing problems later on... Sourcing globally will also bring new requirements for the business – for example in compliance, traceability and financial reporting.')

Crossed wires

('The assumption that there is a common understanding with suppliers from different cultures can result in misunderstanding and dissatisfaction.')

Costs

('Companies can fail to consider all the financial implications of sourcing from abroad: low labour prices are only a small element of the total outlay.')

Yet more regulations

('Service agreements are always sensitive but the global dimension, with different legislation in various nations, adds its own twist of complexity.')

Specification

('Products can be described in different ways across the globe.')

Inspections

('Incorrect assumptions may be made about the ability of a given country to produce quality goods or services.')

Lead times

('Global sourcing increases lead times. To compensate for this, purchasers often increase their minimum order quantity, but financing and carrying this extra inventory is expensive.')

Flexible supply chain

('Delays can be disastrous – especially for companies with limited options to re-route goods.')

Intellectual property

('Fighting counterfeiting is complex and expensive, and it can be difficult to prosecute in emerging markets.')

Are your staff ready?

('Companies that don't train their procurement staff in the specialities of global sourcing increase risk and are more likely to miss out on efficiencies and savings opportunities.')

3 Ethical sourcing in international markets

3.1   The main ethics-related challenges of international sourcing can be summarised as the desire for low-cost sourcing, available from low-cost labour, less onerous compliance burdens and resource availability in international supply markets – *versus* the following constraints.

- The obligation under voluntary ethical or moral standards not to *exploit* suppliers or supplier labour forces, who typically have low power in the supply market and buyer-supplier relationship – ie by paying fair or adequate (Fair Trade) prices; not imposing onerous compliance or investment burdens or risks; and supporting the raising of labour standards and working conditions in developing and low-cost labour countries (eg following the principles of the Ethical Trading Initiative or International Labour Organisation)
- The obligation under voluntary corporate social responsibility standards not to degrade or pollute environments or exhaust resources in developing economies, even though this may be permissible under more lax local environmental protection standards
- The obligation under environmental management standards, environmental legislation and the UK's international commitment (eg to targets for the reduction of carbon emissions) to minimise the environmental impact of operations eg by reducing transport miles, fuel usage and carbon emissions
- The desire to support domestic businesses (for economic and social sustainability and PR benefits), especially in times of economic recession and unemployment
- The desire to protect and enhance the organisation's reputation, image and brand, by buying (and advertising) ethically sourced and produced goods (eg cosmetics not tested on animals, or certified Fair Trade products which guarantee the ethical treatment of labour and suppliers). This is a major trend, with increasing demand for Fair Trade cotton, coffee, tea and chocolate brands, among others. Organisations such as The Body Shop have built high-profile brands on ethical sourcing and production.

13

3.2 There is no real 'answer' to this conflict, since both local and international sourcing can be argued on the basis of ethics and corporate social responsibility (eg the desire to support both local businesses *and* developing economies). Strategies and policies will have to be developed to ensure that the drawbacks of international sourcing – if this is the chosen strategy – are minimised.

3.3 For example, an organisation sourcing internationally will have to pay attention to issues such as fair negotiation and pricing; avoiding over-dependency in supply chains; the monitoring of suppliers' labour and environmental standards (including drilling down to lower tiers of their supply chains); quality management (to protect consumers); and transport planning (to minimise carbon footprint).

Fair Trade

3.4 'Unfair' trading arises when large buyers exert their bargaining power to force down the prices of small suppliers, to levels that bring economic hardship to producers, exacerbating poor wages and working conditions for their workers, and bringing no economic benefit to their communities. In the UK, there have been recent calls for formal regulation of the relationship between large supermarket chains and their much smaller suppliers, for example, because of the allegedly unfair 'squeezing' of prices. More commonly, however, fair trade issues arise in developing economies: the media has recently highlighted the plight of coffee and tea growers, and textile and garment trade workers.

3.5 Started over sixty years ago, Fair Trade has developed into a worldwide concept, seeking to ensure decent living and working conditions for small-scale and economically disadvantaged producers and workers in developing countries. It involves an alliance of producers and importers, retailers, labelling and certifying organisations – and, of course, consumers willing to pursue ethical consumption by support for certified Fair Trade products.

3.6 In August 2009, for example, Cadbury and the Fair Trade Association announced that major brand Cadbury's Dairy Milk Chocolate would go Fair Trade certified in Australia in 2010. A media release by the Stop the Traffik Coalition affirmed: 'This is great news for impoverished cocoa farmers in West Africa and will help greatly in the efforts to end child slavery on cocoa plantations. It is also great news for chocolate consumers, expanding their choice of chocolate that has been certified to be free of child slave labour and labour that has been trafficked onto the cocoa plantations.'

3.7 Ethical sourcing and the fair trade movement were discussed in more detail in Chapter 4.

4 Managing currency and exchange rate risk

4.1 One of the key considerations in international sourcing is the need to manage risks arising from exchange rates: that is, the price of one currency (say, pounds sterling or euros) expressed in terms of another currency (say, US dollars).

4.2 The exchange rate between two currencies is determined by the relative supply and demand for each currency.

- Demand for pound sterling may rise, for example, when foreign buyers need to pay for exports from the UK; or foreign investors want to invest in the UK (perhaps because interest rates are attractively high); or speculators want to buy sterling on the foreign exchange market, in the anticipation that its value is rising.
- Conversely, supply of sterling will rise when people sell their pounds in exchange for foreign currencies: UK residents wishing to buy imports or invest abroad, say, or speculators selling sterling in anticipation of the value falling.

4.3 If demand for a currency, relative to supply, is rising (eg if there is a balance of payments surplus: more exports than imports), the foreign exchange markets will tend to quote the currency at a higher exchange rate. If supply is rising, relative to demand (eg if there is a balance of payments deficit: more imports than exports), the exchange rate will tend to be lower.

Exchange rate risk

4.4 Exchange rates are important for firms in international supply markets. As an example, consider a UK company with extensive importing activities. Suppose that on Day 1 the company contracts with a US supplier to purchase goods valued at US$1m. The exchange rate is such that £1 sterling buys exactly US$2. The credit terms agreed between the two companies are that payment is due on Day 60.

4.5 From the importer's point of view, the key risk is that the exchange rate will move unfavourably (downwards) between Day 1 and Day 60. For example, suppose that on Day 60 the prevailing exchange rate is £1 = US$1.8. A purchase that was expected to cost £500,000 ($1m ÷ 2) will now cost £555,555 ($1m ÷ 1.8). The adverse currency movement has cost the importer £55,555.

4.6 *Importers* want the value of their domestic currency to be as *high* as possible. If the value of sterling is strong or rising against a foreign currency, UK purchasers can acquire more of that currency to pay their foreign suppliers: imports will be cheaper in domestic terms. If sterling weakens, purchasers' ability to acquire overseas currency is reduced, and imports are more expensive in domestic terms. This is the major consideration for international purchasers.

4.7 It is worth noting that for *exporters*, the position is reversed. They want the value of their domestic currency to be as *low* as possible. If the value of sterling is low against a foreign currency, overseas purchasers will be able to buy more pounds to pay for UK goods: UK exports will be more affordable and attractive to overseas purchasers. If the value of sterling is high, UK goods will be more expensive to foreign buyers, and UK suppliers will find it harder to compete with other international suppliers (with weaker currencies).

4.8 Firms producing goods for the domestic market *in competition with foreign imports* similarly want the value of sterling to be *low*, as this makes imports more expensive in domestic terms, favouring domestic suppliers. If sterling rises, imports will be more competitive.

4.9 *Fluctuations in foreign exchange rates* therefore represent a source of financial risk for purchasing organisations. An overseas supplier will normally quote a price in its own currency, and the buyer will need to purchase currency in order to make payment. If sterling weakens between the time when the price is agreed and the purchase of the currency, the buyer will end up paying more. The risk is even greater if staged payments are to be made.

Managing exchange rate risk

4.10 There are a number of ways of managing exchange rate risk.

- The purchaser might be able to transfer the risk to the suppliers, by getting them to quote prices in sterling. (This might be a tough negotiation, unless the purchaser has strong power in the relationship, or can offer concessions in exchange.)
- If fluctuations are not extreme, it may be possible to estimate the rate that will apply at the time of payment, and negotiate prices accordingly (perhaps with a contract proviso that prices will be *re-negotiated* if the exchange rate fluctuates by a stated percentage or reaches a stated rate).
- It may be possible to agree to pay for the goods at the time of contract (ie at today's known exchange rate), without waiting for later delivery. This is an example of a technique called 'leading' (making payment in advance of the due date to take advantage of a positive exchange rate): note, however, that it creates an additional risk for the buyer. A similar technique is 'lagging' (making a payment later than the due date, to take advantage of exchange rate improvements): again, note that this is at the expense of the supplier, and raises ethical, reputational and relationship risks.

13

- Another approach would be to use one of the available tools of currency management, such as a forward exchange contract, which enable the importer to 'hedge' the risk. Under this arrangement, the organisation contracts *now* to purchase the overseas currency at a *stated future date*, at a rate of exchange *agreed now*. For example, the importer might enter a forward exchange contract on Day 1, agreeing to purchase $1m on Day 60 in order to pay its US supplier. The cost of the US dollars will be fixed by the bank on Day 1, the rate being determined by market conditions and expectations of future exchange rate movements. There is a cost to doing this, but for the buyer, the uncertainty is removed: it knows on Day 1 exactly how much its purchase will cost.
- If exchange rate risks are severe, a purchaser may have to consider temporarily sourcing from the domestic market, from a single currency market such as the EU, or from other markets with less volatile currencies.

5   Managing cross-cultural supply chains

5.1   One of the more obvious problems for a UK buyer in dealing with overseas suppliers is that they are not British! This remark is not intended in any racist or xenophobic sense: it is merely intended to make the obvious point that the residents of a particular country, such as the United Kingdom, share a common culture and a common language, which facilitates business dealings between them. When dealing with overseas suppliers, it is necessary to adjust to a different culture and often a different language.

Communication issues

5.2   To deal first with the issue of language, it is clearly vital that commercial agreements are expressed in language that both parties understand. It is an essential element in a binding contract that the parties reach 'agreement', and that element is absent if there is 'misunderstanding': a position in which one party believes it understands what the other has said, but in fact has not done so.

5.3   Meanwhile, before the contract stage is reached, discussions and negotiations will take place. Both the content (what is said, offered, promised and agreed to) and process (how the negotiation is conducted, how agreements are reached, how trust and relationships are developed) have a crucial impact on the final supply relationship. Negotiations are therefore highly subject to differences both in the language of communication and in the *style* and *customs* of communication, which are driven by cultural values and norms.

5.4   An effort on the part of buyers or account/supplier managers to acquire some understanding of the relevant foreign language for a key supply relationship can be helpful, but should be supplemented by use of translation and interpretation services, where required.

5.5   In addition to language barriers, communication challenges may arise from:

- Time zone differences, creating a conflict between the 'business hours' of buyer and supplier, making interactive contact (eg for negotiation, problem-solving and question-and-answer) difficult without compromise
- Communication technology and infrastructure differences (eg lack of access to high-speed internet for web conferencing)
- The use of third parties (eg agents, freight forwarders or logistics providers) lengthening chains of communication, and increasing the risk of messages being lost or distorted in transit
- Pressure to use e-procurement or e-commerce solutions (for which tools, skills and willingness may or may not be available).

Cultural aspects

5.6   Culture has been defined as: 'the collective programming of the mind which distinguishes the members of one category of people from another' (Hofstede). Culture is the shared assumptions, beliefs, values, behavioural norms, symbols, rituals, stories and artefacts that make our society (or ethnic group, or organisation) distinctively 'us' – or as one writer put it, 'How we do things round here'.

5.7 Different countries (or world regions) may have significantly different cultural norms, values and assumptions which influence how they do business and manage people. It is increasingly important to understand this, since procurement professionals are increasingly likely to work in organisations that have multinational or multi-cultural elements – and with multi- or cross-cultural supply chains.

5.8 Culture researcher Geert Hofstede *(Cultures and Organisations)* formulated one of the most influential models of work-related cultural differences, identifying five key dimensions of difference between national cultures.

- *Power-distance:* the extent to which unequal distribution of power and status is accepted or involvement and participation expected
- *Uncertainty-avoidance:* the extent to which security, order, control and predictability are preferred to ambiguity, uncertainty, risk and change
- *Individualism:* the extent to which people prefer to live and work in individualist ('I'-based) or collectivist ('we'-based) ways
- *Masculinity:* the extent to which gender roles are distinct, and whether masculine values (assertiveness, competition) or feminine values (consensus, relationship) prevail.
- *Long-term orientation:* the extent to which thrift and perseverance are valued (long-term orientation) over respect for tradition, fulfilling social obligations and protecting one's 'face' (short-term orientation).

5.9 You should be able to recognise the challenges faced by a purchaser in a country at one end of the spectrum, in dealing with a supplier at the other end of the spectrum, on each dimension. For example, a purchaser in a low uncertainty-avoidance culture such as the UK will be flexible about procedure and forthright about disagreements: a supplier from a high uncertainty-avoidance culture such as Japan may be uncomfortable working without written rules and procedures, and may be offended or stressed by disagreement.

5.10 *Edward Hall* suggested that another dimension of cultural difference is the extent to which the content and understanding of communication is influenced by its context: non-verbal aspects, underlying implications, interpersonal factors and so on.

- **Low-context** cultures (eg Germanic, Scandinavian, North American) tend to take the content of communication at face value: words say what they mean. They prefer clear, written, explicit communication. (The UK is classified as only moderately high context ...)
- **High-context** cultures (eg Japanese, Asian, African, Latin American, Middle-Eastern, Southern European) interpret and exchange more complex messages. They prefer face-to-face and oral communication, and are good at developing networks and using non-verbal cues and unspoken implications. They tend to divulge less information in official or written forms.

5.11 Again, you should be able to appreciate the challenge presented by a sourcing officer in one type of culture, negotiating and collaborating with suppliers in another.

5.12 You should also be able to think of more specific examples of cultural differences which would affect negotiation and supply chain management.

- Attitudes to equal opportunity and participation in business by women (and, by extension, supply chain diversity): equal opportunity is less of a value in some Middle Eastern and Latin cultures, for example.
- Negotiating and conflict styles. Many Asian cultures, for example, have a strong reluctance to lose 'face' or respect, or to cause others to do so, and are therefore reluctant to criticise, question or challenge in public. Some cultures have a long tradition of bargaining, resulting in a high degree of polarisation in initial positions.

13

- Decision-making styles: many Asian cultures seek consensus or group agreement in decision-making, for example, rather than leader-imposed or majority-rule decisions
- The perceived propriety of business gifts and hospitality. These may be considered an important sign of mutual respect in some cultures – where in the West they are regarded as unprofessional and unethical attempts to influence decisions, and are often forbidden in corporate Ethical Codes. This may be a particular issue for purchasers.
- Business customs and formalities. Each culture has its business rituals: eg the importance of business cards in Japan, the importance of social conversation prior to getting down to business in Middle Eastern cultures, or the comparative informality of interpersonal dealings in North America.

Other differences impacting on international sourcing

5.13 There may be a number of other potential differences to take into account.

- Differences in working practices, which can be a source of misunderstanding or frustration for overseas purchasers and managers. Examples might include long lunch breaks in some European countries, and greater (or less) emphasis on worker involvement in decision-making.
- Different standard working hours, wage rates and conditions of employment. This can pose ethical issues and reputational risks for purchasers.
- Different education and skill levels and emphases, and different professional qualification standards: this may affect the selection and management of outsource providers, for example
- Different standard business terms (eg credit periods, standard contract clauses, payment methods) and so on.

Managing diversity and socio-cultural differences

5.14 Schneider & Barsoux *(Managing Across Cultures)* argue that 'rather than knowing what to do in Country X, or whether national or functional cultures are more important in multi-cultural teams, what is necessary is to know *how to assess the potential impact* of culture, national or otherwise, on performance.'

5.15 At the organisational and departmental level, there should be a plan to evaluate this potential impact and to implement programmes to encourage: awareness of areas of difference and sensitivity; behavioural flexibility (being able to adapt in different situations and relationships); and constructive communication, conflict resolution and problem-solving, where differences emerge.

5.16 Another option is to access personnel and local knowledge from the overseas country: employing a local agent, say, or opening a local buying office.

Chapter summary

- There are obvious benefits from sourcing locally, but advantages of overseas sourcing have become very persuasive in recent years.
- Despite this, it remains important to recognise the risks of international sourcing in terms of: price and cost; quality; time, quantity and place; negotiation and relationships; compliance, legal and reputational risks.
- International trading gives rise to particular issues in relation to ethics and sustainability.
- Buyers sourcing from abroad need to manage risks relating to currency and exchange rates.
- International sourcing gives rise to potential for communication and cultural risks.

Self-test questions

Numbers in brackets refer to the paragraphs where you can check your answers.

1   List opportunities presented by international sourcing. (1.3)

2   List benefits and drawbacks of international sourcing. (Table 13.1)

3   List risks of international sourcing in terms of price and cost. (2.2)

4   List risks of international sourcing in terms of quality. (2.5)

5   List compliance, legal and reputational risks that may arise from international sourcing. (2.12)

6   List constraints that firms must manage so as to achieve ethical sourcing from overseas. (3.1)

7   An importer prefers his domestic currency to be strong rather than weak. True or false? (4.6)

8   What communication difficulties may arise in international sourcing? (5.2, 5.5)

9   List the five dimensions of difference between national cultures identified by Geert Hofstede. (5.8)

10 List cultural differences that may affect negotiation and supply chain management in international sourcing. (5.12)

Subject Index